The Politics of Asian Americans
Diversity and Community

Pei-te Lien, M. Margaret Conway, and Janelle Wong

ROUTLEDGE
NEW YORK AND LONDON

Published in 2004 by
Routledge
29 West 35th Street
New York, NY 10001
www.routledge-ny.com

Published in Great Britain by
Routledge
11 New Fetter Lane
London EC4P 4EE
www.routledge.co.uk

Routledge is an imprint of the Taylor and Francis Group.

Printed in the United States of America on acid-free paper.

10   9   8   7   6   5   4   3   2   1

Library of Congress Cataloging-in-Publication Data

Lien, Pei-te, 1957–
    The politics of Asian Americans : diversity and community / Pei-te Lien,
M. Margaret Conway, and Janelle Wong.
        p.   cm.
    Includes bibliographical references and index.
    ISBN 0-415-93464-8 (HC : alk. paper)—ISBN 0-415-93465-6 (PB : alk. paper)
    1. Asian Americans—Politics and government.   2. Asian
Americans—Ethnic identity.   3. Asian Americans—Statistics.   I. Conway,
M. Margaret (Mary Margaret), 1935–   II. Wong, Janelle.   III. Title.
E184.A75L54 2004
324'.089'95073—dc21
                                                    2003013136

Contents

Preface

In late May 2001, U.S. Representative David Wu (D-OR) was invited to speak at the Department of Energy's (DOE) Asian Pacific American Heritage Month program. When Representative Wu and his Legislative Director Ted Lieu—another Chinese American—checked in at security, DOE security guards questioned their citizenship status and the authenticity of Wu's Congressional identification card.[1]

* * * * *

In late May 2002, legislators in Kansas repealed the seventy-seven-year-old "alien land laws" that banned Asian immigrants from owning land and inheriting property in Kansas. The state's legislators acted in response to an information campaign organized by law professor Jack Chin and students working at the Immigration and Nationality Law Review at the University of Cincinnati (Akers, 2002). The Alien Land Law Project led to the successful repeal of the provision in 2001. In Florida and New Mexico, however, similar laws remain on the books. A ballot initiative in New Mexico to strike the laws from the books failed in November 2002.

* * * * *

In early July 2002, mayor David Chiu of San Marcos, Texas narrowly lost his reelection bid by twenty-three votes. Chiu was among the targets of a racist campaign letter just before the runoff election, which also attacked Hispanics, blacks, gays, singles, and abortion rights supporters. The letter, which claimed to be "paid for by San Marcos Citizens for Traditional Values," petitioned its recipients to elect "a council that reflects traditional Texas family values." It attacked Chiu's governing style because of his immigrant refugee background from Communist China.[2]

* * * * *

In November 2002, Democrat Swati Dandekar defeated her Republican opponent by a margin of 57 percent to 43 percent, and became the first Asian to be elected to the state house of Iowa. Dandekar is an immigrant woman from India who has lived in Iowa for the past thirty years. Five weeks prior to the election, her Republican opponent, Karen Balderston, circulated an e-mail questioning Dandekar's loyalty and value as an American.[3] The state's Republican leaders withdrew their support of candidate Balderston after the incident was made public one week prior to the election (Dvorak, 2002).

* * * * *

To what extent have Asian Americans progressed in American politics? These four cases occurring at the dawn of the twenty-first century demonstrate that, although Asian Americans have been settled in this country for at least a hundred and fifty years, and despite profound progress made since their initial arrival as sailors, "coolies," and indentured laborers, their quest toward social and political integration in the United States is still far from over. Their Asian immigrant background, along with their race, ethnicity, class, and gender status, is still the subject of contention and attacks in U.S. society and politics. Regardless of their personal or family histories in the United States and degree of acculturation, their present experiences can be haunted by the anti-Asian sentiment of a racist past.

What characterizes and explains the political and social experiences of today's Asian Americans? How do average Asian Americans think and act politically and why? This book represents an attempt to understand the contours and sources of political attitudes and behavior of Asian Americans—a nonwhite, long-standing, but majority-immigrant American community that is relatively small but rapidly growing. We approach this task from an angle that is slightly different than the majority of the book-length manuscripts on Asian American politics. Our emphasis is on studying mass political opinion and behavior. The main goal is to develop an understanding and conceptualization of Asian American political behavior that challenges popular misconceptions about Asian Americans as politically apathetic, disloyal, fragmented, unsophisticated, and inscrutable. Toward that end, based primarily on a groundbreaking survey, we present a social and political profile of the contemporary Asian American community, and chart the extent to which it is becoming socially integrated and politically incorporated into the U.S. system.

The survey, the Pilot National Asian American Political Survey (PNAAPS),[4] is the direct result of a crosscutting research grant made by the National Science Foundation (NSF—SES 9973435) to Pei-te Lien, the lead author. The NSF

Professional Opportunities for Women in Research and Education (POWRE) is a special program designed to give women scientists who experienced serious disruption in their personal life a lift in career advancement and professional development. Lien became eligible for this grant opportunity because of her background as an adult immigrant woman from Taiwan who reentered graduate school in midlife, and was disadvantaged as a non-native English-speaking scholar in the social and behavioral sciences. One can say that it is based on both her personal merits (as a beginning scholar with a promising record of publication) and persistence (after two failed grant-seeking attempts)[5] that she was awarded the prestigious grant.

The money, which was budgeted to the grant ceiling of $75,000, permitted Lien to conduct a pilot study of the feasibility of randomly surveying the national opinion of a relatively small and scattered population with multiple ethnic and linguistic backgrounds. In hindsight, Lien's attempt shows not only that it is possible to study the Asian population scientifically with advanced sampling and telephone interviewing technology, but that the resultant survey is more than a pilot study. Despite its name, the PNAAPS is a full-scale dataset collected with sophisticated ethnic survey methodology. How a pilot grant conducted on a shoestring budget was turned into a state-of-the-art survey dataset is a story worth much telling and celebration. It shows the possibility of multiracial and crossgenerational partnership with men and women of varied personal and professional backgrounds. The decision to keep "pilot" in the dataset name was made in order to underscore the pioneering nature of this project as well as the likely entrance of a new phase in the empirical study of Asian American politics, thanks in large part to the completion of this survey.

The story behind the making of the PNAAPS should be told, but it is not an easy task to cover more than seven years of research history involving countless named and anonymous organizations and individuals and many angles. For example, it is nearly impossible to recount stages of the survey development without omitting some of the important details and personnel. Below is a genuine but humble attempt to capture some of the vital players and their contributions. Our apologies in advance to those individuals and organizations whose contributions were inadvertently omitted. Our gratitude to them is all the same.

First and foremost, besides the principal investigator, this project was inconceivable without the unfailing partnership of M. Margaret Conway at the University of Florida. A woman of mixed European heritage, Peggy has provided the single most important and steadfast support for Pei-te's research on Asian American politics since her graduate student days in Gainesville, Florida. Peggy Conway, now a distinguished professor emeritus of political science, was both drafted to the project as well as volunteered herself because of her life-long commitment to the advancement of American political behavior research and the incorporation of the experiences of diverse Americans in the curriculum of American government and politics. Both Janelle Wong, a sixth-generation Chinese American and then a Ph.D. candidate at Yale, and Taeku Lee, a first-generation Korean American and then an assistant professor at Harvard, were enticed to participate in the development of the survey because of the joint ambition and shared interest in developing a multimethod and multiracial study based on the pilot project.

Though the dream to take the project to the next stage by including a multiracial sample remains a hope, the "gang of four" toiled and brainstormed in questionnaire design, preliminary data analysis, preparation of preliminary report and press release, and conference presentation on the nation's first multi-ethnic, multi-city, multilingual survey of Asian American political attitudes and behavior. Over the course of the four years (1999–2003), Janelle completed her dissertation and joined the faculty as an assistant professor at the University of Southern California. Despite being the most junior of all, Janelle's dedication, sacrifice, and service to the project are beyond mention. Although Taeku could not join us in the preparation of the book manuscript, the rest of the gang are forever indebted to him for his brilliant ideas, witty insights, and thoughtful foresights.

Polly Kleissas, vice president for account services at the Interviewing Service of America (ISA), is probably the best possible ally an academic can find. Polly was extremely enthusiastic about the NSF grant possibly because she happened to be the same person Pei-te contacted years ago (then as Polly Smith) when Pei-te first began her pursuit for grant support to conduct the survey. ISA was selected to do the fieldwork because of its leadership position in the multilingual, ethnic interviewing field. Polly was extremely generous in sharing her expertise on ethnic sampling, interviewing, questionnaire development, and most responsive to Pei-te's numerous requests for information. In addition, she helped connect Lien with her friends in Survey Sampling, Inc., one of the nation's most respected companies of its kind. Most importantly, Polly helped us find Alice Lee, the research director at KSCI-TV Los Angeles, who shared our common frustration about the marginalization of Asian Americans in standard survey research and persuaded the president and CEO of KSCI-TV Jon Yasuda to donate $10,000 as a community grant to support this research on Asian Americans. This fund was used to double the size of the Los Angeles portion of the project. A Korean immigrant herself, Alice Lee turned out to be an asset of another kind as well when she helped recruit an Asian American–owned company (the Multi-Lingua, Inc.) for multilingual questionnaire translation and helped proofread the Korean version of the questionnaire. She also made invaluable comments on question wording during the pilot-testing stage.

In addition to these key players, we need to acknowledge the invaluable role each of the following played in the interlinked stages that led to the creation of the PNAAPS. Sincere appreciation goes first to Amy Hawbaker, Scott Baston, Linda Pierkarski, and other associates at Survey Sampling Inc. of Fairfield, Connecticut, for providing tireless advice and information necessary for the preparation of the sampling design. Jeff Palish of Marketing System's Group,

Inc. contributed to an earlier stage of sampling development. Chicago-based Multi-Lingua, Inc. was responsible for preparing the Korean and Vietnamese version of the questionnaire. Professor Thanh Troung at the University of Utah helped proofread and advise the Vietnamese version of the questionnaire. Professor Namhee Lee helped look over the Korean translation. Anita Jin of KSCI-TV helped Pei-te translate the Chinese version of the questionnaire. The ISA project team that did the fieldwork deserves special mention because of its high level of professionalism and exceptional enthusiasm for the project. This team includes project manager Hector Levya, account associate Sarah White, CATI programmer Sam Azur, data coding specialist Kevin Kneale, and the multilingual and multiethnic team of supervisors and interviewers. We also wish to thank Melinda Ou of KSCI-TV for helping draft the initial press release. We are grateful as well to University of Utah Ph.D. students Pitima Boonyarak from Thailand and Wan Zheng from the People's Republic of China for helping edit the statistical sheets and preparing the Chinese translation. Last but not least, our thanks go to the panel of anonymous reviewers for the NSF POWRE and Political Science program and the program officers who unanimously favored the approval of the grant.

In the end, the PNAAPS is made possible because so many individuals and organizations showed exceptional care and unconditional support for a Chinese immigrant woman to fulfill her ambition to help advance the study of Asian Americans. Although Lien is extremely grateful for the generous support and advice received from all parties mentioned, any opinions, findings, and conclusions or recommendations expressed in this material are those of the principal investigator and do not necessarily reflect the views of the National Science Foundation or KSCI-TV. To facilitate intellectual exchange and academic advancement, this dataset is to be released for public use in fall 2003 from the Inter-University Data Consortium for Political and Social Research (ICPSR) hosted at the University of Michigan, Ann Arbor. (Methodological details of the survey can be found in Chapter 1.)

For the past twenty-four months between the release of the preliminary report and the completion of a book-length manuscript ready for production, we are indebted to Routledge editor, Eric Nelson for his early interest and strong support of this project. We also wish to thank the three press reviewers who carefully read the entire manuscript and provided invaluable suggestions. Sincere appreciation is extended as well to our colleagues in political science and Asian American studies who expressed a particular interest in the dataset, our findings, and in serving as possible reviewers. These include individuals such as professors Jane Junn, Michael Jones Correa, Don Nakanishi, James Lai, Andrew Aoki, Ling-chi Wang, Him Mark Lai, Madeline Hsu, Carole Uhlaner, Katherine Tate, Louis DeSipio, Paula McClain, John Mollenkopf, Rogers Smith, Jack Nagel, Rosane Rocher, Phil Nash, S. Karthick Ramakrishan, and Michael Chang.

They also include leaders in community organizations such as the National Asian Pacific American Legal Consortium, Asian Pacific American Institute for Congressional Studies, Asian American Legal Center in Southern California, Asian American Legal Education and Defense Fund, Organization of Chinese Americans, Chinese American Voter Education Committee, the 80-20 Initiative, and so on. Last but far from the least, we especially wish to thank Chris Collet of the University of California at Irvine and Pacific Opinions for his extreme generosity in providing critical comments and advice on questionnaire design and in reading the entire manuscript as well as numerous chapter drafts. We are deeply grateful for his insight and constant encouragement.

Writing a book is a challenging task; writing a book with three coauthors can be daunting. This book reflects the knitting together of our individual perspectives, ideas, and approaches. Hopefully, the final product is something more than simply the sum of its parts. We also see the completion of this book as a beginning, rather than an end point. The work here represents an initial analysis and interpretation of the PNAAPS. We hope that researchers are able to use this book as a foundation on which to build a greater understanding of the position, place, and potential political power of Asian Americans in the United States, and the meanings of race, ethnicity, nativity, class, and gender in American politics.

As a study of the public opinion of a nonwhite and majority-immigrant population, our focus on issues of integration and incorporation does not suggest an uncritical acceptance of the extant political and social system. In fact, we begin the exploration by reviewing the historical formation of the Asian American community and the systematic discrimination and other structural forces that result in the disproportionally small and predominantly foreign-born characteristic of the contemporary population. Rather, our approach provides a means to gauge the extent of the gaps between American democratic principles and the reality of contemporary American life for a nonwhite community comprised mostly of immigrants. In the end, this research may contribute to a better understanding of Asian Americans and the role of race and ethnicity in American politics and public opinion.

Throughout this book, we use the term "Asian American" to refer to the respondents in our sample. We consider "Pacific Islanders" to be the indigenous people of the Melanesian (New Guinea, Fiji, and Solomon Islands), Micronesian (Guam, Northern Marianas, Republic of the Marshall Islands, Federated States of Micronesia, and Palau), and Polynesian (New Zealand, Tonga, Marquesa, Tahiti, Hawaii, and Samoa) islands in the South Pacific. Due to limited resources, our study does not explicitly include Pacific Islanders. Thus, we choose not to use the term "Asian Pacific Islander" or "Asian Pacific American" to refer to the PNAAPS sample. For purposes of consistency, we rely on the term "Asian American" or "Asian" to refer to the general U.S. population of individuals whose origins can be traced to East Asia, South Asia, South East Asia, and the Pacific Islands. Thus, the term "Asian American" could be exchanged for "Asian Pacific American," "Asian Pacific Islander," or "Asian Pacific Islander American." We recognize that Pacific Islanders comprise an important segment of the larger Asian American population in the United States.

The term "Asian Americans" is used interchangeably with "Asians" throughout the book. Except where noted, we also use "Chinese," "Japanese," "Vietnamese," "Koreans," "Filipinos," and "South Asians" to stand for "Chinese Americans," "Japanese Americans," "Vietnamese Americans," "Korean Americans," "Filipino Americans," and "Asian Indian/Pakistani Americans," respectively. We use "immigrants" to refer to those respondents born in Asia.

We also intend to clarify our usage of the term "homeland," which is used interchangeably with "country of origin." Although the survey questions on "homeland" contacts are asked only of the immigrant population, we wish to emphasize that our use of the term does not imply that the United States is less of a homeland to immigrants than their previous country or that the United States is not also a "homeland" for Asian Americans.

CHAPTER 1

Introduction

Research Question and Project Outline

The U.S. Census Bureau reports that 11.9 million people in the United States declared themselves Asian (alone or in combination with another race) in 2000. At a growth rate of 72 percent between 1990 and 2000, Asian Americans are among the nation's fastest growing populations by race.[1] This continues a demographic trend that has been observed since the liberalization of U.S. immigration policies in 1965. What is the political significance of the rapid and continuing rise of the Asian American population at the dawn of the twenty-first century? Which party do they feel closer to? Where do their political interests lie? These questions have garnered increasing attention and scrutiny from journalists and politicians in the United States in recent years, in part due to a series of high-profile events concerning international money laundering and campaign finance violations during the 1996 presidential election, and espionage charges against a Taiwan-born Chinese American nuclear scientist working for the Los Alamos National Lab. Yet the answers to date have been incomplete. Popular accounts of the present and future political impact of Asian Americans remain heavily filtered through the stereotypical lens of Asian Americans as a socioeconomically successful and politically acquiescent "model minority," or as the perpetually foreign "yellow peril" who show more interest in their Asian homelands than in American society and politics.

Who are Asian Americans? To what extent and in what ways are they becoming socially and politically incorporated? To what extent do they think and act as a collective political body? And with what theoretical and policy implications? Through the perspective of mass politics, we examine the ways in which the contemporary Asian American population is engaged in debates that involve some of the core issues affecting the shape of the American democracy, as well as identify areas where challenges to community empowerment and full participation are most likely to arise. We undertake this task by showcasing the 2000–2001 Pilot National Asian American Political Survey (PNAAPS), the nation's first multiethnic, multilingual, and multiregional political survey on Asian Americans. This dataset is designed to provide a more comprehensive answer to these central research questions than before. In addition, the PNAAPS achieves a rare feat in contemporary discussions about Asian Americans: It allows ordinary Asian Americans to speak for themselves on vital political questions. For various reasons explained elsewhere and later in the chapter, it has been very difficult to gather survey data that represent the public opinion of Asian Americans in any geopolitical scope or context. The PNAAPS is not, and does not claim to provide, an ideal solution to all of the problems involved in surveying a statistically rare, linguistically diverse, and geographically dispersed population such as Asians. In our view, however, it provides the best possible solution to date for studying the population through survey research.

In this first chapter, after a brief review of the historical and contemporary formation of the population, we present a summary report of descriptive findings to help debunk common mythical perceptions about Asian Americans, and to help reframe theoretical deliberations about the status of the population. Beginning with the second chapter, we examine the contours and sources of ethnic and panethnic (or racial) identities that characterize the contemporary Asian American population. This is followed in other chapters by explorations of the roles of U.S. and non-U.S. socialization, class, gender, ethnicity, immigration generation, homeland contacts, regional context, and political mobilization in the construction of political orientations, partisanship, electoral and nonelectoral participation, and policy preferences. For each issue addressed in the survey, we try to situate the discussion in the larger context of the U.S. census and other data. Importantly, we strive to place the reported statistics and interpretations gathered from this timely survey within the temporal and spatial contexts of discourses on race, ethnicity, gender, and culture in the United States.

In each of the main chapters, we begin with a review of theory and research in both political science and other social science disciplines, as well as in American ethnic studies, that focuses on, or is relevant for, studying Asian American political behavior. We report patterns in Asian American political attitudes and behavior using descriptive statistics from the survey. We then examine these findings with more advanced statistical techniques. To the greatest extent possible, we discuss our research within the extant body of knowledge and compare our findings to large-scale survey data collected over time, such as the American National Election Studies series (ANES, 1952–2000), the Current Population Survey Voter Supplement files (CPSVS, 1990–2000), the *Los Angeles Times* Poll Survey of Asians in Southern California (LATP, 1992–1997), and the General Social Survey (GSS, 1972–2000). Together, these data provide a unique window through which to view the experience of Asian Americans in the U.S. political system, and promise to yield results unprecedented in their diversity and depth.

Who is "Asian" American? An Evolving Population

Evolving Definitions in the U.S. Census

In a general sense, an Asian American is any Asian who resides in the United States on a permanent or long-term basis, regardless of citizenship or other legal status. The definition of who is an Asian, however, has undergone significant expansion over the last hundred and fifty years because of shifts in the racial and ethnic makeup of the U.S. population and changes in social attitudes and political concerns regarding racial and ethnic minorities. The evolving needs of the federal government for data to better address the growing diversity within minority groups and the multiple identities people may hold regarding their race and ethnicity have also resulted in significant changes in the categorization, collection, and tabulation of race and ethnicity data in the U.S. Census (Edmonston and Schultze, 1995; Lott, 1997; Espiritu and Omi, 2000).

A cursory examination of the historical evolution of the census categories into which Asians have been placed helps illustrate the evolving meanings of the term "Asian" in U.S. society and politics. In 1870, more than twenty years after the discovery of gold in California that initiated the first and significant wave of predominantly male labor migration from Asia, "Chinese" became the first Asian category to appear in the U.S. decennial census. A "Japanese" category was added in 1890, within years after banning the Chinese from entry and the subsequent recruitment of Japanese laborers to work on Hawaiian plantations. The categories for Filipinos, Asian Indians (misnamed as Hindus), and Koreans were added in 1920, but only Filipinos were listed, in addition to Chinese and Japanese, in the 1950 census.[2] The categories of Hawaiian and part Hawaiian debuted in 1960. "Korean" reemerged as a category in 1970. "Vietnamese" and "Asian Indian" joined the census definition of "Asian," as did "Guamanian" and "Samoan" for Pacific Islanders, in 1980. In 1990, an umbrella term "Asian or Pacific Islander" and "other Asian or Pacific Islander" was listed, in addition to all the subgroup categories used in 1980.

An "Asian," as defined in the 2000 Census, is a person "having origins in any of the original peoples of the Far East, Southeast Asia, or the Indian subcontinent including, for example, Cambodia, China, India, Japan, Korea, Malaysia, Pakistan, the Philippine Islands, Thailand, and Vietnam" (Office of Management and Budget, 1997). Census 2000 is the first U.S. census that permits the reporting of more than one race. It also breaks apart the "Asian or Pacific Islander" category used in the 1990 Census into two categories—one called "Asian" and the other called "Native Hawaiian or Other Pacific Islander." The latter category refers to any person "having origins in any of the original peoples of Hawaii, Guam, Samoa, or other Pacific Islands." For the purposes of this book, we focus on the "Asian alone" portion of the Asian Pacific American experiences. This emphasis does not imply that the experiences of Pacific Islanders or persons with mixed heritage are any less important than the groups we include here. Rather, the choice is based on data limitations.[3]

By and large, changes in the enumeration of the Asian American population reflect the historical and contemporary formation of the communities in America. This process has been shaped and reshaped by U.S. immigration and other related policies, U.S. race relations, political turmoil and U.S. military engagements in Asia, global labor market conditions, Asian American community activism, and other forces in global economic restructuring (Takaki, 1989; Chan, 1991; Espiritu, 1992; Hing, 1993; Ong, Bonacich, and Cheng, 1994; Okihiro,

1994, 2001; Kitano and Daniels, 1995; Min, 1995; Fong, 1998, 2002; Zhou and Gatewood, 2000; Lien, 2001b). The migration history of Asian groups in the United States clearly varies by major periods and conditions of entry. However, all those who entered prior to 1965 share a common history of overt racial and ethnic discrimination in the application of immigration and citizenship laws, as well and social and economic practices. Some of the most blatant forms of exclusion for Asian Americans were lifted when Congress replaced the racist national origin quota with the hemispheric quota system and created new immigrant preference categories in 1965.

Historical and Contemporary Community Formation—Entering One Group at a Time

The Chinese were the first Asian group that entered in large and persistent numbers. About 52,000 Chinese arrived in 1852 alone. They were lured by the prospects of finding good jobs and fortunes in the western United States. They also arrived to escape homeland problems such as overcrowding, drought, and warfare in southern China. A similar set of push and pull factors explains the early immigration of other Asian groups. Before the passage of the 1882 Chinese Exclusion Act,[4] which closed off Chinese labor migration until after the mid-twentieth century,[5] over 225,000 Chinese laborers arrived. The large and sudden influx of the "heathen Chinese" who were barred from naturalization by law,[6] coupled with language barriers, economic depression, and tight political party competition, created opportunities for politicians to pass the nation's first immigration control act based solely on ethnicity. The destruction of birth and citizenship records in the 1906 San Francisco earthquake as well as the persistent domestic social and economic problems in the politically fractured Chinese homeland had encouraged a continuous stream of Chinese nationals who often entered the United States—both during and after the exclusion era—in strategic and supra legal or illegal ways (Lai, 1992; Salyer, 1995; Kwong, 1997; Chin, 2000). In the contemporary age of globalization and transnational capitalism, the community is steadily infused by new immigrants; some arrive penniless but many others are professionals or venture capitalists. The generational and economic diversity that characterize Chinese Americans is quite unique even compared with other Asian American groups (Kwong, 1987; Wang, 1995; Lin, 1998).

Labor migration from Japan occurred in earnest around the turn of the twentieth century. It came to a halt with the passage of the 1907 Gentlemen's Agreement, in which the Japanese government agreed to stop issuing passports to laborers heading for Hawaii and the United States. In return, the U.S. government allowed the entry of family-arranged wives and brides of laborers. Thus, in the years following the Gentlemen's Agreement and before the prohibition of Japanese women immigration in the 1924 Immigration Act, the Japanese community—in contrast to the Chinese—was able to establish families and assure the continuation of generations of growth in the United States. New immigration resumed in 1952 after the passage of the McCarren-Walter Act, but the miniscule annual quota of 128 was not lifted until 1965. Nevertheless, the horrific internment experience during World War II, incidents of Japan-bashing related to U.S.-Japan trade tensions during the 1980s, and the post war prosperity in the homeland have accounted for the community's relative lack of new immigration in the second half of the twentieth century (Daniels, 1971, 1988; Weglyn, 1976; Ichioka, 1988; Takaki, 1989). The predominance of the U.S.-born is a distinctive feature of the Japanese population in present-day Asian America.

The first major wave of Korean immigration occurred in 1903 and 1905, when over 7,200 Koreans were recruited for plantation labor in Hawaii. The entry of Koreans was subject to the same restrictions placed on the Japanese after Japan's annexation of Korea in 1910. Before the passage of the 1965 Immigration Act, which lifted the miniscule annual quota set for Asian groups in 1924, Koreans entered as political exiles and war brides. Nevertheless, more than three in four of present-day Korean Americans entered the United States only after the late 1960s. Attacks against Korean merchants during the 1992 Los Angeles urban unrest, tense interracial relations between Korean green grocers and their black customers in several other cities, and progress in homeland democratization and economic development have contributed to the slowing down of Korean immigration in the 1990s (Min, 1990, 1995; Abelmann and Lie, 1995; Kim, 2000).

Asian Indians began to immigrate to the United States in large numbers in 1904. Most of the early immigrants came as farmers and laborers; a small portion came as middle-class students, elites, and political refugees. Although the majority of the population in India was Hindu, two thirds of early Indian immigrants were of the Sikh faith. The economic hardships caused by the British colonial rule as well as the prospect of enhancing the Indian independence movement were two important reasons for their emigration. Asian Indian immigration was banned after the creation by U.S. Congress of a "barred zone" in 1917, whereby natives of China, South and Southeast Asia, Afghanistan, Iran, and the Pacific and Southeast Asian Islands were targets for exclusion. Like other Asian groups except the Japanese, the majority of the present-day population arrived after 1965 as highly educated and skilled professionals or relatives of these individuals. They are part of the "brain drain" phenomenon resultant from the global economic structuring in the Pacific Rim region after World War II (Liu and Cheng, 1994; Dirlik, 1996).

Twice colonized, first by the Spanish for 350 years and then by the United States between 1898 and 1946, the Philippines became a major supplier of cheap Asian labor in the early twentieth century. The restrictions on Chinese and Japanese labor migration as well as the economic hardship in the colonized Philippines had sent over 28,000 Filipinos to seek employment on Hawaiian sugar plantations between 1907 and 1919. Because women and children were encouraged to migrate as families after the first years, Filipinos in Hawaii were able to form a stable community beginning in the 1920s. Meanwhile, over 45,000 Filipinos arrived on the West Coast to fill the need for agricultural and domestic labor. They soon formed their own unions to protect themselves from the hostility of the white-controlled labor unions. As U.S. nationals, Filipinos were able to escape immigration exclusion against Asians until the early 1930s, when Congress passed the Tydings-McDuffie Act, which granted commonwealth status to the Philippines but restricted the immigration of Filipinos to fifty persons a year.[7] Although early Filipino immigration included a relatively larger number of students, women, and children than other Asian groups, the majority members of the present-day Filipino American community are part of the new Asian immigration that has mushroomed after 1965. Like Asian Indians, most entered with a degree of English proficiency that is not available to other East Asian immigrant groups.

The Vietnamese (and other Southeast Asians) are the only major Asian American group that does not have a long history and significant presence in America prior to 1965. It is also the only major Asian American group that enters en masse as political refugees—one of the three preference categories set in the 1965 act besides persons with desirable occupational skills and close relatives of U.S. citizens and permanent residents. In 1975, following the end of the Vietnam War, about 130,000 displaced persons from South Vietnam, many professionals or social and political elites, resettled in the United States. Between 1979 and 1982, another 450,000 Indo-Chinese refugees of much more modest background arrived as a result of civil wars in Cambodia and Laos, border war between Vietnam and China, and natural disasters. More recent immigrants include the mostly biracial children of Vietnamese mothers and American fathers, and relatives of resettled refugees. Although arriving in the post-civil rights era, when racial exclusion and discrimination are outlawed, their entry as political refugees suggests that most members have suffered psychological trauma, economic hardship, family disintegration, and social displacement in far more severe ways than any other Asian groups of recent times. To them, economic survival rather than racial discrimination may be a more immediate concern in the host land. The entire community's relative recency in immigration may help anticipate their higher overall interest in and concern about homeland issues than other Asians. The overrepresentation of those under eighteen among the population also suggests that youth-related problems may be more of a concern to them than to some of the more established and older Asian American groups.

Who are Asian Americans? Confronting Popular Myths

The six major ethnic groups reviewed above represent 87.5 percent of the Asian population in Census 2000. Their voices and experiences are the focus of this study. The preceding review suggests that the present-day Asian American population cannot be readily understood as a coherent community with a singular set of history, culture, identity, and politics. Instead, it is a community with diverse origins and multiple—and oftentimes contradictory—concerns related to the variable times and modes of entry, pace of socioeconomic mobility and current status, length of personal and family history in the United States, English proficiency, international relations between the homelands in Asia, divisive "divide and conquer" labor practices, and other factors unique to each community (Lien, 2001b: 42–82). Yet, regardless of the interethnic differences across Asian American groups, they share a common perceived origin—"the Orient" (Said, 1978; Okihiro, 1994), and common experiences of being treated as one and the same—in both positive and negative ways.

As perpetually foreign "Orientals" who are alternately and sometimes simultaneously stereotyped as "the pollutant, the coolie, the deviant, the yellow peril, the model minority, and the gook" (Lee, 1999: 8), Asian Americans share a common legacy of racial exploitation in Asia and exclusion from the U.S. mainstream. They are racially triangulated vis-à-vis whites and blacks in the United States (Kim, 1999). Asian Americans are praised as a "model minority" whose "success" is due to their abilities to overcome disadvantages through hard work, family ties, and emphasis on children's education (Peterson, 1966; Sowell, 1981; Bell, 1985).[8] This stereotype assumes that the relatively high socioeconomic status of Asian Americans is due to innate cultural traits and group beliefs about the importance of education, perseverance, and family. Ignored are external forces shaping Asian American economic achievement, such as U.S. immigration policies that encourage migration among Asians with professional occupation status. The dramatic economic polarization between diverse Asian ethnic groups is also neglected. Asian American success is seen as a product of inherent group traits and values, achieved without group-based political demands. Thus, the model minority stereotype serves to oppress the political activism of other nonwhite groups. Furthermore, even when cast in a positive light, "Asian" cultural values and group characteristics serve as a marker of racial distinction from both nonwhites and whites (Kim, 1999: 118). Moreover, Asian Americans are cast as a "middleman minority" (Blalock, 1967) who function as a political buffer between the dominant and the subordinate and as a group who can be conveniently praised or scorned for their high adaptive capacity and economic success, depending on the social and political context. In addition, because of their perceived racial difference, rapid and continuous immigration from Asia, and on going détente with communist regimes in Asia, Asian Americans are construed as "perpetual foreigners" who cannot or will not adapt to the language, customs, religions, and politics of the American mainstream.

Especially in the realm of civic participation, Kim (1999) argues that these stereotypes, the "model minority" and the "perpetual foreigner," serve to both "valorize" Asian Americans relative to other minority groups and exclude Asian Americans from the social and political mainstream. Furthermore, as political actors, Asian Americans have been characterized throughout history as both hyperactive and apathetic, as well as super-threatening and super-loyal (Chang, 2001). These highly politicized and often contradictory images of the population have put Asian Americans in a precarious position accompanied by an ambivalent status in U.S. politics (Kim and Lee, 2001; Lien, 2001b). Prospects for inclusion in multiracial coalitions with other racial minority groups may be undermined because Asian Americans are viewed as a foreign community that is culturally, socially, and politically inassimilable, but also as a model minority that is unencumbered by social inequities and not in need of government assistance. The revolving and recurring images of Asian Americans as the good, the bad, and the outsider have also created a crisis of identity among some U.S.-born generation members who wish to disown their ethnic heritage and be considered "just another American" (Liu, 1998). Finally, although, many resent racialization processes that gloss over important ethnic group differences, Asian Americans share a common need to confront, protect, and advance the larger pan-Asian group interests (Espiritu, 1992). Whether or not members of the community share a common racial or ethnic identity and consciousness for political action is an empirical question to be assessed.

In the following pages, we debunk some of the prevailing myths about the population by presenting summary findings of the political attitudes and opinions of Asian Americans through a randomly drawn, large-scale sample survey, bolstered by data collected by the U.S. Census Bureau and findings from other studies.[9] We show that the experiences and status of the present-day Asian American community can be examined, represented, and understood from a number of angles. However, no matter the vantage point one adopts, it is clear that the community is neither the model minority, nor the perpetual foreigners, nor the oriental yellow peril. Rather, at the dawn of the twenty-first century, the Asian American experience can be represented by at least the following thirteen broad observations.

Observations 1–13

1. *The Asian American population is ethnically and socioeconomically diverse, with uneven population size, growth rate, and socioeconomic achievement.*

Although the Asian populations in the United States have often been lumped together as a single, undifferentiated entity by U.S. society and government, Asian American populations are made/up of people of multiple ethnic origins who encompass a wide range of population sizes, growth rates, and income and education levels.[10] A total of twenty-five distinct ethnic origins were tabulated in the Census 2000 Brief for the Asian population (Barnes and Bennett, 2002). Among the 11.9 million Asians who reported belonging to either a single ethnic origin or at least one other racial or ethnic origin in 2000, Chinese was the largest ethnic group (2.73 million), followed by Filipino (2.36 million), Asian Indian (1.90 million), Korean (1.23 million), Vietnamese (1.22 million), and Japanese

(1.15 million). Comparing these figures with the 1990 Census data, Asian Indians experienced the highest growth rate (133 percent), followed by the Vietnamese at 99 percent, the Chinese at 75 percent, Filipinos at 68 percent, Koreans at 54 percent, and the Japanese at 36 percent over the last decade. From 1990 to 2000, Asians as a population grew by 5 million or 72 percent.[11]

On the socioeconomic front, although Asian Americans were characterized by higher educational attainment and median family income than non-Hispanic whites and other racial groups in Census 2000 on average, their per capita income of $21,823 was lower than the $24,819 of non-Hispanic whites, and their percentage of persons living below poverty level (13 percent) was higher than that of non-Hispanic whites (8 percent). Among major Asian American groups in 1990, socioeconomic status varies, however. The per capita income of the Vietnamese was less than half of the Japanese; the percentage of persons living below poverty level varied between 6 percent for Japanese to 28 percent for Vietnamese Americans; that for college degree holders varied from 17 percent for Vietnamese to 58 percent for Asian Indian Americans.

2. *The Asian American community is mostly made up of the foreign-born and recent arrivals, but the majority are also U.S. citizens by naturalization or birthright.*

Seven out of ten (69 percent) Asians counted in Census 2000 were foreign-born.[12] More likely than not, these foreign-born persons are also recent arrivals. Of all the documented immigrants from Asia who entered between 1820 and 2000, every three in ten arrived after 1990, another 31 percent entered between 1981 and 1990, and 20 percent entered between 1971 and 1980 (U.S. Immigration and Naturalization Service, 2002). Among recent arrivals, or those who entered between 1991 and 2000, 528,893 (28 percent) came from China, Taiwan, and Hong Kong, 503,945 (26 percent) came from the Philippines, 363,060 (19 percent) came from India, and 286,145 (15 percent) came from Vietnam. These recent arrivals accounted for as much as 44 percent of all immigrants from India, 38 percent from Vietnam, 33 percent from the Philippines, but only 13 percent of all immigration from Japan, throughout recorded U.S. immigration history. In contrast, only 3.5 percent of the total European immigration between 1820 and 2000 entered in the 1990s and more than half (54 percent) entered between 1881 and 1920.

Although the Asian population is predominantly foreign-born, this does not mean that the majority of the population consists of foreigners or noncitizens. Longitudinal data from the Immigration and Naturalization Service (2002) show that Asian immigrants tend to become naturalized much earlier and at much higher rates than immigrants from other world regions—a phenomenon observed since the 1970s (Barkan, 1983; Portes and Rumbaut, 1996). In November elections held between 1994 and 2000, an average of 79 percent of adult Asians in the Current Population Survey (CPS) were foreign-born; an average of 46 percent of these foreign-born adult Asians were naturalized U.S. citizens.[13] Overall, close to six in ten adult Asians in these national surveys (58 percent) were U.S. citizens. In the PNAAPS, an average of three out of four adult respondents were born in Asia; 59 percent are naturalized citizens. The citizenship rate for the total sample is 68 percent, with as high as 71 percent of noncitizens expecting to become U.S. citizens in the next few years.

These statistics demonstrate that this immigrant majority population is by no means a foreign population by citizenship, and there is a strong desire to become U.S. citizens among those who are not yet citizens.

3. *The Asian American community is linguistically diverse, but most members are proficient in English.*

Of the 9.52 million Asian persons age five or over enumerated by the 2000 Census, only 21 percent did not speak a language other than English at home. This does not mean, however, that the majority of Asian Americans are non-proficient in English. In fact, about eight in ten persons who spoke other languages at home indicated that they spoke English either "well" or "very well." The same pattern is observed in the 1990 Census where the majority in each of the Asian ethnic groups, including the foreign-born segment, identified themselves as relatively fluent in the English language (Jiobu, 1996).[14]

In the PNAAPS, 26 percent of all respondents report using English, 48 percent using a language other than English, and 24 percent using a mixture of English and another language to communicate at home with other household members. Outside of the home, English use is much higher. Among all Asian American respondents, almost two-thirds (71 percent) used English to conduct personal business and financial transactions. English language use also varies greatly across different Asian American ethnic groups. English language use in the home is lowest among Vietnamese (2 percent), Chinese (4 percent), and Korean (10 percent) samples. But a much higher percentage of respondents from these groups (71 percent Koreans, 59 percent Vietnamese, and 33 percent Chinese) rely on the English language to conduct personal business and financial transactions.

4. *Rather than being politically apathetic, the Asian American community has shown a high interest in U.S. governmental and ethnic politics.*

Contrary to a public image of political docility and complacency, Asian Americans have a long history of participation in American politics. In addition to formal participation in elections, they have participated through indirect means such as lobbying, litigation, petitioning, protesting, boycotting, civil disobedience, contacting public officials and the media, and contributing to political campaigns in the United States (Lien, 2001b). The rallying points for such political activism have been rampant legal, political, economic, and social discrimination on the domestic front as well as concerns for the people and welfare of the overseas homeland. However, prior to the repeal of discriminatory immigration and naturalization laws during and after World War II, only the U.S.-born generation, the majority of whom were of Japanese origin and under the voting age, were eligible to vote. Even decades into the post-1965 era, despite monumental reforms in the nation's immigration and voting rights policies, the community's prospect for full franchise has been impeded by citizenship and voting registration requirements and by unfair electoral practices.[15]

To explore whether the apparent lack of participation by Asian Americans in the American electoral process is due to their lack of interest, participants in the PNAAPS were asked how interested they are in politics and what's going on in government in general. We find that a majority are, in fact, interested in politics. The proportion of respondents reporting that they are very interested or somewhat interested in politics ranges from 52 percent among Vietnamese respondents to 72 percent among South Asians. Overall, 61 percent of those interviewed indicate that they are either very interested or somewhat interested in what goes on in government. Only 13 percent of the respondents indicate that they are not interested in politics at all.

Their level of political interest is also indicated by the amount of attention paid to news stories regarding Asians in the United States and in Asia. Overall, 53 percent of the respondents pay either very or fairly close attention to news on Asian Americans; 13 percent indicate having paid no attention at all. Roughly eight in ten Korean and Chinese Americans pay either very or fairly close attention to news about Asian Americans, but as much as 30 percent of Vietnamese and 23 percent Japanese indicate no interest at all. A comparable distribution of interest in news about Asians in Asia is reported in the next observation.

5. *Asian Americans are concerned about politics both in their countries of origin and the United States.*

Because of their predominantly foreign-born status and the continuing influx of new immigrants from Asia, Asian Americans may have a higher interest in politics related to their home country origins than to the United States. Over half of our respondents (56 percent) report paying very close or fairly close attention to news events that happened in Asia. This attention to Asian news is particularly high among Korean (80 percent) and Chinese (68 percent) respondents. Because less than one-fourth (22 percent) of the Japanese respondents were born in Japan, they are the least likely to follow news and current events related to Asia (38 percent). It is interesting to note that, except for the Vietnamese and Filipinos, respondents are just as likely or even more likely to follow news events about Asian Americans as they are to keep up on stories about events in Asia. A much higher percentage of the Vietnamese report having paid very close or fairly close attention to news events involving people in Asia than involving Asians in the United States.

Most of the Asian immigrants who took part in the survey also maintain strong social ties with people in their countries of origin. For example, a quarter of the Asian-born sample make contacts with people back in their home country of origin (either by mail, phone, or in person) at least once a week. Among South Asians, 44 percent would contact someone in India or Pakistan at least once a week. Twenty percent of Filipino immigrants and 22 percent of Chinese and Korean immigrants also maintain contacts with people in their countries of origin at the same frequency. A large majority of respondents in each ethnic group report having contacted individuals in their country of origin at least once a month. Moreover, about a quarter of the Asian-born respondents paid their most recent visit to their country of origin less than twelve months ago; close to seven in ten immigrant respondents visited their home country within the last four years.

These connections with the country of origin do not necessarily suggest that Asian Americans are preoccupied with politics related to the Asian homeland at the expense of participation in politics in the United States. We asked the PNAAPS immigrant sample if they had ever participated in any activity dealing with the politics of their home countries after arriving in the United States. A lofty 94 percent answered "no" to the question, which ranges from 4 percent for Chinese and Korean to 10 percent for Vietnamese American respondents. These figures are much lower than the foreign-born sample's rates of voting (38 percent) and registration (46 percent) in the United States.

Taken together, these summary results suggest that interest and participation in homeland politics do not necessarily interfere with interest and participation in U.S. mainstream politics. The two may have no relationship to each other or they may mutually reinforce each other. We return to this point in a later chapter.

6. *Asian Americans are far from ignorant of the U.S. democratic system and politics, but their levels of news awareness may vary by issue and by the survey context.*

How much do Asian Americans know about the U.S. democratic system? The 2000 Florida election debacle gave us a unique opportunity to examine this question. We asked the PNAAPS respondents, both voters and nonvoters, about their familiarity with the process of electing the U.S. president. An overwhelming majority (79 percent) report either being very or somewhat familiar with the process. South Asians report the highest level of knowledge at 93 percent and the Vietnamese report the lowest level at 65 percent.

Both self-perception of knowledge and news saturation of the election outcome may account for the extremely high level of knowledge. In contrast, few respondents report knowledge of a political movement to organize the Asian American vote in the 2000 presidential election. Only about one in five respondents report having heard of the 80-20 Initiative, a nonpartisan organization that aims to increase political empowerment among Asian Americans. There is also a great deal of variance across groups in their familiarity with this campaign for pan-Asian unity, with Chinese (39 percent) and Koreans (28 percent) most familiar, and less than 10 percent of South Asians, Filipinos, and Japanese showing such familiarity. Those who are knowledgeable about 80-20 are more likely to support the group's efforts to organize Asian Americans politically.

Respondents indicate, however, a high level of awareness and concern for current community affairs dealing with Dr. Wen Ho Lee, the Taiwan-born

Chinese American nuclear scientist charged by the U.S. government with downloading "classified" data for China. Lee spent nine months in jail before the presiding judge in New Mexico dropped 58 of the 59 charges in September 2000. Roughly three out of five respondents are familiar with the Wen Ho Lee case, with Chinese (84 percent), Koreans (73 percent), and Japanese (63 percent) more familiar and South Asians (43 percent), Vietnamese (34 percent), and Filipinos (33 percent) less familiar. More than half (53 percent) of respondents who are familiar with the case disapprove of the government's handling of it, while 19 percent approve and 21 percent report no opinion on the matter. Not surprisingly, Chinese respondents are conspicuously more negative about the government's handling of the case (67 percent disapprove, 8 percent approve).

7. *Most Asian Americans vote if and when they are eligible to vote.*

Voting participation is a three-stage process that involves possessing birthright or naturalized citizenship, becoming registered to vote, and turning out to vote (Lien, Collet, Wong, and Ramakrishnan, 2001). Because of historical discrimination and continuing institutional hurdles of citizenship and voting registration requirements (see *Observation 4*), only a minority of the adult Asian American population are voters. About a quarter of adult Asians voted in elections of the 1990s, according to CPS data.[16] In the PNAAPS, 44 percent of the respondents report having voted in the November 2000 presidential election. Japanese respondents voted at the highest proportions (63 percent), compared to, say, Filipinos (47 percent), the next highest group in voting turnout. Koreans have the lowest turnout rate at 34 percent. Noncitizenship is the most commonly cited reason for not voting. This is mentioned by nearly six out of ten respondents who failed to cast a vote in the 2000 presidential election. Not having registered to vote is the second most commonly cited reason, mentioned by a quarter of the nonvoters. Not having time is the most frequent reason for those who are both citizens and registered.

When voting rates are calculated only among the eligible (citizens who are registered), 82 percent of Asians reported having voted. The turnout rate is highest among South Asians (93 percent), followed by the Vietnamese (91.5 percent). The turnout rates for Koreans and Filipinos are lower, but still fairly high at 71 percent and 76 percent respectively. (More discussion on the extent and sources of political participation among Asians is found in Chapter 5.)

These voting statistics provide a direct and clear set of evidence of Asian Americans' desire to become politically integrated and vote. Their low overall voting levels do not reflect apathy, but are mostly due to lack of satisfaction with the citizenship and voter registration requirements. Once these institutional constraints are overcome, some may vote at rates higher than non-Latino whites, who traditionally vote at the highest rates of any major racial or ethnic group (Lien, 2000, 2001b).

8. *Among Asian Americans donating to political campaigns is not among the most popular acts of participation other than voting; community work is the most common form.*

Past research suggests that a combination of relative affluence, strong home-land connections, and lack of U.S. citizenship and the vote may compel the politically interested among Asians to rely on checkbooks rather than ballots to express their political opinions (Nakanishi, 1991, 1998; Erie and Brackman, 1993). Although this observation refers to the behavior of a small number of in-dividuals, one might jump to the mistaken conclusion that a majority of Asians, especially the foreign-born, make more frequent use of political donations than other means of political expression to influence U.S. politics. Extensive news coverage of illegal Asian money pouring into the 1996 presidential campaign and subsequent congressional hearings certainly helped feed this image (Wu and Nicholson, 1997; Wang, 1998).

When the PNAAPS respondents were asked if they had ever participated in a variety of political activities in their community other than voting during the preceding four years, only 12 percent of all Asians report having donated money to a political campaign. The most common mode of political partici-pation reported was working with others in the community to solve a problem (21 percent), followed by signing a petition for a political cause (16 percent), and attending a public meeting, political rally, or fundraiser (14 percent). Among donors, it is Japanese (20 percent), rather than Chinese (8 percent), who are more likely to report such participation. Moreover, the percentage of donors among the foreign-born (10 percent) is lower than the percentage among the U.S.-born (17 percent)—a pattern true with practically all types of political activities except for voting among the naturalized. Last but not least, while past research has emphasized donations to political campaigns as an important aspect of Asian American political behavior (Nakanishi, 1998; cho, 2001; Lai, Cho, Kim, and Takeda, 2001), both non-Latino whites and blacks are observed to report higher rates of campaign contributing than do the Asian Americans in the PNAAPS (Uhlaner, Cain, and Kiewiet, 1989; Verba, Schlozman, and Brady 1995; Lien, 1997).

9. *Most Asian Americans do not live a clannish, segregated social life but are part of an interracial social network.*

We use three measures to indicate respondents' degree of interracial connec-tions: crossracial friendships, perceived racial make up of their neighborhood, and approval of intermarriage. Contrary to the "clannish" profile (Lee, 1999), most respondents in the survey are part of an interracial social network. In terms of crossracial friendships, though many respondents (46 percent) men-tion having a close friend who is Asian, 31 percent mention having a close friend who is white, 27 percent mention having a close friend who is black, and 26 percent report having a close friend who is Latino, also.[17] Close to half of the respondents report living in a pretty evenly mixed-race neighborhood

(45 percent). A quarter of the respondents report having mostly white neighbors, but less than 5 percent of them report having mostly black or mostly Latino neighbors. Only one-fifth of the respondents reside in mostly Asian neighborhoods (20 percent). In fact, a dissimilarity index study shows that, compared to other nonwhite groups, Asians hold the highest level of residential integration with whites nationwide (Hum and Zonta, 2000).

When queried about their attitudes about someone in their family marrying a person of different ethnic background than their own, few respondents express disapproval (11 percent). The highest disapproval rate of 24 percent is found among Koreans. The lowest disapproval rates are found among Japanese (4 percent), Filipinos (5 percent), and Vietnamese (7 percent). In fact, close to three quarters of the respondents from these three groups either approve or strongly approve of intermarriage, which is higher than the average response of 54 percent among all. None of the results suggest that Asians only make friends with, live near, or support marriage to others within the ethnic community alone.

10. Each ethnic community within Asian American populations has a unique set of issues and priorities, but all share concerns about racial discrimination.

When asked to mention the most important problem facing their respective ethnic community, mentions of specific issue concerns and issue priorities seem to vary by ethnic community. For the Chinese, the top community issues include language barriers, racial and ethnic relations, and unemployment or inadequate job opportunities. For Koreans, many share a concern over language, but they are also concerned about the lack of cohesion inside the community and problems dealing with teenagers. Vietnamese respondents prioritize their concerns over gangs, drugs, employment, and housing opportunities. Yet, at least four out of ten Japanese (49 percent), South Asians (47 percent), and Filipinos (41 percent) report seeing no problem facing their respective ethnic community, while at least another 20 percent of respondents in these ethnic groups are unsure if there is a problem. When a problem is reported, the most frequently mentioned among the Japanese is discrimination; for Filipinos, language barriers and the break down of family structures; for South Asians, unemployment or job opportunities.

Importantly, although English-speaking respondents of Japanese, Filipino, and South Asian descent are much less likely to identify community problems as an important political concern, they are not less likely to report being a victim of hate crimes. Between 15 to 19 percent of respondents in these three communities had been verbally or physically abused or had properties damaged due to racial- or ethnic-based discrimination. Neither are members of these three communities less likely to report ever being personally discriminated in the United States. An average of four in ten respondents from each ethnic group have experienced racial and ethnic discrimination. Thus, even though each of the ethnic communities may face a different degree and type of problems, all share concerns about racial discrimination.

11. Asian Americans are ideologically moderate and identify more as Democrat than as Republican, but up to half do not identify with either of the major parties.

Are Asian Americans more likely to consider themselves conservative or liberal? Overall, 36 percent of the PNAAPS respondents classify themselves as either very or somewhat liberal, 32 percent as middle of the road, and 22 percent as somewhat or very conservative. When asked about their party affiliations, 36 percent of the respondents identify themselves as Democrat, 14 percent as Republican, and 13 percent as Independent. Critically, overall 20 percent do not think of themselves in partisan terms and 18 percent are either uncertain about their party identification or refuse to give a response. Put another way, half of Asian Americans in the survey do not identify with a major American political party. Among independents, a higher percentage lean toward the Democratic party (32 percent) than the Republican party (21 percent); again, close to half refuse to think in traditional partisan terms.

Group differences exist in patterns of party affiliation. Between the two major parties in the United States, Japanese (40 percent to 9 percent), Chinese (32 percent to 8 percent) and South Asians (44 percent to 13 percent) are most likely to affiliate with the Democratic Party over the Republican Party. Filipinos and Koreans favor the Democratic Party over the Republican Party by a two-to-one margin. Only Vietnamese identify more as Republican than as Democrat (15 percent to 12 percent).

At the dawn of the twenty-first century it is clear that the majority of Asian Americans are neither conservative in political ideology nor Republican in political party identification. In terms of political ideology, they are most likely to be middle of the road and more likely to be liberal than conservative. In terms of political partisanship, they are most likely to have none and, among those who did exhibit partisanship, they are more likely to be Democrats than Republicans. They are the "median voters" whose attitudes sit squarely between the attitudes of whites and those of other minorities; they are also a genuine swing group whose votes are not bound by a strong sense of partisanship (Cho and Cain, 2001).

12. Asian Americans are not necessarily politically fragmented, but evidence of their tendency to vote as an ethnic bloc is not compelling.

We assess the evidence of Asian Americans' tendency to vote as a bloc with two questions in the PNAAPS. The first is presidential vote choice among voters in the November 2000 election. In this historic election, 55 percent of Asian American voters report casting a vote for Al Gore, 26 percent for George Bush, and 1 percent for Ralph Nader. Eighteen percent of respondents either refuse to report their vote choice or are not sure.[18] The percentage of voters favoring Gore ranges from 44 percent among Koreans to 64 percent among the Chinese. Nevertheless, Gore receives a higher proportion of the presidential vote than Bush in every ethnic group. Although of all Asian ethnic groups in our survey Vietnamese voters report the highest percentage of support for Bush (35 percent), it is almost 20 percentage points below the group's support for Gore (54 percent). Among respondents who report their vote for president, two-thirds prefer Al Gore to George Bush. Support for Gore is highest among Japanese and Chinese Americans, who favor Gore to Bush by more than a three-to-one margin.

The second question, asked of all the respondents, voters or not, is a hypothetical scenario on candidate choice between an Asian or a non-Asian, when the two are equally qualified. Sixty percent of respondents answered favorably for the Asian candidate; support is especially high among the Vietnamese, Chinese, and Korean respondents. When these respondents are asked of their willingness to vote for an Asian American, even if he or she is less qualified, only a quarter answer affirmatively to this and support is particularly low among the Vietnamese. This suggests that, for current or potential Asian American voters, ethnicity may be an important factor in vote choice, but candidate quality may be an even more important consideration.

13. Most Asian Americans prefer ethnic- rather than panethnic-based identities, but they show evidence of panethnic solidarity in policy concerns affecting the minority community.

A crucial challenge for any emergent community is the development of a sense of common fate among rank-and-file members. Do average Asian Americans share a common sense of identity? We assess this issue by asking a set of questions on (pan)ethnic self-identity, perceived shared culture, and (pan)ethnic shared fate. First, given a choice of identifying oneself as American, Asian American, Asian, ethnic American (e.g., as Chinese American), or simply in terms of one's ethnic origin (e.g., as Chinese), the PNAAPS respondents are most apt to indicate an ethnic-specific identity. Among all respondents, 34 percent choose to identify as ethnic American and 30 percent by ethnic origin alone. Only 15 percent identify themselves as "Asian American" and 12 percent as "American." However, when respondents who do not choose "Asian American" are asked to indicate if they have *ever* thought of themselves as Asian American, about half of respondents report such panethnic identification. Thus, cumulatively, close to six out of ten respondents may identify with the panethnic "Asian American" label in some contexts. This panethnic identification is most strongly felt among South Asians and least strongly among Koreans and Japanese.

We also examine panethnic group identity as a function of having a sense of shared culture among Asians and a sense of common destiny with fellow Asians (see more in Chapter 2). Typically, about half of respondents see different Asian groups in America as culturally very or somewhat similar to each other. An equal proportion of respondents believe that what happened generally to other groups of Asians in the United States would impact what happened in their life.

A third window into the sense of common identity among Asians is their public policy concerns. Respondents were queried about their opinion on language policy, immigration, affirmative action, and campaign contributions. We find that Asian Americans are decidedly supportive of affirmative action policies, campaign contributions by legal permanent residents, and bilingual provision of government services and public information to immigrant communities. Seventy percent who report an opinion on affirmative action are in favor of it; 73 percent favor bilingual services and public information; respondents approve rather than disapprove of political contributions by legal immigrants by more than a two-to-one margin. On immigration, a plurality of Asian Americans (45 percent) support a quota on legal immigration to the United States, but up to a third do not have a preference or an opinion.

Thus, although indicators of panethnicity provide some evidence of a sense of common identity and consciousness among the mass Asian Americans, advocates for solidarity will find greater hope in their policy orientations. Given the strength of the ethnic-specific orientation and the tremendous heterogeneity within the Asian American community, these results not only provide grounds for optimism about the possibilities of forming a pan-ethnic coalition among Asian Americans, but, more importantly, they spell out areas of challenges and the need for political leadership to address these challenges.

These analyses of summary statistics show that, at the dawn of the twenty-first century, Asian Americans are ethnically and racially diverse, socially connected with other groups in American society, and are interested in becoming politically integrated into the U.S. mainstream. Although most immigrants maintain a strong ethnic bond with homeland cultures and peoples and are more concerned about language barriers than other issues, the majority of community members do not show a deficiency in using English outside of the home nor a greater interest or involvement in homeland politics. Rather, an overwhelming majority of Asian Americans believe they are informed politically, show some or higher interest in U.S. than in homeland politics, pay attention to news regarding Asians on both sides of the Pacific, and turn out to vote once they have met the citizenship and voter registration requirements. Among those who are citizens and registered to vote, the majority are not fragmented, but exhibit similar patterns in terms of voting behavior and political attitudes. Far from belonging to a monolithic, issue-free community, members in each ethnic group have a different degree and set of issue concerns, but they also share a similar level of experience with racial and ethnic discrimination. Although most prefer an ethnic-specific rather than a panethnic identity, the majority respondents are also amenable to the panethnic Asian American label under certain conditions. The potential for unity is shown as well in their favoring the election of political candidates of Asian American descent and public policies addressing the concerns and needs of the nonwhite immigrant community.

Unique Challenges and Opportunities for Studying the Mass Political Behavior of Asian Americans

Debating Conceptual Frameworks

How distinct is the Asian American experience? To what extent can the Asian American experience be understood with the extant theoretical frameworks developed to explain and predict the social and political incorporation of ethnic and racial minority Americans? From the perspectives of both their historical entries into America and the contemporary community opinion as expressed in the data reported above, Asian Americans comprise a population and an electorate that are historically, socially, culturally, politically, and ideologically distinct from both the majority white and each of the major nonwhite populations.[19] It follows that the present-day political attitudes and behavior of this rapidly expanding and majority-immigrant population may not be readily understood with any of the conventional conceptual frameworks informed mostly by studying the native-born, non-Hispanic white population and their European ancestors (e.g., assimilation). Neither may it be studied with theories informed by observing the experiences of black Americans, including the native-born descendants of former black slaves or black immigrants from Africa or the West Indies (e.g., racism and racial segregation). Nor may it be interpreted with hypotheses formulated by studying the indigenous population native to the North American continent or immigrants from today's Mexico and South and Central America (e.g., internal colonialism or two-tiered pluralism). Contemporary Asian immigration is either voluntary or, for political refugees, semivoluntary. For the most part, their history of becoming American cannot by explained by forced entry, as in the case of black slavery or Mexican annexation or internal colonization.[20] They do not suffer from the same types of persistent income inequality and de facto social segregation as a result of past and present prejudice and legalized discrimination as experienced by other nonwhite minorities. Furthermore, they appear to be more culturally diverse than other major U.S. racialized groups—all of which encompass considerable ethnic, religious, and linguistic diversity—because no particular language, religion, or other elements of culture dominates the much-evolved Asian America of the present day.

Nonetheless, and importantly, the diverse origins and destinies of the Asian American population also provide an ideal group for studying debates about the continuing significance of race, ethnicity, nativity, and class as well as the openness of the U.S. society and system to incorporate a relatively affluent, predominantly foreign-born, and nonwhite population. To what extent and in what ways are Asian Americans similar to or different from the experiences of other major American racial and ethnic groups? Below, we introduce a number of leading conceptual frameworks that intend to capture the processes of social adaptation and political incorporation among immigrants and nonwhite

Americans. We then assess their adequacy in understanding the Asian American experience.

Assimilation/Acculturation

For European immigrants and their descendants, the prevailing paradigm used to describe their American experiences is assimilation, which prescribes uninterrupted social mobility and acceptance over time. Classic theories posit that old ways associated with the country of origin and ethnic community will eventually be replaced with new "American" ways (Park, 1928; Warner and Srole, 1945). Assimilation theory assumes that distinct ethnic groups will eventually share a common culture over time and achieve access to the social, economic, and political institutions of society. One key aspect of assimilation theory is that adaptation to the host society is linear (and one-way) across all dimensions of American life (for a good discussion of this assumption, see Rumbaut, 1997). Thus, in terms of political assimilation, as immigrants learn English and move up the socioeconomic ladder, they would also be expected to adopt an "American" identity, abandon their attachments to the country of origin, and move into the mainstream political arena.

This dominant paradigm has been revisited and revised over time to reflect the reality of the persistence of ethnicity, the existence of group-based discrimination, as well as the differential rates of incorporation in different spheres of social and political life (Park, 1950; Glazer and Moynihan, 1963; Gordon, 1964; Alba and Nee, 1997; Rumbaut, 1997). In particular, its presumption of equal opportunities for all in a fair and open democratic system cannot be supported by a cursory reading of U.S. history, and its legacy of institutional discrimination based on race, ethnicity, gender, class, religion, and other social attributes (e.g., Dinnerstein, Nichols, and Reimers, 1996; Smith, 1997; Feagin and Feagin, 1999). Moreover, even if the prediction of acculturation and amalgamation may ring true for some, success in one adaptation stage does not automatically lead to success in another or the natural abandonment of homeland or ethnic ties. More importantly, the a priori assertion and privileging of a dominant U.S. mainstream culture have relegated all non-White Anglo Saxon Protestant cultures, including Asian-influenced cultures, to a second-tier or lower place in American society and disregarded their experiences as racial minorities.

Segmented Assimilation

One response from critics of the assimilation paradigm is segmented assimilation, which posits that assimilation in America may lead to different outcomes depending on group resources and settlement contexts. Segmented assimilation theories recognize that the society into which distinct groups enter is segregated and unequal (Portes and Zhou, 1993). It proposes that identification with certain American subcultures, for instance, may be associated with limited socioeconomic mobility (Gans, 1992; Portes and Rumbaut, 2001). Instead of a straight-line model, proponents of segmented assimilation argue that ethnic identity and economic success should be decoupled. The theory posits three major trajectories: upward economic mobility and the shedding of distinctive group traditions and cultural practices; downward economic mobility and the development of an "oppositional culture;" and upward economic mobility and the retention of group values and practice (Zhou, 1997). The adaptation pattern exhibited by a group will depend in large part on social and residential class context.

For immigrant groups entering with a strong family, ethnic networks, access to capital, and few ties to American nonwhite groups, resisting acculturation may provide better economic opportunities for the second generation (Portes and Zhou, 1994). For immigrant groups that face severe discrimination and limited socioeconomic mobility, and who possess strong social ties to nonwhite natives, Americanization may suggest the development of adversarial or oppositional identities (Portes and Bach, 1985; Portes and Rumbaut, 1996, 2001). However, for the U.S.-born, more experience with or perceptions of racial and ethnic discrimination may forge the development of "reactive ethnicity," which in turn may mobilize participation for ethnic causes.

Segmented assimilation theory often presumes that the experience of Asian Americans in the United States is an example of the last trajectory: upward economic mobility coupled with the retention of group values and cultural practices. In fact, the retention of group norms and values is thought to be critical for economic advancement and educational achievement among some Asian American groups (Caplan, Whitmore, and Choy, 1989; Rumbaut, 1997). The assumption of an embedded cultural advantage for certain nonwhite immigrant groups has opened up the segmented assimilation approach to criticism because of the theory's unfounded assumptions about both immigrants and urban black Americans who live in poverty. In particular, the behavior of immigrants is compared with or juxtaposed against an image of poor urban blacks that is based on stereotypes about their pathological behavior and perpetuates notions about a black "culture of poverty" (Tang, 2000).

Transnationalism

One assumption embedded in the assimilation theory is that ties to the homeland inhibit some ethnic groups' integration into American life (Zhou, 2001: 199). Connections to the country of origin are expected to fade over generations and time as groups shed their old orientations for new ones (Dahl, 1961). Although many European immigrants did not actually return to their countries of origin, according to some researchers, first-generation European immigrants were not interested in American politics because they were focused on their homelands and the idea of returning to their countries of origin in the future (Portes and Rumbaut, 1996). The sole goal of these peasants was to save enough money so as to buy land in their home villages back in Europe (Portes and

Rumbaut, 1996: 101). The idea that preoccupation with the country of origin interferes with interest in American politics continues to have currency in studies of contemporary immigrant groups (Harles, 1993; Portes and Rumbaut, 1996: 108).

Both acculturation and segmented assimilation espouse "a container concept of space—adaptation of immigrants within nation-states is considered to be a process not significantly influenced by border-crossing transactions" (Faist, 2000: 200). Some have thus suggested abandoning the ideas of acculturation and assimilation altogether, adopting instead notions of transnational boundaries and diasporic cultures to explain the experiences of recent practitioners of international migration (Gilroy, 1993; Glick-Schiller, Basch, Blanc-Szanton, 1995; Dirlik, 1996, 1998; Lowe, 1996). Because of technological change and global economic restructuring, immigrants do not make an abrupt change from one society to another by abandoning social ties to the homeland altogether.[21] Instead, people frequently maintain strong social, economic, symbolic, and political transnational ties that enable the formation of multiple identities, particularly in nation-states with multicultural or polyethnic rights.

There have been critiques of the transnational perspective. Waters' (1999) study of black West Indian immigrants, for example, raises doubts regarding the formation of a deterritorialized, universal identity. In fact, her research finds transnationalists' claims to be quite exaggerated. Although most of her informants had not become citizens and maintained close contacts with their homelands, they mostly wanted to be seen as American and most did not see themselves as loyal to their homelands. However, the high ambition and expectations of West Indians to be accepted as equal Americans were swamped over time by the structural realities of American race relations.

Panethnicization and Racial Formation

To understand the possibilities of a pan-Asian American community or any American community that contains a multiplicity of ethnicities and cultures, proponents of racial formation and panethnicity stress the role of the state and organized opposition to that state in structuring ethnicity over the influence of socioeconomic status and transnational forces. They conceive of ethnic or racial group formation as an unfixed, elastic phenomenon that is formed through the interaction between subjective identification and objective conditions and is constantly shaped and reshaped by social, cultural, legal, and political forces in the environment (Lopez and Espiritu, 1990; Omi and Winant, 1994; Espiritu and Omi, 2000). Through racial lumping, racial violence, and bureaucratic racial categorization, as well as through panethnic organizing by community-based or candidate-centered organizations, previously unconnected and ethnically distinct peoples may find themselves forging a sense of belonging to the imposed larger, panethnic community out of political and situational needs (Espiritu, 1992; Lai, 2000; Lien, 2001b; Ngin and Torres, 2001). The assumption of this theory for mass politics is that internalized racial experiences may be transformed into group consciousness and serve as a catalyst for community mobilization. By nature, panethnicity is contingent upon both situational and personal factors. By definition, it is not set to account for the variations across groups of individuals or segments of the population, such as between women and men or between the U.S.- and the foreign-born in their reactions to racial experiences.

This brief review suggests that each of these theoretical frameworks presents both possibilities and limitations in terms of understanding the Asian American political experience. On the one hand, summary statistical accounts reported earlier in the chapter profile an American ethnic community in which a substantial portion of the population is socially connected, culturally adapted, and politically interested, informed, and engaged, while maintaining a high level of ethnic-specific identities and high volume of contacts with homeland people and culture. The pluralistic group outlook provides some evidence of support for the assimilationists' claim of an open society in the contemporary era as well as the desire for the majority of the community to become incorporated into the American system. Transnationalism receives initial support in the evidence of the high levels of contact immigrants maintained with peoples and cultures in their respective homeland and subsequent differences across ethnic groups on many opinion fronts. The persistence of group-specific differences and experiences of group-based discrimination suggest support for segmented assimilation's argument of the need to decouple economic success and ethnic group identity. Last but not least, the rather common experience of racial discrimination and unified political orientations among the politically engaged also suggest support for the possibility of a racialized, panethnic group identity and consciousness.

On the other hand, the preliminary report of survey findings contains grounds for suspicion about the adequacy of each of the traditional frameworks for explaining the Asian American experience. To begin with, the experience of Asian Americans in the political sphere appears to challenge the assimilationists' assumptions of a linear progression across multiple aspects of American life. While Asian Americans have made substantial progress in terms of average economic and educational attainment, they continue to struggle for acknowledgement and representation in the American political system, especially through mass politics. Despite the higher median income reported by Asian Americans than other major racial groups (see *Observation 1*), their aggregate participation in the most common of political activities, voting, remains the lowest of any major racial group among the voting age population (see *Observation 7*).[22] Their lack of political representation in the American system is not anticipated by segmented assimilation, which extols Asian Americans for their ability to benefit from culture-based strengths. Moreover, transnationalism's assumption of immigrants' continuing interest and involvement in homeland political issues is also suspect because discussion in *Observation 5* shows that, although Asian immigrants maintain a high level of homeland contact, their interest and participation in homeland politics is much lower than their interest and participation in American electoral politics. Finally, despite the coercive forces of racialization and assimilation within the U.S. context, evidence shown in *Observation 13* suggests that panethnic self identity among contemporary Asian Americans is still a rare thing, compared to the popularity of ethnic-specific identities.

Can the political attitudes and behavior of Asian Americans be understood within the context of the traditional theoretical frameworks reviewed? This preliminary appraisal shows that, although each of the conceptual approaches may illuminate some aspect of Asian American politics, none of the aforementioned theoretical frameworks provides a sufficient basis for interpreting the multi-faceted dynamics contained in contemporary Asian American experiences. We do not deny the potential contribution of each of the extant frameworks to explain some aspects of the Asian American experience. However, the combined and uneven progress of the population in economic, social, and political fronts points to the special need to reappraise and disentangle the effects of factors such as race, ethnicity, class, gender, immigration generation, and citizenship on the political attitudes and behavior of Asian Americans. A focus on the contours, sources, and impacts of the social and political identities, orientations, and participation of Asian Americans presents unique opportunities to advance understanding of the dynamics of the interplay of these factors in structuring the adaptation and incorporation concerning a non-European and largely non-native population. The profound diversity within the Asian American population also stipulates the need of a composite theoretical model that incorporates features of the aforementioned frameworks to help answer the questions raised. In the chapters to follow, the relative efficacy of these conceptual frameworks and the unique contribution of the specific components within each framework in understanding the various aspects of Asian American public opinion are examined. We discuss the theoretical underpinnings of our findings in the concluding chapter.

Overcoming Practical Difficulties in Research Methodology with the PNAAPS

In addition to the need to identify a viable conceptual framework or at least a set of useful factors in interpreting Asian American political attitudes and behavior, researchers of the Asian American population also face challenges in the practical difficulties of scientifically studying a statistically small and extremely diverse population. Minimally, the population can be characterized as diverse along cleavages of race, ethnic origin, nationality, socioeconomic status, place of settlement, residential patterns, religious orientations, out-marriage rates, and home language use. Each of these characteristics adds a layer of difficulty in survey research design, and collectively these difficulties have been used as an excuse to not include any Asians or a large enough number of Asians for analysis in conventional large-scale sample surveys. Consequently, past studies of Asian American political behavior have relied on case studies and other research methods that investigate either only a specific segment of the adult population who reside in a certain locality or localities or with a very limited scope and number of research questions.[23]

To advance understanding of the political attitudes and behavior of this rapidly growing and uniquely diverse population en masse and to permit hypothesis-testing, it is imperative to adopt a scientific research design based on notions of randomization and representation to improve the validity and reliability of results. The *PNAAPS* is designed to address some of the above-mentioned challenges in researching Asian Americans. It strives to achieve the best possible alternative of a nationally representative sample given the population and available resources by surveying a broad spectrum of social and political attitudes and activities across six major Asian American groups who reside in the five major communities of the Asian American population. In fact, the *PNAAPS* is the nation's first survey dataset of its kind to help us comprehend the political world of Asian Americans and their potentials in shaping the future of American racial and ethnic politics. Presented below is a description of the survey methodology, followed by a discussion of the limitations of the survey approach in general and those specific to this research. Next, we introduce the survey respondents by profiling some of their major attributes.

Description of Survey Methodology

A total of 1,218 adults of Chinese, Korean, Vietnamese, Japanese, Filipino, and South Asian descent residing in the Los Angeles, New York, Honolulu, San Francisco, and Chicago metropolitan areas were randomly selected and interviewed by phone between November 16, 2000 and January 28, 2001. Households with telephones in these five metropolitan areas—chosen for their large Asian ethnic populations, geographic location, and concentration of particular ethnic groups—were sampled using a dual-frame approach consisting of random-digit dialing (RDD) at targeted Asian zipcode densities and listed-surname frames. Only households with telephones occupied by adults self-identified as belonging to one of the six major Asian American ancestries were included in this study. For our New York and Chicago samples only the listed-surname approach was used. Within each sampling area, the selection probability for each ethnic sample was to approximate the size of the ethnic population among Asian Americans according to the 1990 Census. However, we over-sampled Vietnamese and South Asian populations to generate sufficiently large sample sizes. Within each contacted household, the interviewer would ask to speak with an adult eighteen years of age or older who most recently had a birthday. To increase the response rate, multiple call attempts were made at staggered times of the day and days of the week, with break-offs and refusals recontacted.

This design yielded a final sample of 308 Chinese, 168 Korean, 137 Vietnamese, 198 Japanese, 266 Filipino, and 141 South Asians or an average of 200 completed interviews from each Metropolitan Statistical Area (MSA) and an additional 217 interviews from the Los Angeles metropolitan area. Based on the English proficiency rate of each Asian subgroup and practical cost concerns, English was used to interview respondents of Japanese, Filipino, and South Asian descent; respondents of Chinese, Korean, and Vietnamese descent were interviewed in their language of preference. Among the Chinese, 78 percent chose to be interviewed in Mandarin Chinese, 19 percent in Cantonese, and 3 percent in English. Close to 9 out of 10 Koreans (87 percent) chose to be interviewed in Korean. Nearly all Vietnamese respondents (98.5 percent) chose to be interviewed in Vietnamese. The average interview length is 27 minutes for interviews conducted in the respondent's non-English language and 20 minutes for interviews conducted in English. The average incidence rate for interviews drawn from the listed surname sample is 41 percent, with a range from 14.5 percent for the Filipino sample to 81 percent for the Chinese sample. The incidence rate for RDD interviews is 15 percent, which ranges from 4.6 percent for the Korean to 24 percent for the Japanese sample. The average refusal rate is 25 percent, with 34 percent in the listed sample and 3.5 percent in the RDD sample.

Limitations of the Survey

The margin of sampling error for the general sample in this survey is plus or minus 3 percentage points. The margin of error is higher for certain subgroups. In addition to random errors innate to a scientific survey, the representativeness of the PNAAPS may be limited by the sampling design, which may omit households with unlisted telephone numbers or persons who do not bear identifiable surnames in the targeted study areas. Samples generated with the RDD frame may not allow coverage of households located in zip codes that rank below the top ten ethnic density areas or with less than 10 percent ethnic density for a targeted Asian subgroup in each zip code. In addition, because a survey is often a snapshot of the public opinion at the time when the interviews took place, the views expressed may be affected by what happened in the environment. For example, because our survey was fielded right after the 2000 presidential election, respondents' views on their presidential choice may be impacted by events in Florida.[24] More generally, survey response has been known to be susceptible to the specific race and gender of the interviewer and the way a question is worded, ordered, and translated.

While every effort has been made to generate data that is as valid and reliable as possible, we acknowledge the likely existence of the following imperfections and ask readers to use caution when making inferences about the results: (1) the sample size remains modest for certain subgroups, in particular, Vietnamese, South Asians, and Koreans; (2) our multilingual interviews are not available for Filipino, South Asian, and Japanese respondents; (3) the PNAAPS only surveys the opinions of Asian Americans, and the implications of our findings vis-á-vis interracial politics and race relations would be improved with samples of African Americans, Latinos, and whites; (4) our sample draws from five major population centers, which obviously limits our ability to draw inferences about Asians in the United States writ large; (5) finally, the allocation of ethnic quotas in our sampling design is based on information in the 1990 Census (but see below for the extent of this bias).

To assess how representative our sample is of the Asian American population, we compare the percentage distribution of selected demographic variables in the PNAAPS to those reported by the U.S. Census (see Table 1.1). Overall, the Asian population in the five MSAs surveyed accounted for 37 percent of its nationwide population in 1990. Although direct comparison is not theoretically possible because of differences in racial counting and categorization between the two data sources, we find that the demographic characteristics of our sample generally approximate the Asian (and Pacific Islander) population structure found in the 1990 census. Typical of opinion surveys, our adult-only sample is better educated, older, and has a higher percentage of foreign-born people than in the census (Groves and Kahn, 1979; Groves et al., 1988). There's an underrepresentation of females among the South Asian and Vietnamese samples. Importantly, except for the Japanese, our sample respondents do not necessarily have higher family income than found in the 1998 Current Population Survey among adults of the first two immigration generations. However, the distribution of ethnic group makeup in each MSA and the rank orderings of ethnic groups in educational achievement, family, income, citizenship, and immigrant naturalization are similar in both data sources.

Who Participated in the Survey? A Profile of Respondents

The survey respondents are of multiple Asian ethnic origins and from five major cities around the nation with sizable Asian American populations. One-third reside in Los Angeles, the rest are equally distributed in San Francisco, Chicago, New York, and Honolulu. Exactly one-fourth of the respondents are of Chinese descent; of them, about seven out of ten can trace their ancestral homes to Mainland China, about two out of ten originated from Taiwan, and about one-tenth were from Hong Kong. Over one-fifth of the respondents are of Filipino descent (22 percent); one-sixth are of Japanese descent (16 percent), and the rest are of Korean (14 percent), South Asian (12 percent), and Vietnamese (11 percent) descent. Most of Korean, Vietnamese, and Filipino respondents reside in the Los Angeles area. About six out of ten Chinese respondents reside in either Los Angeles or San Francisco. Close to half of all Japanese respondents reside in Honolulu and 39 percent of South Asians reside in the Chicago area.

Table 1.1 Comparing Distribution of Demographic Characteristics across Major Asian American Groups between the 1990 Census and the PNAAPS

	CHINESE		FILIPINO		JAPANESE		KOREAN		INDIAN		VIETNAMESE	
	(a)	(b)	(a)	(b)	(a)	(b)	(a)	(b)	(a)	(b)	(a)	(b)
percent among Asians	27	25	23	22	14	16	13	14	13	12	10	11
median age	32	44	31	36	37	49	29	44	29	33	26	43
percent female	50	54	54	48	54	56	56	56	46	41	47	36
percent citizen	61	61	70	79	76	86	57	55	50	50	54	66
percent foreign-born	69	91	64	68	32	21	73	94	75	86	80	98
percent Education (for Census, among Persons 25-Years-Old and Over)												
less than 9th grade	17	9	10	1	6	1	10	6	7	1	20	7
9th–12th grade	10	6	7	2	7	5	10	2	8	1	19	15
high school graduate	15	20	16	16	26	16	25	18	12	6	18	33
some college	18	13	27	28	27	27	21	10	15	18	26	11
bachelor's degree	41	50	39	45	35	44	35	59	58	69	17	33
percent Earned Family Income, 1997*												
less than $20k	21	20	12	10	21	7	18	20	13	14	22	34
$30k–39,999	9	15	16	15	15	18	20	16	7	11	9	25
$40k–59,999	17	12	25	33	16	29	10	17	23	27	28	14
more than 60k	37	28	35	31	33	35	34	31	50	39	30	19

Note: Entries under column (a) are figures from the 1990 census; those under column (b) are figures from the PNAAPS.

Source: U.S. Bureau of the Census (1993, Tables 1, 3–5).

*Reported by adults of the first two immigration generations in U.S. Bureau of the Census (1998).

Nativity and Immigration Generation.   The majority of the respondents were born in Asia (76 percent), 14 percent of all respondents were U.S.-born but have Asian-born parents, another 10 percent were, along with their parents, born in the United States. Less than one-fourth (22 percent) of the Japanese respondents, however, were born in Japan and over four in ten among them are of the third generation or more. The Filipino sample is the only other group that includes 10 percent or more third generation respondents. Overall, 91 percent of Chinese, 94 percent of Koreans, 98 percent of Vietnamese, 86 percent of South Asians, and 68 percent of Filipinos or an average of three in four respondents were born in Asia.

Length of U.S. Stay.   For the U.S.-born, their length of U.S. stay is equal to their age (see below). For the foreign-born, the average number of years they live in the United States on a permanent basis is 13 years, with about half of the respondents living in the United States for at least 10 years. Japanese immigrants have the longest overall U.S. stay of 17 years; South Asians have the shortest overall U.S. stay of 11 years. Both Chinese and Vietnamese immigrants report an average U.S. stay of 12 years.

Length of Local Residence.   The respondents lived an average of 12.8 years in their present city or town. The average length for the Japanese is significantly higher at 26.7 years; that number is significantly lower for South Asians at 7.9 years and for Koreans at 8.8 years. Besides the Japanese (47 percent), both Filipinos (16 percent) and Chinese (12 percent) also include a significant proportion of the respondents who have lived in the local area for 21 or more years.

Age and Sex.   The average respondent age is 44, but a typical South Asian respondent is significantly younger at age 36 and a person of Japanese descent is older at age 49. The sample is equally divided between male and female respondents, but more males than females are represented in the Vietnamese and South Asian subsamples.

Education.   About half of the sample has a college or more advanced degree. The educational achievement among South Asian respondents is especially astonishing with over one-fourth holding a postgraduate degree. Even among the Vietnamese, the group reporting the lowest levels of educational achievement, one-third report having a college degree or more. With the exception of the Japanese sample, the majority of respondents in each ethnic group received education mainly outside of the United States. An even percentage of Filipinos received education in and outside of the United States.

Income.   Many respondents are reluctant to report income. However, among those who report their income, the results defy an image of overall affluence. Respondents in each ethnic group differ somewhat in terms of the "most common" categories of family income they indicated. For example, the most common category for the Chinese is "between $10,000 and $19,999." The average income category for Japanese and Filipinos is "between $40,000 and $59,999." The two most common categories for Koreans and South Asians are "between $40,000 and $59,999" and "over $80,000." However, for the Vietnamese, the two most common categories are "between $10,000 and $19,999" and "between $30,000 and $39,000."

Religion.   The respondents also differ greatly in religious beliefs. Close to seven out of ten (68 percent) Filipinos are Catholic and a similar proportion of Koreans are Christians. Close to half (49 percent) of Vietnamese respondents are Buddhist and 46 percent of South Asians are Hindu. However, over one-fourth of Japanese (26 percent) and close to 40 percent of Chinese respondents do not have a religious preference.

Conclusion

This book focuses on Asian Americans and their political attitudes and behavior. In this opening chapter, we present thirteen observations to help debunk the popular myths about a U.S. population group with a rich history that is expanding rapidly, but remains relatively small due to institutionalized racism and exclusion. Although we argue that the Asian American experience is uniquely complex and cannot be readily understood with any of the leading theoretical frameworks discussed in this opening chapter, we believe by studying Asians this project can contribute to improving understanding of American minority political behavior, racial and ethnic politics, and the shape of the American democracy in general.

First, Asian Americans have been and will continue to be a critical component of American political life. Asian Americans have historically played a key, though often unrecognized, role in American politics through worker organizing, fighting Asian American immigrant exclusion, and expanding naturalization laws through the courts. Their growing numbers in the population, along with their involvement at different levels of government and in various civic institutions, further ensures the continued importance of Asian Americans in American politics today.[25]

Second, focusing on Asian Americans allows a unique perspective through which to view the American political system. We argue that focusing on Asian Americans, an ethnically and linguistically diverse, nonwhite, and predominantly immigrant population, highlights both the value and limits of current understandings of American identity, political orientation, partisanship, participation and policy attitudes among the nation's nonwhite peoples. Using Asian Americans as the lens through which to view American politics suggests the ways in which most research on these topics, based on the majority racial group, non-Latino whites, must be expanded to account for the experiences of growing numbers of people in the United States who are not white and who may not be native born.

Our main dataset, the PNAAPS, provides a unique window to appreciate the dimension and scope of the political behavior of Asian Americans. It offers insights into how they conceptualize their experiences in the United States as members of a racial minority group that is dominated by immigrants and characterized by a multitude of ethnic groups that speak different languages, follow different spiritual paths, live in a variety of metropolitan areas and neighborhoods, and identify themselves in a various ways. The PNAAPS taps as well into the ways in which different Asian American groups are likely to take part in the American political discourse as well as the ways that they are likely to act in concert or in conflict with each other and with other racial groups within the U.S. political system.

In the next chapter, we take the first steps toward understanding Asian American political behavior and the role of Asian Americans in the larger political system by examining the sources and contours of ethnic group-based identities among Asian Americans. We first describe the different conceptualizations of the term "ethnic identity" in a multidisciplinary context. We then review major research on the formation of ethnic and panethnic identity among Asian Americans. Given the internal diversity and rapid expansion of the population, a major empirical question is whether the panethnic term "Asian American" is recognized and has meaning among individuals of Asian descent in America. If yes, who among Asian Americans adopt this term as an aspect of their self-identity and with what degree of intensity? If not, what other identity modes are preferred and why?

CHAPTER 2

Who Am I? Mapping Ethnic Self-Identities

In this chapter, we seek answers to the following questions: (a) How do individuals of Asian descent identify themselves and why? And (b) How much and under what conditions do Asian Americans choose to coalesce into a political bloc based on a common panethnic American identity? These are questions of central concern to followers of the Asian American community and U.S. racial and ethnic minority politics. The presence of a panethnic identity among ordinary community members may have important implications for their political behavior and policy preferences.[1] Because of the pronounced internal diversity and constant expansion of the population, many wonder if the term "Asian American" is recognized and has meaning among individuals of Asian descent in the United States. If yes, who among Asian Americans would adopt this term as an aspect of their self-identity and to what degree? If not, what other identities are preferred and in what ranking order?

Although a number of researchers have investigated the issue of Asian ethnic identity,[2] most focus on the second generation. Only one major survey prior to our study produces some direct empirical evidence of the scope of panethnic self-identification among Asian Americans, but it is restricted to the children of immigrants. Moreover, when the issue of group identity and political behavior is discussed empirically, much of the research relies either on census statistics, qualitative data, or both. In rare instances when raw public opinion survey data files are accessed and analyzed, because of inadequacies in the existing pool of publicly accessible survey data, researchers can at best report indirect evidence of the possible existence of panethnicity among Asian Americans. In this context, the PNAAPS not only allows us to look beyond sociodemographics and address the social and political diversity within the nation's Asian American population; it permits us to explore relationships among indicators of diversity and the formation of ethnic group-based self identities at the individual level. Further, it allows us to test long-standing assumptions and theories about panethnic identity in a systematic, more generalizable way than previous studies.

Our analysis begins with a review of past research explaining the formation and contours of ethnic identity. Then we look into research on Asian Americans and point out the possibilities and difficulties for members of the nation's Asian population to conceive themselves as belonging to one socially and politically meaningful community. This is followed by a summary review of the modes of self-identity and the intensity of panethnic identification among PNAAPS respondents. We discuss the possible effects of survey context on the pattern of responses to these questions. Next, we report percentage distributions of several major components of ethnicity by Asian American ethnic groups. This is followed by a summary review of key indicators of cultural, social, and political adaptation by self-identity types to help explain the formation of identity choices among Asian Americans. Last, we report multivariate results that assess the competing forces shaping the ethnic self-identification of the survey respondents.

Theorizing the Formation and Contours of Ethnic Identity

One of the basic challenges to understanding ethnic group-based identities and their relationship to political attitudes and behavior is that little agreement exists about the basic concept of ethnic identity. In fact, a major review of ethnic identity literature reports a great deal of confusion over conceptual and operational definitions and inconsistency in findings across studies (Phinney, 1990). Often, one's country (or place) of origin is taken as an indication of primordial affective ties and synonymous to ethnic identification without presenting any attitudinal evidence consistent with such an assumption. In addition, theoretical refinement appears to far outweigh empirical research on ethnic identity, with much of the empirical work concentrated on U.S.-born children rather than immigrant adults. Research on patterns of ethnic self-identification among children of immigrants reports a different process of ethnic self-identification than that occurring among their immigrant parents (Portes and Rumbaut, 2001). Our research incorporates analyses of both foreign-born adults, who are the most rapidly growing sector of the Asian America population, and their American-born counterparts.

We consider ethnic identity formation for individuals in an immigrant majority community of color as part of the multifaceted process of developing new attachments and affiliations in the host society. How individuals identify themselves in ethnic terms is a product not only of primordial ties or individual characteristics and preferences but also of social and political construction of the concepts of race and ethnicity. In addition to distinct ethnic group culture and human capital factors, this process can be influenced by domestic racial and social conditions, transnational events, global economic structuring, community organizing efforts, U.S. immigration, citizenship, and racial enumeration and categorization policies, among others. The ethnic self-identity labels preferred by individual Asian Americans are likely to be the negotiated outcome of several competing forces, such as between assimilation and ethnic retention, and between identification with a specific ethnic or a panethnic, racialized entity. To understand how at the nexus of these forces Asian Americans make their ethnic identity choices, we hypothesize that this process is likely to be influenced by the following set of factors mostly derived from the major conceptual frameworks introduced in Chapter 1.

Primordial Ties. To scholars of primordialism, ethnicity is considered first and foremost an extension of a premodern social bond or a common sense of belonging to a particular ancestry or origin and the sharing of common cultural characteristics and historical experiences (Min, 1999). For an immigrant majority community, a central element in this perspective is the strong and lingering effect of emotional ties to the country of origin or ancestral homeland. The affective bond is often sustained by adopting ethnic language, religion, food, dress, holidays, customs, values, and beliefs—even though recent research suggests that maintaining ethnic traditions is not a necessary component for strong ethnic identification among U.S.-born Asian Americans (Tuan, 1998). Nevertheless, the intensive transpacific flow of capitals, skills, and goods in recent decades may help sustain cultural distinctiveness of many contemporary Asian American groups and imply the continuing significance of primordial ties in drawing ethnic boundaries. Differences in ethnic culture and history among Asian American communities, however, may predict different roles of primordial ties in shaping ethnic identification among individuals of various Asian descents.

Sociopsychological Engagement. Most studies in (social) psychology treat ethnic identity as part of a social identity or a self-concept derived from an individual's knowledge of his or her "membership in a social group (or groups) together with the value and emotional significance attached to that membership" (Tajfel, 1981: 255). According to social identity theory, having developed cognitive, evaluative, or emotional attachment to an ethnic group may increase the sense of belonging to that group. Tajfel (1982) also suggests that the belief in a common, linked fate plays a critical role in the formation of group identification. The role of sociopsychological engagement in structuring ethnic identification is attested to in a recent study by Jackson and Smith (1999) in which they find that "attraction to the in-group" or emotional attachment to one's own ethnic culture and people and "interdependency of beliefs" or belief in common or linked fate among group members are among the dimensions conducive to the formation of identification with one's own group. This theory, however, has not paid enough attention to possible differences in ethnic boundaries and modes of self-identification found among our respondents.

Acculturation and Social Integration. Ethnic identity can also be conceptualized as consisting of two aspects: internal and external identity (Isajiw, 1990). The former refers to the dimensions of self-perception mentioned by Tajfel. The latter refers to observable social and cultural behaviors such as language use, media preference, friendship patterns, spousal choice, and so on. The external indicators of ethnicity overlap with the cultural and social assimilation stages of immigrant adaptation to America proposed by Gordon (1964). The formation of an assimilated nonethnic American identity ("American") may be associated with the level of English language use at home, in business transactions, or in consuming mass media products. It may also correlate with the level of supportive attitude toward intermarriage. Residing in a mostly white neighborhood or having close friends who are white may also facilitate the formation of an unhyphenated American identity.

Reactive Ethnicity and Racial Formation. It is not clear, from theories of assimilation and social identity, whether and how these external indicators impact the formation of hyphenated U.S.-based identities among nonwhites. It seems, for nonwhite immigrants, having encountered discrimination by race or ethnicity may help forge a sense of alienation from the host society and hinder the formation of U.S.-based ethnic and panethnic identities. For the U.S.-born, the theory of reactive ethnicity predicts that experiencing racial discrimination mobilizes the formation of panethnic ("Asian American") identities. Panethnic identification may be engendered by a sense of community and group consciousness from either personally experiencing discrimination or perceiving persecution or threats to the interest of one's ethnoracial group (Portes and Rumbaut, 1996, 2001). This theory echoes the racial formation theory introduced in Chapter 1, in which panethnicity can be a strategic response to racially coercive forces imposed by governmental and social institutions. The theory on racial formation does not, nevertheless, distinguish between responses by nativity as does the theory of segmented assimilation.

Political Integration and Civic Participation. One of the final stages in immigrant adaptation to U.S. mainstream society and polity is becoming politically integrated into the system (Gordon, 1964; Alba and Nee, 1997). By developing affiliation with major political parties, adopting mainstream political ideological jargon to express one's political views, and by acquiring or seeking to acquire citizenship, one is expected to possess a stronger sense of attachment to U.S.-based identities. In addition, participation in American politics to advance ethnic community interests may facilitate the development of identification with both the American mainstream and the politicized panethnic community in the United States. Being active in civic institutions, such as those related to religion and ethnic communities, may influence ethnic identity choice because these organizations often function as important conduits of political information and social networking (Wald, Owen, and Hill, 1988; Huckfeldt and Sprague, 1995; Jones-Correa and Leal, 2001). Specifically, being active in ethnic churches and community organizations may reinforce ethnic or panethnic identity rather than an unhyphenated "American" identity.

Socialization and Social Ties. Last but not least, recent literature on transnationalism (Glick-Schiller, Basch, and Blanc-Szanton, 1995; Vertovec, 1999; Faist, 2000) and segmented assimilation (Portes and Zhou, 1994; Portes and Rumbaut, 1996, 2001) emphasizes the importance of prior socialization and social networks in shaping immigrant adaptation. Having received one's education mostly outside of the U.S. context may limit U.S.-based identity formation.

Conversely, having greater exposure or ties to U.S. society because of gains in age, immigration generation, and work-related opportunities may have the opposite effect. Because women of color often bear the majority of household responsibility and have limited opportunities in the U.S. labor market, they may have fewer prospects for networking and developing social ties to the U.S. mainstream than their male counterparts. Thus, being an Asian female may have a negative impact on the formation of U.S.-based identities.

Section Summary and Discussion

As the first part of this chapter suggests, ethnic identity can be studied in multiple, and sometimes overlapping, complementary, or even contradictory, ways. Social identity theory tells us that ethnic identity is a subjective self-concept influenced by internal factors such as one's emotional attachment to ethnic ties, cognitive awareness of one's group well-being, belief in common fate or group cohesion, concern with group interest over self interest, and assessment of intergroup relations. By contrast, racial formation theory tells us that ethnic identity is both an involuntary, externally imposed identity and a strategic response to institutionalized categorization and to prejudice and discrimination against an ethnoracial group. To further complicate matters, acculturation theory tells us that the strength and direction of ethnic identity can be influenced by indicators of social and cultural integration such as language use, media preference, friendship patterns, and organizational membership. However, proponents of segmented assimilation argue that this relationship may be affected by an individual's immigration generation, social class status, experience of racial and ethnic discrimination, and racial and ethnic makeup of the neighborhood context. Finally, proponents of transnationalism tell us that we cannot fully understand ethnic identity without taking account of ties to and involvement in home country society and politics.

Regardless of which conceptual framework we embrace, there is general agreement that ethnic identity is a fluid, malleable, contextual, and layered phenomenon. Scholars differ in assessing the relative influence of the underlying mechanisms to anticipate and explain the formation of ethnic identity. Adherents of assimilation and cultural pluralism theories differ over whether group identity is a one-dimensional, bipolar phenomenon or a two-dimensional phenomenon. Proponents of social identity and transnational perspectives go even further, conceiving of identity as a heterogeneous, hybrid, multidimensional construction. Moreover, these theoretical debates have thus far centered around predicting the strength of ethnic resilience and the degree of adaptation to the American mainstream. What is largely missing from this debate is a careful consideration of whether predominantly immigrant communities of color are more likely to express U.S.- or country-of-origin-oriented uniethnic or panethnic identities, or to abandon any notion of a hyphenated American identity and adopt an assimilated American identity.[3]

Table 2.1 Possibilities of Ethnic Choices among Asians in America

	ASSIMILATION	ETHNICITY
Panethnic	"Asian American"	"Asian"
Uniethnic	"[Ethnic*] American"	"[Ethnic*]" only
Nonethnic	"American" only	N/A

*May be of any ethnic-specific descent such as Japanese, Filipino, Korean, Vietnamese, Asian Indian, or Chinese. These are the six major Asian ethnic groups targeted in our survey.

Based on the literature reviewed above, we expect individuals of Asian descent in the United States—who are at the nexus of the above-mentioned cross-cutting and contending forces—to self-identify in multiple and variable forms, which may be expressed in at least five distinct types. A typology of the possible modes of self-identification among Asian Americans is shown in Table 2.1. Under the "assimilation" column are ethnic identity types that, according to the literature described above, would suggest that individuals perceive greater Americanization as a desirable goal. Under the "ethnicity" column are identity types that, by the same token, suggest that individuals value the retention of ethnic culture over becoming more assimilated. Each set of identities differs as well among themselves in terms of the degree of receptivity to the panethnic notion. In the context of opinion polls, we also expect that the ethnic labels Asian Americans choose, and the intensity with which they choose that label, will vary by survey-specific factors such as question wording, the language of the interview, and survey sampling method. The empirical question that follows is: Who among Asians would identify with which label, to what extent, and under what survey context?

How Asian Americans Report Their Ethnic Self-Identity

Most of the past research on ethnic self identification among Asian Americans focuses on the experiences of the U.S.-born and their identification with the panethnic concept (e.g., Gibson, 1988; Kibria, 1997, 2000; Rumbaut, 1997; Zhou and Bankston, 1998; Hong and Min, 1999; Min and Kim, 1999; Thai, 1999). With few exceptions, these studies usually adopt qualitative interview or ethnographic data to describe the process of ethnic identification among high school or college students of various Asian ethnic origins. In the first wave of the Children of Immigrants Longitudinal Study (CILS) in 1992, second generation Asian American middle and high school students in San Diego, mostly of Filipino or Southeast Asian origin, were evenly divided in their choices between national-origin and nation-specific hyphenated American labels (Rumbaut, 1997). National origin identifiers outweighed hyphenated American identifiers in the second wave survey conducted in 1995–1996. Only .3 percent of respondents in 1992, but 4.5 percent of respondents in 1995–1996, identified themselves panethnically as "Asian" (Portes and Rumbaut, 2001). Although each ethnic group reported an increase of its percentage of panethnic identifiers and a reduction in its percentage of American identifiers in the second wave, the percentages vary widely among ethnic groups—as high as 38 percent of Hmong Americans and as low as 1.9 percent of Filipino Americans would identify with the panethnic label. The authors surmise that the shift in identity patterns over time toward ethnicization and panethnicization among the U.S.-born generation can be explained with the theory of reactive ethnicity. In a survey of Korean junior and senior high school students in the New York area, the authors report a similarly low level of panethnic Asian American identity (3 percent) and a very high level of hyphenated Korean American identity (72 percent) among the second generation respondents (Hong and Min, 1999). The percentage of unhyphenated "American" identifiers was 3.5 percent in both surveys.

The relative popularity of the national origin or ethnic-specific identities and the relative obscurity of the panethnic identities observed above may be attributable to a number of factors unique to the Asian American experience (see Lien, 2001b). They include the lack of historical precedents of interethnic cooperation because of white labor management practicing the "divide and conquer" rule; the practice of "ethnic disidentification" by some Asian Americans to avoid being misidentified as members of another ethnic group and thus perceived as less respected Asian Americans, and the belated emergence in the late 1960s of a pan–Asian American racial identity. They also include the simultaneous strengthening of homeland ethnic ties and further diversification of the polyethnic population along class, ethnic origin, race, ideology, religion, and other lines of cleavage occurring after the 1965 immigration reform; U.S. military involvement in East and Southeast Asia; and global economic restructuring in the past four decades.

The notion of panethnicity is situational and unfixed, and is thus constantly shaped and reshaped by coalescing forces both inside and outside of the multiethnic community. Internal forces fostering panethnic identity formation include the increasing frequency of interethnic marriages and aggressive coalition-building efforts by community activists, political candidates, and organizational elites to forge a united front. Examples of external forces include government policies on racial counting and media stereotyping that lump Asians of diverse origins together. They also include headline-making political events such as the campaign finance controversies involving immigrant Asian American donors in the 1996 presidential election, and the 1999 Los Alamos "spy" charge leveled against a naturalized Chinese American nuclear physicist, Dr. Wen Ho Lee. Many people in the Asian American community view these incidents as racial attacks and racial profiling. The increasing prominence and frequency of these anti-Asian events reported by the mainstream media may heighten panethnic consciousness among Asian Americans. Alternatively, the immigrant-targeted, Chinese-centered nature of events may foster ethnic distinctions and disidentification, particularly among those who wish to distance themselves from the controversy that such events bring.[4] We suspect that these events may yield different identity patterns by nativity and ethnicity among our survey respondents.

The Mode and Extent of Ethnic Identification among PNAAPS Respondents

In this chapter we treat the concept of ethnic identity as both a subjective and an objective phenomenon that can be measured both directly and indirectly. Objectively, it can be directly indicated by one's personal or ancestral country of origin. We estimate the influence of distinct ethnic group culture or primordial ties by assigning each respondent a unique ethnic origin code based on his/her response to the country of origin question.[5] (For details on the question wording and coding scheme, see the appendix of this book.) We then create a set of dummy variables of Asian American subgroup identity based on the ethnic origin codes.

To study ethnic identity as a subjective phenomenon, we use both direct and indirect indicators. In this section, we measure ethnic self-identity among Asian American adults with a set of three questions on the type of self-identity, identification with the pan–Asian American label, and intensity of pan–Asian American identification. We also distinguish between a preferred self-identity and a secondary self-identity as a result of forced choice. Responses to the first self-identity question are treated as the preferred or primary identity. Responses to the follow-up questions on pan–Asian American identification are treated as the secondary identity. A dummy variable of panethnic self-identity is then created based on these responses. Individuals who self-identify as Asian American either as a first or a secondary preference are assigned a score of 1 and all others are assigned a score of 0. We measure the intensity levels of respondents' pan–Asian American self-identification by a four-point scale.[6]

Table 2.2 reports the type and extent of Asian American self-identification. While outsiders often view Asian Americans as a homogenous group, there is a tremendous level of heterogeneity within the Asian American community writ large as well as within each constituent Asian ethnic group. As shown in responses for Q1, given a choice between identifying oneself as American, Asian American, Asian, ethnic American (e.g., as Chinese American), or simply in terms of one's ethnic origin (e.g., as Chinese), respondents are most apt to indicate an ethnic-specific identity as their preferred identity. Among all respondents, 34 percent chose to identify as ethnic American and 30 percent by ethnic origin alone. The prevalence of ethnic American identification is fairly consistent across all groups, with Filipino American (40 percent) the most common and Japanese American (26 percent) the least common. Ethnic-only identification varies considerably more, with Chinese (42 percent), Vietnamese (42 percent), and Korean (41 percent) respondents much likelier to identify ethnically than Filipino (21 percent), Indian (21 percent), and Japanese (12 percent) respondents. Only 3 percent of all the respondents are not sure of how to answer this question.

Among the other categories of primary self-identification, a fairly consistent minority of respondents in all groups, ranging from 12 percent of Chinese respondents to 23 percent of South Asians, self-identified as "Asian American." The degree of identification simply as "American" is astonishingly varied across groups. On the high end, more than 40 percent of Japanese respondents identify as American, with roughly one in seven Filipinos and Indians in the middle, and almost no Korean, Chinese, or Vietnamese identifying as American (3 percent, 1 percent, and 1 percent, respectively). This variance appears to be due largely to the high proportion of Japanese Americans in our sample from Hawaii. Almost 40 percent of our Honolulu respondents choose the "American" only label, and among Japanese respondents from Honolulu, fully 55 percent identify as "American."[7]

Assessing Impacts of Survey Context on Ethnic Self-Identification

Question Wording

The choice of identifying as "Asian American" (or other ethnic labeling) may be a function of the survey's question wording, which includes specific mentions of possible ethnic choices. Although our wording in Q1 is implicitly open-ended and offers options for choosing other self-identities or non-identification, the explicit mention of the panethnic term as distinct from other ethnic identity terms may artificially boost the percentage of "Asian American" identifiers.[8] Alternatively, the open-ended question used in the CILS may account for the low percentage of panethnic identifiers among Asians.[9] However, when our respondents who did not choose "Asian American" were asked to indicate in Q2 if they *ever* think of themselves as Asian American, about half of respondents report such a panethnic American consciousness. As high as six out of ten Filipino (59 percent) and Vietnamese (56 percent) respondents, compared to four out of ten Korean (41 percent) and Chinese (43 percent) respondents, who previously did not identify themselves as panethnic American do so after the follow-up probe. Among those who do not self-identify as Asian American in the first question, those who identify themselves by an ethnic American label are most likely to adopt the panethnic American label (65 percent). Just over half of those who identified as "American" or "Asian" would adopt the panethnic American label; about one-third of those who either identified only as "ethnic" (33 percent) or were previously uncertain about which label to choose (29 percent) would do the same. Those who previously refused to identify with an ethnic label are most reluctant to adopt the panethnic American label (14 percent).

Table 2.2 Percentage Distribution of Ethnic Self-Identity by Ethnic Origin

Q1. *People think of themselves in different ways. In general, do you think of yourself as an American, an Asian American, an Asian, a [R's ETHNIC GROUP] American, or a [R's ETHNIC GROUP]?*

	ALL	CHINESE	KOREAN	VIETNAMESE	JAPANESE	FILIPINO	SOUTH ASIAN
"American" only	12	1	3	1	41	14	14
"Asian American"	15	12	15	13	15	16	23
"Asian"	4	4	5	7	2	4	3
"[Ethnic] American"	34	34	33	34	26	40	33
"[Ethnic]" only	30	42	41	42	12	21	18
not sure	3	4	1	3	2	2	7
refused	2	1	2	1	2	3	2
Column Total	1218	308	168	137	198	266	141

Q2. (Asked of those who did not self-identify as "Asian American" in Q1.) *Have you ever thought of yourself as an Asian American?*

	ALL	CHINESE	KOREAN	VIETNAMESE	JAPANESE	FILIPINO	SOUTH ASIAN
yes	49	43	41	56	50	59	48
no	41	41	56	34	46	32	43
not sure	5	9	2	8	1	4	5
refused	4	7	1	2	3	4	3
Column Total	1027	270	143	119	168	221	106

(*cont.*)

42

Table 2.2 (*Continued*)

Q3. (*Asked only if respondent answered "Asian American" in Q1 or yes in Q2.*) *How often do you think of yourself as an Asian American? Is it very often, often, or not that often?*

	ALL	CHINESE	KOREAN	VIETNAMESE	JAPANESE	FILIPINO	SOUTH ASIAN
very often	21	28	14	17	16	21	31
often	39	47	48	64	17	33	29
not that often	37	19	36	20	66	43	36
not sure	3	6	3	–	2	3	4
Column Total	694	153	84	84	113	175	85

Note: Cell entries are percentages. Cell values *within each column* may sum up to over 100 percentage points because of rounding errors. The categories of "Aethnic American" and "Aethnic" labels refer to the respondent's respective ethnic origin.
Source: PNAAPS 2000–2001.

Table 2.3 Percentage Distribution of Ethnic Choices by Nativity and Ethnic Origin

	Row Total	AMERICAN		ASIAN AMERICAN		ETHNIC AMERICAN		ASIAN		ETHNIC	
		(a)	(b)	(a)	(b)	(a)	(b)	(a)	(b)	(a)	(b)
All	1218	12	6	15	57	34	12	4	2	30	20
U.S. born	305	33	16	17	63	33	12	3	1	7	3
Asia born	913	5	2	15	55	34	12	5	2	37	25
Chinese	308	1	–	12	50	34	15	4	2	42	27
Filipino	266	14	6	16	66	40	10	4	2	21	22
Japanese	198	41	21	15	57	26	10	2	1	12	9
Korean	168	3	1	15	50	33	12	5	4	41	31
South Asian	141	14	8	23	60	33	14	3	1	18	11
Vietnamese	137	1	–	13	61	34	10	7	1	42	27

Note: Entries under column (a) are responses in percentages to Q1 in Table 2.2; entries under column (b) are reconstructed percentages of ethnic self-identification after respondents were asked to make a forced choice regarding the panethnic question (Q2 of Table 2.2). Cell values *across each row* may not sum up to 100 percentage points because of the omission of "not sure" and "refused" categories. A dash means less than 0.5%. *Source:* PNAAPS, 2000–2001.

Table 2.3 shows that, as a whole, close to six out of ten respondents (57 percent) have considered themselves panethnically Asian American. This significant jump from 15 percent in the first question is a direct result of the forced choice imposed by the second question. About one out of five respondents would still self-identify as ethnic-only (compared to 30 percent in response to the first question). Only 12 percent of respondents would self-identity as ethnic American (compared to 34 percent in the first question). And the percentage points for both American-only and Asian-only identifiers were cut in half in response to the second query. Table 2.3 also shows that, when segmented by nativity, a much higher percentage of the U.S.-born would identify themselves as "American" and a much higher percentage of the Asia-born would identify themselves as "ethnic" only. In terms of percentage point distributions, there's not much of a difference between the U.S.-born and the Asia-born among "Asian American," "ethnic American," or "Asian" identifiers. The distribution pattern by nativity under each identity choice remains very much the same after the panethnic probe except that a higher percentage of U.S.-born individuals would identity themselves as "Asian American" and a quarter of the Asia-born individuals would still identify themselves only as "ethnic."

Within each of the six Asian origin groups, Table 2.3 shows that although South Asians originally had the highest percentage of pan–Asian American identifiers (23 percent), Filipinos registered the highest percentage of that identity mode after being asked if they ever thought of themselves as Asian Americans. Most of this identity shift among Filipinos came from a 30-percentage-point drop of "Filipino American" identifiers after the probe and not from a change among "Filipino" identifiers. The Chinese respondents also registered a similar percentage-point drop for "Chinese American" identifiers, but there is also a 15-percentage-point drop among "Chinese" identifiers when asked if they ever thought of themselves as Asian Americans. Among the Japanese, the increase in the percentage share of pan–Asian American identifiers came mostly from a 20-percentage-point drop among "American" identifiers and a 16-percentage-point drop among "Japanese American" identifiers. Although about an equal share (40 percent) of Chinese, Korean, and Vietnamese respondents identified themselves only as "ethnic" in the first question, as many as 31 percent of the Koreans respondents maintained that identity after the follow-up question.

These results suggest that, even though only one out of six respondents would do so as their first and foremost ethnic choice, Asian American adults were more receptive to the pan–Asian American notion at the dawn of the twenty-first century than the limited results suggested in previous surveys. Confirming the conditional nature of responses to survey items, our survey shows that ethnic self-identity is highly susceptible to the context structured by the survey item. Furthermore, it demonstrates that the contours of ethnic identity may vary greatly from one ethnic group to another. However, we also find that immigrant background is significant in shaping some, but not all, modes of self-identity.

Interview Language and Sampling Method

Besides question wording, the direction of ethnic self-identification may vary by the language of interview and survey sampling method. As shown in Table 2.4, English language respondents reported a much higher percentage of identification with the "American" label and a slightly higher percentage of identification

Table 2.4 Percentage Distribution of Ethnic Choices by Interview Language and Sampling Method

	Row Total	AMERICAN	ASIAN AMERICAN	ETHNIC AMERICAN	ASIAN	ETHNIC
Interview shape Language						
English	637	22	18	35	3	17
other	581	1	13	33	5	44
Sampling Method						
random Digit Dialing	312	26	16	27	2	25
listed Surname	906	8	15	36	5	31

Source and Note: See Table 2.3.

with the "Asian American" label than those among non-English respondents. By contrast, English language respondents reported a much lower percentage of identification with the ethnic-only label compared to that among non-English respondents. Interview language does not seem to make much difference in identification for those who choose ethnic American and Asian-only labels. The same table also displays significant differences in self-identity according to sampling method. For example, respondents selected by RDD method had a much greater percentage of identification with the U.S.-only identity compared to those selected using the listed surname frame. Conversely, those selected from the listed surname frame had a higher likelihood to self identify as ethnic American or Asian ethnic than those selected using RDD method. However, sampling method does not seem to impact the percentage distribution of pan–Asian American identifiers.

In addition to discrete measurements of ethnic self-identification, we consider the intensity of panethnic identification in Q3 of Table 2.2. Every six out of ten respondents who were willing to consider themselves Asian American did so either very frequently or frequently. This panethnic consciousness was most strongly felt among South Asians and Chinese and least strongly among Koreans and Japanese. A crosstabulation analysis comparing the intensity of panethnic self-identification to responses in the ethnic identity question finds about one-third of respondents who initially self-identified as "Asian American" would very often think of themselves in this panethnic American term. This percentage was not much higher than the 30 percent among those self-identified as "Asian" and the 23 percent among those self-identified as ethnic American. However, in the first question, about six out of ten "American" identifiers, but only one out of four "Asian American" identifiers, would not often think of themselves as being Asian American.

While we found sampling method to be related to making ethnicity-related choices, it does not seem to be associated much with the intensity of panethnic self-identification as an Asian American. More than twice the proportion of English than non-English language respondents (43 percent versus 20 percent), however, reported that they did not often think of themselves as Asian American. Whereas half of the non-English respondents (50 percent) often thought of themselves as Asian American, that percentage dropped by 20 percentage points among respondents who were interviewed in English. We suspect that the lack of representation of certain ethnic groups among the RDD respondents (Vietnamese and South Asian) and among non-English interviewees (Japanese, Filipino, and South Asian) may explain most of the skewed distribution patterns. This is supported by results of a multivariate analysis, which examines the net effect of interview language and sampling method while simultaneously controlling for a list of possible confounding factors reported later in the chapter.

Gauging Subjective Ethnic Identity with Sociopsychological Measures

To assess the contours of ethnicity other than through self-identification or objective ascription based on ancestry or country of origin, we examine several sociopsychological measures of ethnicity along cognitive, affective, evaluative dimensions expressly designed to approximate the extent of panethnic and ethnic-specific identification. The cultural, affective component of ethnic group identification is measured with a question on whether Asians in America share a common culture. The moral or evaluative component of ethnicity is estimated by asking respondents whether they consider their fate in life to be intimately linked to the fate of other Asians or their coethnics in America. The cognitive component of ethnic group identification is assessed by two questions on the degree to which respondents follow news stories and other information about Asians in the United States or countries in Asia.

Common Culture

We first examine panethnicity or pan–Asian group identity as a sense of shared culture. As shown in Table 2.5, in the full sample, only about one out of every ten respondents agree that different Asian groups in America are "very similar" culturally. Four out of ten respondents (41 percent), however, believe that different Asian groups in America are somewhat similar culturally. There is a remarkable uniformity among several ethnic groups on this question.

Shared Fate

We then examine panethnic identity as a sense of a common destiny. Cumulatively, about half of respondents (49 percent) believe that "what happens generally to other groups of Asians in this country will affect what happens in your life." But there is considerable variation across groups. Although Koreans are least likely to believe that Asian Americans share a common culture, they are most likely to perceive a general linked fate (61 percent) among Asian Americans. Filipinos (54 percent) and South Asians (53 percent) also exhibit high levels of a panethnic linked fate. Less than half of Chinese and Japanese and only 36 percent of Vietnamese view Asians as sharing a common destiny. Groups also differ in how strongly this sense of shared panethnic destiny is felt. For example, a third of Vietnamese, but only 4 percent of Koreans, who believe that they share the same fate with other Asians think that they are not very much affected by issues and events happening to other Asians.

We also asked our respondents if and how much they believe that what happened to their coethnics in America would affect what happens in their lives. Generally, individuals feel somewhat more strongly about *ethnic* shared fate (55 percent) than about *panethnic* shared fate (49 percent). As in the panethnic case, Koreans are most likely to express ethnic solidarity (76 percent) and Vietnamese are the least likely to do so (38 percent). With Chinese, Japanese,

Table 2.5 Percentage Distribution of Sociopsychological Indicators of Ethnicity by Ethnic Origin

Common Culture

Some say that people of Asian descent in the United States have a great deal in common culturally, others disagree. Do you think groups of Asians in America are culturally very similar, somewhat similar, somewhat different, or very different?

	ALL	CHINESE	KOREAN	VIETNAMESE	JAPANESE	FILIPINO	SOUTH ASIAN
very similar	9	9	9	12	7	8	8
somewhat similar	41	45	29	45	39	46	37
somewhat different	29	29	36	35	26	24	29
very different	16	11	23	3	17	19	24
not sure	5	6	3	4	11	3	1

Panethnic Linked Fate

Do you think what happens generally to other groups of Asians in this country will affect what happens in your life (probe, if answer is "it depends")?

	ALL	CHINESE	KOREAN	VIETNAMESE	JAPANESE	FILIPINO	SOUTH ASIAN
yes	49	44	61	36	44	54	53
no	43	47	33	58	43	37	37
not sure	9	8	5	7	12	9	10

If yes, will it affect it a lot, some, or not very much?

	ALL	CHINESE	KOREAN	VIETNAMESE	JAPANESE	FILIPINO	SOUTH ASIAN
a lot	22	18	23	29	16	22	32
some	56	63	72	29	62	47	51
not very much	18	17	4	33	21	24	15
not sure	4	3	1	10	1	6	3

(cont.)

48

Table 2.5 (*Continued*)

Ethnic Linked Fate

What about the [R's ETHNIC GROUP] people in America? Do you think what happens generally to [R's ETHNIC GROUP] Americans will affect what happens in your life (probe, if answer is "it depends")?

	ALL	CHINESE	KOREAN	VIETNAMESE	JAPANESE	FILIPINO	SOUTH ASIAN
yes	55	54	76	38	54	50	57
no	37	36	22	55	38	40	37
not sure	8	10	2	7	8	9	6

If yes, will it affect it a lot, some, or not very much?

	ALL	CHINESE	KOREAN	VIETNAMESE	JAPANESE	FILIPINO	SOUTH ASIAN
a lot	31	27	30	36	27	31	42
some	54	57	65	36	56	50	45
not very much	11	11	4	17	14	17	6
not sure	4	5	2	10	3	2	6

Attention Paid to News—Stories on Asian Americans

How closely have you followed news stories and other information of Asians in the United States—very closely, fairly closely, not too closely, or not at all?

	ALL	CHINESE	KOREAN	VIETNAMESE	JAPANESE	FILIPINO	SOUTH ASIAN
very closely	20	32	34	7	7	15	14
fairly closely	33	46	49	12	27	22	36
not too closely	33	18	13	46	43	45	38
not at all	13	2	3	30	23	15	12
not sure	2	2	1	6	1	2	1

(*cont.*)

Table 2.5 *(Continued)*

Attention Paid to News—Stories from Asia

How closely have you followed news stories and other information about what happened in Asia, such as a story from Japan, Korea, China, India, Vietnam, and the Philippines—very closely, fairly closely, not too closely, or not at all?

	ALL	CHINESE	KOREAN	VIETNAMESE	JAPANESE	FILIPINO	SOUTH ASIAN
very closely	18	20	27	10	9	22	22
fairly closely	38	48	53	31	29	28	33
not too closely	34	26	20	42	49	35	33
not at all	9	3	1	16	14	14	11
not sure	1	3	–	2	–	2	1

Source and Note: See Table 2.2.

Filipinos, and South Asians alike, roughly three out of every five respondents believe in an ethnic shared fate. Groups differ widely, again, in the strength of this shared ethnic fate. For example, more than four out of ten South Asians (42 percent) but less than three out of ten Chinese and Japanese (27 percent) who believe that they share the same fate with their coethnics think that they are very much affected by issues and events happening to other individuals in their own ethnic groups.

News Attention

We estimate our respondents' cognitive attachment to the panethnic American identity by asking them to indicate the amount of attention they pay to news stories and other information regarding Asians in the United States. Overall, one-fifth of our respondents pay very close attention and one-third pay fairly close or not too close attention to Asian American news. However, there is significant variance across the six ethnic groups. About one out of three Chinese and Koreans, but less than one out of ten Vietnamese and Japanese, report having paid very close attention to Asian American news. About four out of ten Filipinos and South Asians do not closely follow newsstories on Asians in America.

To estimate Asian Americans' cognitive ties to their ethnic origin, we asked respondents to indicate the degree of attention they give to news stories about current events in Asian countries. As in panethnic news attention, a higher percentage of Koreans (27 percent) than other groups follow news stories from Asia very closely. However, about one-fifth of Filipinos, South Asians, and Chinese also follow Asian news very closely. Although Vietnamese and Japanese respondents still report the lowest news attention, their level of attentiveness to Asian news is higher than that paid to Asian American news. For example, four out of ten Vietnamese respondents report having followed news stories and other happenings in Asia very or fairly closely; only 19 percent do so concerning news of Asians in America. It is interesting to note that, except for the Vietnamese and Filipinos, respondents are just as likely or even more likely to follow current events about Asian Americans in the United States as they are to keep up on stories about events in Asia.

Explaining the Formation of Ethnic Self-Identities: Percentage Distribution of Possible Correlates

According to our literature review, the underlying reasons explaining ethnic identification are likely to be the multidimensional result of cognitive, affective, and evaluative factors and cultural, social, and political attachments to both one's country of origin and the United States. We expect the degree of sharing a perceived common culture and linked fate as well as the possession of (pan)ethnic news interest and concerns to be associated with the making of ethnic choices and to correlate with the strength of (pan)ethnic identification among Asian Americans. We also expect that the degree of acculturation in the

United States, the nature and degree of racial interaction, and the degree of political and social integration into the mainstream system may be associated with the nature and extent of ethnic identity formation. Additionally, we expect the process of ethnic formation for Asia-born immigrants to be associated with their past and current social and political ties to their homeland in Asia as well as their personal comparison assessment of the U.S. government and the government of their respective Asian country of origin. Stronger homeland ties may help retain Asia-based ethnicity, whereas greater trust and self-efficacy may correlate with greater assimilation and the formation of U.S.-based identities. In the next section, we examine the relationships between modes of self-identity and these possible correlates of self-identity at the bivariate level using crosstabulation statistical procedures appropriate for estimating the significance of relationships involving a categorical variable: ethnic (self-identity) choice.

Sociopsychological Indicators of Ethnicity

Table 2.6a reports the frequency percent distribution of selected response categories within each sociopsychological indicator of ethnicity. Of the five independent variables used, only the cognitive measures tapping ethnic news attentiveness are significantly related to ethnic self-identity choices. Those who do not follow news regarding Asia or Asian Americans are more likely to self-identify as "American"; those who follow the news closely are more likely to

Table 2.6a Percentage Distribution of Sociopsychological Indicator of Ethnicity by Ethnic Choices

	Row Total	AMERICAN	ASIAN AMERICAN	ETHNIC AMERICAN	ASIAN	ETHNIC
Perception of Common Culture among Asian People in America						
very different	195	13	14	33	4	31
very similar	107	11	20	27	6	31
Sense of Panethnic Linked Fate with Other Asians in America						
none	516	13	13	34	3	31
very high	132	12	20	38	6	23
Sense of Ethnic Linked Fate with Other Coethnics in America						
none	455	13	15	33	3	30
very high	207	12	14	39	3	29
Follow Asian American News*						
not at all	156	21	15	27	4	30
very closely	237	6	17	39	4	29
Follow News from Asia*						
not at all	112	19	13	30	2	24
very closely	225	6	15	35	4	36

Note: Cell values *across each row* may not sum up to 100 percentage points because of the omission of >not sure = and >refused = categories.
*Chi-sq tests of differences in ethnic choices for each measure are significant at $\alpha = .05$ level.
Source: PNAAPS, 2000–2001.

self-identify as "Asian American." Perceptions of common culture and a sense of panethnic linked fate with other Asian groups are not significantly related to one's ethnic choices. Neither does individual Asians' sense of shared fate with fellow Asians from the same ethnic origin have any statistically discernible impact on making ethnic choices.

Political Integration/Civic Participation

Turning to political indicators, we measure the degree of integration into the mainstream political system by the direction and strength of political partisanship and ideology. The effect of ideological strength is measured by one's degree of identification with the liberal ideology. Individuals' adaptation to the mainstream political system is assessed by their citizenship status or, for noncitizens, the expectation or plan to acquire U.S. citizenship. It is also measured by a cumulative index of one's political participation in activities involving Asian American candidates or issues. One's degree of social integration and civic ties to the Asian American community is measured by membership in ethnic community-based organizations. We also gauge social integration by the extent of frequency of attending religious services.

Table 2.6b shows that ethnic self-identity among Asian Americans may be associated with political partisanship and political ideology, but the relationships are not strong. Republicans, compared to other partisan groups, are most likely to self-identify as "ethnic American" and least likely as "ethnic." Persons not identifying with a major party are less likely to identify as "Asian American." Persons who are somewhat liberal are least likely to self-identify as "American." Persons who are very conservative are most likely to self-identify as "ethnic American" and least likely as "ethnic" only. Whether or not one is a U.S. citizen, or expects to become one, matters greatly in ethnic self-identification. A much higher percentage of citizens than noncitizens who do not expect to become naturalized identify with the U.S.-based ("American," "Asian American," and "ethnic American") modes; the reverse is true for identification with the "ethnic" mode. A similar but less strong effect is observed of political participation in Asian American activities and of an individual's membership in Asian American organizations. Attendance at religious services is also associated with ethnic identity choice. Attendeding religious services on a more frequent basis may be associated more closely with being "Asian American" than with being "ethnic" only.

Acculturation

The degree of acculturation or cultural adaptation to the U.S mainstream is assessed by respondents' language-use patterns both at home and in business settings. The relative frequency with which one uses ethnic language media as compared to English media is also examined for its effects on choice of ethnic identity. Table 2.6c shows that these three measures are significantly related to ethnic self-identity choices. Those Asian Americans who use English to communicate at home or do business and those who do not use ethnic media

Table 2.6b Percentage Distribution of Political and Social Integration by Ethnic Identity

	Row Total	AMERICAN	ASIAN AMERICAN	ETHNIC AMERICAN	ASIAN	ETHNIC
*Political Partisanship**						
Democrat	434	12	19	35	4	27
Independent	158	13	15	31	2	34
Republican	195	15	17	39	6	18
no/not sure	431	11	11	32	4	36
*Political Ideology**						
very liberal	101	18	18	33	3	22
somewhat liberal	338	10	17	34	4	31
middle	385	13	14	33	4	32
somewhat conservative	225	16	17	37	5	22
very conservative	45	18	16	42	2	18
*Citizenship**						
No, not expected	116	1	10	12	4	63
yes	824	16	17	39	3	19
*Participation in Activities on Asian Americans**						
none	976	11	14	33	4	32
at least one or more act	242	15	19	38	4	20
*Membership in Ethnic Organization**						
no	1037	11	14	33	4	32
yes	181	15	19	38	4	20
*Frequency of Attending Religious Services**						
never	273	11	14	28	4	38
weekly	355	12	16	36	6	28

Source and Note: See Table 2.6a.

very often are more likely to self-identify as "American" or "Asian American." Conversely, those who mostly use a non-English language at home or in business transactions or use ethnic media most of the time are more likely to self-identify only as "ethnic."

Racial Interaction

We examine the possibility that ethnic group identification is facilitated (or enabled) by the experiences of racial interaction: attitude toward intermarriage, the racial composition of the neighborhood of residence, and the racial background of close personal friends. The quality of interracial contact is assessed by asking respondents if they have any personal experiences with racial discrimination and, if so, whether they think it is based on their ethnic background, and whether they have been victims of a hate crime.

Table 2.6c Percentage Distribution of Acculturation and Racial Interaction by Ethnic Choices

	Row Total	AMERICAN	ASIAN AMERICAN	ETHNIC AMERICAN	ASIAN	ETHNIC
*Language Used at Home with Family**						
other	579	2	13	32	6	45
English	322	36	21	30	2	9
*Language Used in Business or Financial Transactions**						
other	158	1	14	28	8	46
English	863	17	16	36	4	23
*Ethnic Media Use**						
not very often	424	14	16	38	4	24
most of the time	264	3	15	34	4	39
*Attitude toward Intermarriage**						
strongly approve	156	25	17	32	5	17
approve	496	14	17	36	3	25
neither approve nor disapprove	350	7	14	35	5	35
other	216	7	13	29	2	39
Ethnic Makeup of Neighborhood (multiple response)						
mostly white	301	11	15	35	5	31
mostly asian	248	10	16	32	4	34
mostly mixed	552	15	16	33	3	26
Race of Close Personal Friends (multiple response)						
white	382	14	16	38	4	23
Asian	555	12	16	34	4	30
mixed	604	15	16	36	4	26
Experienced Discrimination by Ethnic Background						
no	810	12	15	34	3	30
yes	408	12	16	34	6	29
Hate Crime Victim						
no	1032	11	15	34	4	30
yes	186	17	17	32	5	25

Source and Note: See Table 2.6a.

The percentage distribution of these indicators of racial interaction across modes of ethnic self-identity is found at the bottom half of Table 2.6c. The Chi-square tests of significance indicate that individuals who are more supportive of interracial marriage are more likely to self-identify as "American" and less likely to self-identify as "ethnic." Having close friends who are white or of other race(s) than Asian is related to having a higher probability of self-identifying as "Asian American" or "American" and a lower probability of self-identifying as "ethnic" only; however, having close friendships with other Asians does not seem to have an impact. At the aggregate level, an experience with discrimination based on ethnic background is not significantly associated with ethnic choices. Neither do measures of victimization by hate crimes and the racial makeup of one's neighborhood appear to impact one's ethnic choices.

Homeland Ties

The impact on ethnic self-identity formation of immigrants' social and political ties to their Asian homeland is assessed using a series of survey questions asked only of immigrants born in Asia. The extent of involvement with homeland political institutions is measured by asking if they had been members of any political or partisan organization prior to their emigration to the United States. Also examined is their current involvement in homeland politics. Respondents' attachment to their homeland country and people is gauged by asking if they plan to move back to Asia in the long run and their frequency of contact with homeland people. Foreign-born respondents were also asked to compare their personal trust of government officials and their ability to influence government decisions in the United States and Asia; the impacts of these evaluations on ethnic self-identity are assessed.

As Table 2.6d shows, among Asian immigrants, ethnic self-identity choices do not have a significant relationship with an individual's prior membership in homeland political or party organizations, participation in U.S. homeland

Table 2.6d Percentage Distribution of Homeland Ties by Ethnic Choices among Immigrants

	Row Total	AMERICAN	ASIAN AMERICAN	ETHNIC AMERICAN	ASIAN	ETHNIC
Prior Membership in Homeland Political or Party Organizations						
no	828	5	15	34	4	37
yes	75	8	12	33	8	35
Participation in Homeland Politics in the U.S.						
no	860	4	14	34	4	38
yes	53	15	17	34	6	24
Frequency of Contact with Homeland People in the Past 12 Months						
none	128	9	15	35	6	28
once a week or more	230	6	13	29	6	44
*Expect to Return to Home Country**						
no	863	5	15	35	5	36
yes	50	0	10	16	4	62
Trust More of U.S. Government Officials						
no	413	4	12	36	5	39
yes	500	6	17	33	4	35
*Feel Having More Influence on Decisions Made by U.S. Officials**						
no	554	4	12	34	5	41
yes	359	7	20	34	3	32

Source and Note: See Table 2.6a.

politics, frequency of contacts with homeland people, or the comparative level of trust in government officials. Nevertheless, an expectation to eventually return to an Asian homeland may decrease identification with U.S.-based identities ("American," "Asian American," and "ethnic American") while increasing identification with Asia-based identities. A sense of efficacy through having more influence on U.S. government officials may also increase self-identification as "American" or "Asian American"; but lower self-efficacy may increase self-identification with ethnic-based identities ("ethnic American," "Asian," and "ethnic").

To sum up, at the aggregate level, the only sociopsychological factor that has a suggested significant relationship with ethnic self-identity is interest in ethnic and panethnic news. All the indicators of political integration and civic participation are significant, but citizenship status appears to have the strongest relationship. Ethnic choices may also be strongly linked to English language use and to attitude towards intermarriage, but not to other measures of racial interactions. Among indicators of homeland ties, only the intent to return to Asia and sense of relative efficacy may be related to ethnic choices.

Understanding Ethnic Self-Identity Choices: Multinomial Regression Results

The bivariate results presented in the previous section help us establish relationships at the aggregate level between modes of ethnic self-identity and their possible correlates. In order to understand if and how those correlates can make a difference in predicting the direction and extent of identity choices while considering the potential effects of all other variables simultaneously, we performed a series of multivariate regression procedures and report the results in this section. Our first task is to sort out factors that influence a respondent's decision in making his/her primary ethnic identity choice (Q1 in Table 2.2). Because the dependent variable is categorical and has more than two values, we used multinomial logistic regression, a maximum likelihood-estimation (MLE) based procedure that allows simultaneous analysis of determinants of the various modes of ethnic self-identification. This procedure requires selecting one of the dependent variable categories as a referent point. Effects are then computed and assessed in comparison to that category. To make the results more interpretable, the dependent variable is restricted to four categories[10] and identification as "ethnic" only is assigned as the category of reference.[11] Cell values in Tables 2.7 and 2.8 are logistic coefficients (b) or log odds; standard errors (s.e.) are in the columns to the right of b. Because the impact of any given factor in a MLE model is not constant across values and cannot be interpreted independently of other factor scores, discussion of results and comparison of effect size is facilitated by estimating the parameters with rescaled independent variables where all the scores vary between only 0 and 1.

To recap from the previous section, the following sets of explanatory variables are used in the analyses: respondent's ethnic or country of origin; measures of the affective, cognitive, and evaluative bases of (pan)ethnic identity (belief in a shared culture and a common fate and interest in ethnic news); respondent's political profile as indicated by his/her identification with the mainstream political party and ideology,[12] acquisition of U.S. citizenship or expectation of citizen status, membership in Asian American organizations, level of activism in political campaigns involving Asian American candidates or issues, and level of participation in religious services; respondent's level of acculturation as indicated by his/her reliance on English to communicate at home and in business and to receive information and entertainment from the mass media;[13] four measures of personal interracial interactions (experience with ethnic discrimination,[14] attitude toward intermarriage, residence in a mostly white neighborhood, and intimate friendships with whites); and respondent's socialization in the United States (whether their primary education was outside the United States and the length of stay as a proportion of one's life in the United States). In addition, controls for sociodemographic background characteristics such as education, family income, gender, age, length of residence in a community, employment status, and marital status are included in the analyses.

Table 2.7 presents the multivariate results. The "American" columns report respondents' likelihood to prefer the "American" identity to an "ethnic" only identity. Here, ethnic origin in and by itself appears to strongly matter in the identity choice of Asian Americans. Specifically, other conditions being equal, Filipinos, Japanese, and South Asians are more likely to identify as "American" than the Chinese. Those who are more politically assimilated in terms of partisan identification as Republican, citizenship status, or involvement in Asian American political events; those who are more acculturated in terms of their ability and preference in English language use and supportive attitude toward intermarriage; and those who are older in age, employed, or spent a higher proportion of their life in the U.S. are more likely to self-identify as "American" than those who do not share these attributes. Conversely, those who are more involved in ethnic organizations, have experienced racial discrimination, are female, or have received most of their education outside of the United States are less likely to self-identify as "American" than as "ethnic."

The middle columns in Table 2.7 report results for choosing the "Asian American" identity relative to choosing an ethnic-only identity. Here, respondents of South Asian descent may be more likely than those of other Asian descents to prefer a panethnic American identity to an ethnic-only identity. Those who perceive a shared culture among Asians in America are more politically assimilated in terms of partisan identification as Republican, citizenship status, and involvement in Asian American political events; and older in age or employed have a higher likelihood of self-identifing as "Asian American." Conversely, those who have experienced racial discrimination,

Table 2.7 Predicting Ethnic Identity Choices among Asian Americans

	AMERICAN		ASIAN AMERICAN		ETHNIC AMERICAN	
	b	s.e.	b	s.e.	b	s.e.
(Intercept)	−8.249	1.462	−3.328	.807	−2.535	.652
Ethnic Origin or *Primordial Ties (ref = Chinese)*						
Filipino	2.279*	.947	.300	.517	.628	.419
Japanese	2.891**	1.006	.596	.632	.389	.544
Korean	−.340	1.315	.036	.448	.157	.343
South Asian	3.567**	.959	1.617**	.534	1.022*	.462
Vietnamese	−.761	1.314	−.913^	.527	−.477	.407
Socio psychological Engagement						
shared culture	.239	.551	.853*	.437	.102	.357
linked fate	−.051	.500	.166	.392	.346	.323
ethnic news interest	.499	.716	.575	.582	.602	.490
Political Integration and Civic Participation						
Democratic partisanship	−.263	.475	.555	.368	−.056	.304
Republican partisanship	1.368*	.625	.959*	.492	.420	.416
liberal ideology	−.549	.549	−.344	.422	−.702*	.350
citizenship status	2.845**	.893	1.741**	.486	2.289**	.377
religious attendance	−.607	.476	.088	.378	−.214	.311
ethnic organization membership	−1.167*	.460	−.681^	.376	−.164	.306
participation in Asian American causes	3.662*	1.523	2.812*	1.229	1.364	1.098
Acculturation/Racial Interaction						
English language use	2.438*	1.160	.975	.719	.563	.582
support intermarriage	1.878**	.618	.853^	.468	.682^	.382
white neighborhood	−.115	.388	−.314	.302	−.072	.238
white close friends	.028	.351	.104	.283	.456*	.234
experience with discrimination	−1.161*	.499	−.886*	.387	−.712*	.317
Socialization and Social Connectedness						
education	−.295	.718	−1.057*	.513	−.010	.419
female	−.832*	.329	−.766**	.262	−.497*	.215
age	2.903**	.891	1.438*	.732	1.604*	.615
employed	.777*	.374	.646*	.297	.347	.235
proportion of life in U.S.	1.495*	.766	.784	.592	.503	.501
non-U.S. education	−1.597**	.477	−1.072**	.341	−.972**	.291

N = 774
−2 Log Likelihood (Intercept only) = 2018.76
Model Chi-Sq = 476.96
Nagelkerke R-sq = .497; McFadden = .236

Note: The dependent is a categorical variable with four possible responses. The reference category is R's self-identity as "ethnic" only. The parameters are estimated using multinomial regression procedures with rescaled independent variables where scores are to vary only between 0 and 1. Excluded variables are family income, length of community residence, and marital status. b=unstandardized but re-scaled logistic coefficient, s.e.=standard error   ^.05< p ≤.10   *.005< p ≤.05   **p ≤.005
Source: PNAAPS 2000–2001.

are less educated, female, or have received most of their, education outside of the United States are significantly less likely to self-identify with the pan–Asian American label. In nine out of ten instances, being Vietnamese and a member of an ethnic organization may be associated with less, but having a more favorable attitude toward intermarriage may be associated with higher, incidence of panethnic identification.

The two columns under "Ethnic American" in Table 2.7 report results for respondents' chance of choosing the "ethnic American" identity over an ethnic-only identity. Here again, being South Asian alone may be associated with more identification as "ethnic American" (South Asian American) than "ethnic" (South Asian). This is not the case with other Asian Americans. Although this identification appears to be positively associated with greater political assimilation in terms of citizenship status and being older in age and greater racial integration in friendship patterns, it can be negatively associated with having a conservative ideology, experiencing racial discrimination, being female, being married, or having received most of one's education outside of the United States. In at least nine out of ten instances, having a more favorable attitude toward intermarriage may also correlate with the likelihood of self-identification as "ethnic American" (e.g., "Korean American") over "ethnic" (e.g., "Korean").

Together, these multinomial results suggest that the ethnic self-identity choices Asian Americans make for adopting each of the three American-based identities rather than an ethnic-only label can be significantly associated in different ways with the sets of factors suggested by previous research. Other conditions being equal, we note that a respondent of South Asian descent is more likely to self-identify as either "American," "Asian American," or "South Asian American" than as "South Asian." This would not be the case with other Asian ethnic groups, even though a person of Japanese or Filipino descent may also be more likely to self-identify as an "American" as compared to a Chinese respondent of equal status.

Among the sociopsychological indicators of ethnicity, only the perception of a common culture is significant enough to predict self-identification as "Asian American" over "ethnic." Although Democratic partisanship and the frequency of attending religious services have no independent relationship with ethnic decisions, being or expecting to become a citizen is positively associated with the likelihood of self-identification with each of the U.S.-based identities. Stronger identification as Republican and greater participation in Asian American causes are associated with a greater likelihood of identification as "American" or "Asian American." Political ideology may not matter except for predicting identification as "ethnic American." Being a member of an ethnic organization is negatively associated with the odds of identifying as "American" and perhaps "Asian Americans," but not as "ethnic American."

Turning to indicators of social and cultural adaptation, an experience with discrimination because of ethnic background is negatively associated with the odds of adopting U.S.-based identities, while being supportive of intermarriage is positively associated with it. A preference for using English to communicate at home and in business is linked to a greater likelihood of self-identifying as "American." Having close friends who are mostly white may be linked to a greater identification as "ethnic American" over "ethnic." However, residing in a majority white neighborhood does not seem to be related to ethnic decision-making.

In terms of sociodemographic background, particularly one's socialization and social ties, we find that being female and receiving a mostly non-U.S. education are associated with a lower likelihood, while being older is associated with a greater likelihood, of preferring each of the three U.S.-based self-identity modes to "ethnic." Greater educational achievement in and of itself is associated with a lower likelihood of identification as "Asian American," but connection to a social network via employment is associated with a greater likelihood of identification with two of the American modes. Spending a higher percentage of one's lifetime in the U.S. is associated with a greater likelihood of identification as "American" but not with other U.S.-based identities. Nevertheless, neither family income, length of residence in a community, nor marital status has a discernible effect on making ethnic choices.

Predicting the Adoption and Intensity of Pan–Asian American Identity: Multivariate Results

Our analysis in a previous section demonstrates that although many Asian Americans may not choose panethnic American terms as their primary identity, they are certainly willing to identify as Asian American when forced to make a choice. This section explores the forces beneath the formation of this mostly secondary but politically critical panethnic orientation in this polyethnic minority population. Past research on ethnic identification comparing immigrant parents and their children reports different and contrasting paths of identity formation. Whereas adult immigrants may feel the pressure of becoming assimilated Americans, their U.S.-born children tend to develop a stronger sense of ethnic identity and consciousness over time because of personal and situational experiences dealing with racial discrimination (Portes and Rumbaut, 2001). Because immigrants may possess a different set of orientations and reactions to the same situation and context than their U.S.-born counterparts, we conduct separate analyses for the foreign-born and the U.S.-born to understand the sources of their panethnic orientation.

The "Asia-born" column of Table 2.8 presents results among the Asia-born using logistic regression, a procedure appropriate for analyzing effects with dichotomous dependent variables. Interpretation of the cell values is similar to those for Table 2.7, except that the reference category for the dependent variable is among those who do not self-identify as Asian American as either their primary or secondary identity. Because our focus in this section is on the panethnic

Table 2.8 Predicting the Adoption of Panethnic Self-Identification by Nativity

	ASIA-BORN		U.S.-BORN	
	b	s.e.	b	s.e.
(Constant)	−.387	.641	.193	1.194
Ethnic Origin or *Primordial Ties (ref=Chinese)*				
Filipino	.960*	.420	−1.902*	.957
Japanese	.417	.591	−1.570^	.916
Korean	−.550^	.327	.231	1.397
South Asian	.340	.402	−.580	1.199
Vietnamese	.271	.462	6.641	22.269
Sociopsychological Engagement				
shared culture	.705*	.340	1.518*	.617
panethnic linked fate	.591*	.282	.540	.507
attention to Asian American news	.932*	.398	1.436*	.712
Political Integration and Civic Participation				
Democratic partisanship	.747*	.299	.689	.524
Republican partisanship	.353	.382	1.002	.808
liberal ideology	−.808*	.331	−.040	.632
citizenship status	.263	.355		
religious attendance	.270	.296	.547	.545
ethnic organization membership	.317	.309	−.191	.473
participation in Asian American causes	2.072^	1.155	.750	1.704
Acculturation/Racial Interaction				
English language use	−.419	.575	1.069	1.144
support intermarriage	.089	.365	1.499*	.646
white neighborhood	.071	.221	−.387	.458
white close friends	.038	.218	.344	.380
experience with discrimination	−.633*	.304	1.824**	.588
Socialization and Social Connectedness				
education	−.243	.411	−2.441**	.856
female	−.932**	.211	−.706*	.361
age	−.189	.612	−2.298*	.901
employed	.264	.224	.111	.384
proportion of life in U.S.	.359	.662		
non-U.S. education	−.334	.269		
Homeland Ties				
active in homeland politics	.406	.487		
maintain homeland contact	−.409	.374		
plan to return to Asia	−.418	.483		
prior partisanshipence	−1.197*	.496		
more trust and influence in U.S.	.496*	.251		
N	555		220	
−2 Log Likelihood	637.49		217.65	
Model Chi-sq(31,26)	117.57		54.43	
Negelkerke R-sq	.257		.309	

Note: The dependent variable is a dichotomous variable indicating the presence of R's self-identification as Asian American both as a primary and secondary preference. The parameters are estimated using logistic regression procedures with rescaled independent variables where scores are to vary only between 0 and 1. Excluded variables are family income, length of community residence, and marital status.
Source: PNAAPS 2000–2001.

phenomenon, we use three sociopsychological indicators of panethnicity to tap into one's predisposition toward a pan–Asian American self-identity. The results show that each of the indicators—the degree of perceiving a shared culture, sense of a panethnic linked fate, and interest in Asian American news—are positively associated with the odds of panethnic self-identification. We also find that the likelihood of choosing a panethnic identity is relatively high among Filipinos, but—nine in ten times—less prevalent among Koreans, all else being equal. The adoption of panethnicity among Asian-born respondents appears to correlate with the strength of identification with the Democratic Party and the perception of having a greater say in U.S. than homeland government decisions.[15] In nine out of ten times, greater participation in Asian American causes is associated with the adoption of such identification. However, an Asian immigrant is less likely to adopt the panethnic identity if he or she is more conservative in political ideology, experienced racial or ethnic discrimination, female, or had been active in a political or party organization while in Asia.

Among the U.S.-born (shown in the "U.S.-born" column of Table 2.8), being Filipino (and, in nine out of ten times, Japanese) may be associated with a lower likelihood of adopting the panethnic identity. Perceiving a shared culture among Asian Americans and having an interest in Asian American news—two of the sociopsychological indicators of identity—as well as having a supportive attitude toward intermarriage may be positively related to the adoption of panethnic identity. Importantly, personal experiences with racial discrimination may be positively, rather than negatively, associated with adopting a panethnic identification among the U.S.-born. However, being female, in addition to being more educated and older in age, may be negatively associated with the likelihood of U.S.-born Asians to self-identify as "Asian American." None of the indicators of political and civic institutional ties are significant enough to predict the adoption of panethnicity among the U.S.-born.

Turning to predictors of the intensity of the panethnic Asian American identity (Q3 in Table 2.2), we report results of ordinary least squares-based (OLS) regression analysis, a procedure appropriate for estimating effects on a continuous dependent variable, for the foreign born sample in the "Asia-born" columns of Table 2.9. Here, greater intensity of panethnic identification among the foreign-born may be associated with higher attention to Asian American news and participation in Asian American affairs. In at least nine out of ten times, respondents who possess a greater sense of a common culture and stronger identification with the Democratic Party are also more likely to have a higher sense of panethnic identification. However, being Korean, more conservative in ideology, female, educated mostly outside of the U.S. context, or being formally active in a homeland political party or other organization may be associated with having a weaker sense of panethnicity. Experience of racial discrimination, nevertheless, is insignificant, along with other indicators of cultural- and social-structural adaptation.

Table 2.9 Predicting the Intensity of Panethnic Self Identification by Nativity

	ASIA-BORN			U.S.-BORN		
	b	s.e.	t-statistic	b	s.e.	t-statistic
(Constant)	.630	.365	1.725	.547	.542	1.008
Ethnic Origin or *Primordial Ties (ref = Chinese)*						
Filipino	.160	.192	.836	−.486	.323	−1.504
Japanese	.061	.276	.220	−.756	.313	−2.420
Korean	−.395	.154	−2.572	−.130	.414	−.314
South Asian	.187	.188	.995	−.115	.371	−.309
Vietnamese	.090	.213	.422	1.149	1.051	1.093
Socio psychological Engagement						
shared culture	.090	.053	1.713	.137	.079	1.727
panethnic linked fate	.051	.043	1.186	.107	.064	1.654
attention to Asian American news	.123	.060	2.037	.241	.089	2.697
Political Integration and Civic Participation						
Democratic partisanship	.086	.045	1.900	−.006	.067	−.090
Republican partisanship	.026	.058	.440	.003	.104	.029
liberal ideology	−.114	.050	−2.267	.047	.081	.584
citizenship status	.052	.084	.625	.345		
religious attendance	.002	.137	.016	−.011	.182	−.059
ethnic Organization membership	.053	.034	1.545	.059	.050	1.175
participation in Asian American causes	.148	.061	2.447	.016	.076	.211
Acculturation/Racial Interaction						
English language use	−.079	.089	−.883	.084	.141	.591
support intermarriage	.039	.056	.696	.112	.085	1.323
white neighborhood	−.016	.102	−.153	.185	.176	1.049
white close friends	.026	.100	.260	.139	.144	.970
experience with discrimination	−.109	.139	−.780	.259	.208	1.248
Socialization and Social Connectedness						
education	−.021	.036	−.574	−.107	.059	−1.810
female	−.356	.097	−3.654	−.076	.136	−.558
age	.001	.003	.429	−.005	.004	−1.180
employed	.078	.105	.742	−.057	.152	−.377
proportion of life in U.S.	.408	.300	1.359			
non-U.S. education	−.240	.123	−1.953			
Homeland Ties						
active in homeland politics	.022	.210	.106			
maintain homeland contact	−.049	.038	−1.274			
plan to return to Asia	−.042	.211	−.199			
prior partisanship	−.143	.056	−2.558			
more trust and influence in U.S.	.185	.117	1.590			
N	555			220		
F	3.35**			2.21**		
Adj-R-sq	116			.113		

Note: The dependent variable is a 4-point scale measuring the intensity of panethnic identification among Asian Americans. b = unstandardized ordinary least squares regression coefficient, s.e. = standard error.
Source: PNAAPS 2000–2001.

Among the U.S.-born in Table 2.9, being attentive to Asian American news may be related to having a stronger sense of identification with the pan–Asian American concept. Having a greater sense of common fate with fellow Asian Americans may be marginally significant to achieve the same effect. However, other conditions being equal, being U.S.-born Japanese is associated with a weaker sense of panethnic identity. Nine in ten times, having more years of education is also negatively related to the intensity of panethnicity. Many factors significant in predicting the strength of panethnic identification for the foreign-born such as political ideology, gender, and level of participation in pan–Asian American community affairs are not found to be useful for predicting the behavior of the native-born.

Findings reported in this section suggest that nativity matters greatly in understanding the formation of panethnic identity. Results in both Tables 2.8 and 2.9 show that immigration experiences may mold and shape the formation of ethnic self-identification so that it differs from patterns among the native-born. For example, Filipinos who are foreign-born are more likely, but those born in the U.S. are less likely, to adopt panethnicity. U.S.-born Japanese are less likely than their foreign-born counterparts to adopt panethnicity. Conversely, foreign-born Koreans are less likely than their U.S.-born counterparts to adopt panethnicity. Strength of Democratic partisanship, ideology, and level of involvement in Asian American affairs may be positively related to the adoption of panethnicity, but only for the Asia-born. Experience with discrimination may be negatively related to the adoption of panethnicity among the Asia-born, but the two may be positively related among the U.S.-born. More education and being older are associated with a lower likelihood of adopting panethnicity, but this is true only among the U.S.-born. However, regardless of nativity, the likelihood of adopting panethnicity may be positively associated with the perceptions of a shared fate among Asians and with paying more attention to Asian American news. Being female may be associated with a lower chance of adopting panethnic identity, but indicators of acculturation and structural adaptation have little impact. A similar effect of nativity is found in predicting the intensity of panethnic identification, except that experiences of discrimination and age may not matter, and U.S.-born women may not have a significantly lower level of panethnicity than U.S.-born men.

Among immigrant-only measures, having prior membership and participation in a homeland political party or organization may interfere with the formation of panethnic identification in both direction and strength. The perception of having more trust and a greater say in the U.S. system may be associated with a higher likelihood, and having received education mostly outside of the United States may be associated with a lower likelihood, of adopting panethnic identification. However, neither participation in homeland politics, maintaining contacts with homeland people, nor the future intent to return to the Asia homeland is significant enough in predicting the adoption or the strength of an immigrant's self-identification as "Asian American."

Discussion and Conclusion

In this chapter, we explore the contours and sources of ethnic self-identities among Asian Americans. We find that two-thirds of the respondents prefer to identify themselves in ethnic-specific modes, with the percentage of ethnic American identifiers (e.g., "Chinese American") being slightly higher than that of ethnic only identifiers (e.g., "Chinese"). Although only one-sixth of respondents would identify themselves first and foremost as "Asian American," close to six in ten respondents were able to identify with this panethnic term after probing. Furthermore, the distribution of self-identity varies by interview language and sampling method. These results demonstrate that ethnic identity among Asian Americans is multilayered and prone to influence by the survey and the social context.

Findings at the aggregate level show that ethnic self-identification varies greatly by ethnic origin. Japanese Americans are most likely to identify only as "American"; Chinese, Korean, and Vietnamese are most likely to identify only as "ethnic." While both Filipinos and South Asians are most likely to identify as "ethnic American," South Asians have the highest percentage of "Asian American" identifiers. When other conditions are controlled, South Asians, compared to Chinese, are more likely to self-identify not only as "Asian American" but also with the two other American-based identities. This is not the case with respondents of other ethnicities, except that a person of Japanese or Filipino descent is also more likely to identify only as "American" than as "ethnic." Primordial ties matter but only for some groups and selected identity modes. The failure to entirely reject this theory also points to the necessity in future research to identify missing factors that may better account for ethnic differences.

Indicators of sociopsychological engagement are generally very useful for predicting the acquisition and the intensity of panethnic identification. However, they do not seem to matter much in distinguishing identity choices between ethnic-only and other American-based identity modes either at the bivariate or multivariate level. In fact, only the perception of a common culture is statistically significant as a predictor and is positively associated with the panethnic "Asian American" identity. This may point to the limitations in extant conceptualization and operationalization of the social identity theory in understanding ethnic options for a multiethnic nonwhite majority immigrant population.

Turning to indicators of political integration and civic participation, the findings underscore the importance of conducting separate analyses for predicting ethnic choices and for predicting the acquisition and strength of panethnicity. Often, the same variable may play a different and sometimes contrary role in impacting outcome. Although stronger identification as Republican but not Democrat may structure ethnic choices for two of the U.S.-based identities, stronger identification as Democrat but not Republican is positively associated with the acquisition and strength of panethnicity among immigrant respondents. Other conditions being equal, being or expecting to become a citizen is associated with a higher likelihood of self-identification with each of the U.S.-based identities, but it may not be associated with the acquisition and the intensity of panethnicity. Membership in an ethnic organization is negatively associated with the identification as "American" and potentially "Asian American," but it has little relationship with either the adoption or the strength of panethnicity. This suggests that many Asian American organizations are ethnic-based and may emphasize ethnic group interests over the larger U.S. society-based interests in general. However, participation in ethnic organization activities may be associated with a heightened awareness of the pan–Asian American group identity and interest. Possessing a more liberal ideological outlook, on the other hand, may be associated with lower odds of identification as "ethnic American" over "ethnic," as well as the adoption and strength of panethnicity among the Asia-born. Greater participation in Asian American political affairs may be associated with higher odds of identification as "American" or "Asian American" as well as the adoption and strength of panethnicity among the Asia-born. The frequency of religious attendance does not show an independent impact on any of the identity models.

Indicators of acculturation and social structural adaptation are more useful for predicting ethnic choices than the acquisition and strength of panethnicity. Both a preference for using English in different settings and a supportive attitude toward intermarriage may be associated with a greater likelihood to identify only as "American," but attitudes toward intermarriage may also be associated with higher odds of choosing two other U.S.-based identities. Crossracial friendship may be associated with identification as "ethnic American" over "ethnic," but neighborhood racial makeup may not matter in deciding the direction of ethnic identification. None of these indicators may be associated with the adoption or the intensity of panethnicity, except perhaps holding a supportive attitude toward intermarriage.

One surprising finding, which contradicts predictions based on readings of racial formation theory, is that experiences with discrimination because of ethnic background may be associated with a lower likelihood of adopting any of the three American-based identity modes. A further analysis by nativity suggests that the effect of racial experiences may differ between the U.S.-born and the foreign-born. Specifically, the experience of racial discrimination may contribute to the process of racialization and mobilize panethnic identification among the U.S.-born; such experiences may impede the process of racialization and discourage the formation of panethnicity for those born in Asia. Our results suggest support for the reactive ethnicity hypothesis and the need for revising the racial formation theory to understand the process of forming new American identities among immigration-impacted non-white populations. They also underline the importance of recognizing that the *processes* of identity formation may be very different for the U.S.-born compared to immigrants. Rather than becoming politicized and mobilized, immigrants who experience racial discrimination may feel alienated or petrified in the host society.

Turning to indicators of socialization and social ties, these factors are more useful in predicting the direction of ethnic identification than the acquisition and strength of panethnicity, even though place of birth or nativity and gender consistently matter in making these predictions. Being female or having received education mostly outside of the United States may be negatively associated with a respondent's likelihood of adopting any of the three U.S.-based identity modes. Being older in age has exactly the opposite effect. Being employed may be associated with a higher chance of identifying oneself as "American" and "Asian American." Likewise, having a longer family history in the United States may be associated with a higher likelihood of adopting the "American" identity mode, but not the panethnic or ethnic American modes. Regardless of the place of birth, women are less likely to adopt panethnicity than men. However, U.S.-born Asians who are better educated and older in age are less likely to adopt panethnicity, while only Asia-born, but not U.S.-born, women are likely to have a weaker draw to panethnicity than their male counterparts. This last result suggests that the role of gender in structuring ethnic identity may differ by nativity among Asian Americans.

Finally, among immigrants, indicators of homeland ties may lend at best partial support to the theory of transnationalism or the persistence of transnational influence, either at the bivariate or multivariate level. At the aggregate level, only two of the five indicators—plan to return to the homeland and relative efficacy within the United States—are associated with the mode of ethnic identification. Other conditions being equal, prior partisanship may be negatively associated with the acquisition of new ethnic identity (panethnicity), but having more trust and feeling more efficacious about one's influence on government decisions in the host land than in the homeland may be positively associated with the adoption of panethnicity. Neither frequency of homeland contact, participation in homeland politics in the United States, nor one's plan to return to Asia has an independent impact on the adoption of a panethnic identity. Prior membership and participation in a political party and other political organizations may also have the unique impact of weakening the intensity of panethnicity, but not any other indicators of homeland ties.

Overall, our findings confirm that ethnic identity among Asian Americans is a multilayered, socially constructed phenomenon. Indicators of primordial ties related to ethnic origin and prior socialization, in addition to indicators of cultural, social, and political integration, may play an important role in structuring ethnicity identity preferences among contemporary Asian Americans. Indicators of sociopsychological attachment are only marginally useful in understanding the ethnic identity choices of this immigrant population, but they are very useful in predicting the acquisition and the strength of panethnicity. On the other hand, indicators of acculturation and social-structural adaptation as well as of socialization and social ties appear to be less useful in understanding the adoption and the intensity of panethnicity. And then, certain indicators of political integration and civic participation have opposite effects in structuring the making of ethnic choices as well as the acquisition and strength of panethnicity. While we started out this chapter aiming to provide a clear understanding of ethnic identity, our findings point to the incredibly complex nature of identity and identity formation. These findings underscore the need to distinguish between models for the two and highlight the need for reconsideration and expansion of the extant conceptual frameworks on studying ethnic identity formation for this nonwhite, multiethnic, multilingual, and transnational population.

CHAPTER 3

Political Orientations: Beliefs and Attitudes about Government

How do Asian Americans think and act politically? In this chapter, the directions and sources of Asian Americans' political orientations toward the U.S. political system and government are examined. The political attitudes of central concern to this chapter are interest in what goes on in government in general, trust in local and state government officials, beliefs about local public officials' responsiveness to citizen complaints, and political ideology. We also examine the perceived influence of Asian Americans on local government decision making. For those born in Asia, we compare their relative levels of political trust in local U.S. and homeland government and their perceptions of their relative abilities to influence government decisions in the United States and in the homeland.

Differences in political attitudes and beliefs among ethnic groups based on country of personal or family origin are examined.[1] Also assessed is whether political orientations differ significantly by whether the respondent was born in the United States or in Asia. Those who immigrated to the United States have experiences with government and politics in another country, which may be quite different from the experiences of lifelong residents of the United States. Among those who were born outside of the United States, the proportion of their life lived in the United States, among other factors, could affect opportunities to acquire knowledge of the U.S. political system and develop the beliefs and attitudes examined in this research. Three-fourths of the survey respondents were born in Asia; their average length of years living in the United States is 13, while their average age is 44. Immigrants' political beliefs and attitudes may also vary with whether or not they have attained American citizenship. Among noncitizens, attitudes and beliefs may differ between those who expect to become citizens and those who do not. In our sample, 59 percent of immigrants are citizens and 29 percent are immigrant noncitizens who expect to become citizens. Twelve percent of the immigrants are not citizens and do not expect to become citizens.

Differences in socioeconomic resources may also affect patterns of political attitudes and beliefs. Basic socioeconomic status measures such as education and income, which have been found to have a major influence on political behavior in studies of the general American population, are expected to play a role in structuring Asian Americans' political orientations. However, their effects may not be the same as those observed in the general population. In addition to these basic sociodemographic characteristics, other variables may play an even larger role in impacting the extent and direction of Asian Americans' political orientations.

Factors Influencing the Acquisition of Political Orientations

The conceptual frameworks introduced in Chapter 1 and the crossdisciplinary examination of ethnic identity theory in Chapter 2 provide a useful guide to the conceptual approaches used here to examine factors that may help structure the political orientations of Asian Americans. Primarily, proponents of primordial ties argue that some aspects of ethnicity or ethnic culture may not be readily explained away by individual or contextual factors. Social identity theory suggests that emotional ties, concerns with a common fate perceived as shared by group members, and panethnic ties may be significant in structuring political attitudes. Acculturation theory suggests that language and ethnic media use patterns, friendship patterns, the extent of ethnic integration in the residential neighborhood, and political and civic organizational ties may influence political attitudes and beliefs. Transnationalism implies a number of other variables that might impact attitudes; these include measures of continued contact with the country of origin, such as recency of visits to the home country, contact with the home country, involvement in politics in the home country, and attention to media coverage of the home country. The formation of a racialized or panethnicized identity may also influence interest in and attitudes toward government and that may be stimulated by political events (such as the government's scapegoating of an ethnic or racial group member) and personal experiences such as discrimination based on race or ethnicity.

We start with the premise that political learning is a lifelong process, with beliefs and attitudes being formed and modified as a result of interaction with a myriad of socializing agents (Beck, 1974; Jennings and Niemi, 1981; Jennings and Markus, 1984; Jennings, 1987, 1996; Sigel, 1988; Beck and Jennings, 1991; Damico, Conway, and Damico, 1998; Conway and Damico, 2000; Damico, Conway, and Damico, 2000; Sigel and Jenkins, 2001). Those agents include the family, friends, peers, schooling, the mass media, and representatives of the political system (Conway, 2000), with political education beginning in early childhood. Children first learn beliefs and attitudes by overhearing conversations of family members about political subjects. The influence of friends, acquaintances, and peers on individuals' attitudes, beliefs, values, and behavior occurs both through personal interactions and participation in formal organizations. Formal schooling serves to inculcate political orientations through the school's curriculum, classroom rituals, and the values and attitudes unconsciously transmitted by its staff as well as by the school's social climate, student organizations, and extracurricular activities. The mass media may also significantly structure beliefs and attitudes toward government processes, institutions, and authorities (Eveland, McLeod, and Horowitz, 1998; McLeod, Scheufele, and Moy, 1999; Eveland

and Scheufele, 2000; McLeod, 2000; Shah, McLeod, and Yoon, 2001). Engaging in political activities such as voting, campaigning, or protest demonstrations can influence individuals' subsequent evaluations of internal political efficacy and ideological position (Finkel, 1986; Jennings, 1987). For adult immigrants, messages sent by television or other mass media may be particularly influential in the processes of acquiring political attitudes and beliefs in the new country (Black and Leithner, 1988; Chaffee and Yang, 1990; Chaffee, Nass, and Yang, 1990; Viswanath and Arora, 2000).

John Zaller (1992) suggests that political awareness is a necessary condition for the formation of political attitudes and beliefs. He argues that "every opinion is a marriage of information and predisposition" (1992: 6), with political information provided to the public through elite discourse that is conveyed most often through the mass media. However, information can also be distributed through other channels of political socialization, both personal and organizational. By "information," Zaller means stereotypes, frames of reference, and elite leadership cues. The extent to which information is received and retained is a function of individuals' political attentiveness and existing values. Zaller asserts that political awareness is best measured by simple tests of factual information about politics. According to Zaller, such tests indicate what has been learned and serve as the best possible indicator of cognitive engagement with public affairs.

What Zaller calls political awareness is measured in the analysis presented here by a summed index of political knowledge composed of responses to three questions: familiarity with the U.S. presidential election process, awareness of a prominent event of concern to the Chinese and also to other Asian American communities (such as the Wen Ho Lee case), and knowledge of a panethnic political movement that sought to organize the presidential vote of Asian Americans in Election 2000 (the 80-20 initiative). Those who score higher in political awareness are expected to differ from those who score lower on the index in their levels of political interest and other political attitudes.

To examine the relationship at the bivariate level between the list of factors informed by the literature and measures of political orientations, the results of a series of cross tabulations are presented. The independent effect of these explanatory variables on political interest, political ideology, and the acquisition of other political orientations are then assessed using multivariate analyses.

Political Orientations and Their Correlates

Political Ideology

Central to research on American voting behavior, political ideology is considered "a symbol for the systems of political belief—however enriched or impoverished—that ordinary citizens espouse." Chief among its functions is "to provide structure, organization, and coherence to one's thinking with regard to matters that the ideology defines as relevant to politics" (Miller and

Shanks, 1996: 121). Thus, political ideology is often thought to have unparalleled influence over the direction of political party identification and policy preferences.

How much and how do Asian Americans identify themselves in conventional ideological terms? Table 3.1 shows that, in general, Asian Americans indicate that they are more liberal than conservative. Overall, 8 percent of the PNAAPS respondents classify themselves as very liberal, 28 percent as somewhat liberal, 32 percent as middle of the road, 18 percent as somewhat conservative, and 4 percent as very conservative. Only 10 percent are not sure where to place themselves. Although in each ethnic group the percentage of liberals is higher than that of conservatives, significant ethnic group differences exist. For instance, Filipinos (40 percent) and South Asians (61 percent) are more likely to identify themselves as very liberal or somewhat liberal than are Japanese (34 percent), Koreans (33 percent), Chinese (30 percent), and Vietnamese (22 percent). Thirty-four percent of Filipinos place themselves in one of the conservative categories, as do 31 percent of Koreans and 24 percent of the Japanese. Only 17 percent of South Asians, 13 percent of Chinese, and 9 percent of the Vietnamese consider themselves conservative.

Even though nine out of ten Asian American respondents are able to place themselves along the liberalism-conservatism scale, this may not indicate that they have a deep understanding of the meaning of the labels. When a small group of respondents are asked to define the labels,[2] even though almost all could place themselves along the liberal-conservative continuum, about half gave conventional meanings, but others appeared more uncertain of the meanings.[3]

Contrary to popular notions, Asians with higher incomes are not necessarily more conservative in ideological self-placement. In fact, a higher percentage of Asians with family income at or over $60,000 identify themselves as very or somewhat liberal. In contrast, a larger percentage of Asians with family income at or lower than $30,000 identify themselves as somewhat or very conservative. A significantly larger percentage of respondents in the lower income groups as well as those who fail to indicate income are unsure of their ideological self-placement. Those with at least some college education are more likely to self-identify as very or somewhat liberal, while those with no college education are more uncertain of their ideological identity than those with at least some college education. Nativity matters in that a larger share of the U.S.-born (23 percent) are more likely to be somewhat conservative than the foreign-born (17 percent) and a greater share of immigrants (11 percent) are unsure of their ideological identification than the natives (6 percent). There is no significant difference in the patterns of ideological self-placement between citizens and noncitizens. Consistent with studies of the general population, a strong association exists between ideology and party identification. Those Asians who are very or somewhat liberal are more likely to be Democratic Party identifiers and those who are very or somewhat conservative are more likely to be Republican Party

Table 3.1 Percentage Distribution of Political Orientations by Ethnic Origin

Political Ideology

How would you describe your views on most matters having to do with politics? Do you generally think of yourself as very liberal, somewhat liberal, middle-of-the-road, somewhat conservative, or very conservative?

	ALL	CHINESE	KOREAN	VIETNAMESE	JAPANESE	FILIPINO	SOUTH ASIAN
very liberal	8	4	4	12	9	8	18
somewhat liberal	28	26	29	10	25	32	43
middle-of-the-road	32	42	28	47	37	18	16
somewhat conservative	18	11	27	5	20	29	14
very conservative	4	2	4	4	4	5	3
not sure	10	15	8	21	4	6	6

Political Interest

How interested are you in politics and what's going on in government in general? Are you very interested, somewhat interested, only slightly interested, or not at all interested in politics and what goes on in government?

	ALL	CHINESE	KOREAN	VIETNAMESE	JAPANESE	FILIPINO	SOUTH ASIAN
very interested	24	18	28	21	21	24	38
somewhat interested	37	46	43	31	38	29	34
slightly interested	24	24	24	27	25	26	16
not at all interested	13	10	4	18	16	20	11
not sure	1	2	1	3	1	1	–

(cont.)

Table 3.1 (*Continued*)

Political Trust in Local Public Officials

Next, I have a few questions concerning your view of U.S. government officials: How much of the time do you think you can trust your local and state government officials to do what is right—just about always, most of the time, only some of the time, or none at all?

	ALL	CHINESE	KOREAN	VIETNAMESE	JAPANESE	FILIPINO	SOUTH ASIAN
just about always	7	2	10	15	4	9	4
most of the time	30	28	33	23	28	32	39
some of the time	44	35	44	45	54	45	48
none at all	8	10	5	6	8	8	5
not sure	11	25	8	11	6	6	5

(Asked of immigrants) Do you feel you can generally trust U.S. government officials more, about the same, or less than government officials in your home country?

	ALL	CHINESE	KOREAN	VIETNAMESE	JAPANESE	FILIPINO	SOUTH ASIAN
more	55	39	72	67	29	58	60
about the same	26	33	18	13	46	22	30
less	6	7	2	2	15	11	6
not sure	13	21	7	18	10	7	5

(*cont.*)

Table 3.1 (*Continued*)

Perceived Local Government Officials' Responsiveness to Citizen Complaints

If you had some complaint about a government activity and you took that complaint to a local public official, do you think that he or she would pay a lot of attention to what you say, some attention, very little attention, or none at all?

	ALL	CHINESE	KOREAN	VIETNAMESE	JAPANESE	FILIPINO	SOUTH ASIAN
a lot	9	6	6	12	7	14	10
some	33	25	25	23	39	40	45
very little	27	20	42	34	30	25	23
none at all	14	18	21	8	13	14	10
not sure	16	31	5	23	12	7	13

Perceived Personal Influence over Local Government Officials' Decisions

How much influence do you think someone like you can have over local government decisions—a lot, a moderate amount, a little, or none at all?

	ALL	CHINESE	KOREAN	VIETNAMESE	JAPANESE	FILIPINO	SOUTH ASIAN
a lot	6	1	5	7	6	10	8
some	20	10	21	17	23	26	24
very little	41	37	38	36	48	40	48
none at all	27	43	33	26	20	18	16
not sure	7	9	4	15	4	4	4

(Asked of immigrants) Do you feel you can generally influence decisions made by U.S. government officials more, about the same, or less than those made by government officials in your home country?

	ALL	CHINESE	KOREAN	VIETNAMESE	JAPANESE	FILIPINO	SOUTH ASIAN
more	39	19	59	56	32	44	38
about the same	24	24	18	13	46	25	33
less	17	25	12	4	20	19	18
not sure	19	32	11	25	2	12	11

Note: Column totals may not equal to 100 percentage points due to rounding errors and omitted categories.
Source: PNAAPS, 2000–2001.

identifiers. Moreover, 70 percent of Asians who fail to place themselves along the liberal-conservative continuum and 38 percent of Asians who call themselves middle-of-the road also do not classify themselves as Democrat, Republican, or Independent.

Is there a relationship between political ideology and the policy orientation of Asian Americans? The possible influence of ideology on policy opinion is examined with several policy questions on the general attitude toward affirmative action and support for *specific* affirmative action programs targeting Asian Americans. Other policy preferences examined are respondents' opinions about government-sponsored bilingual services, limiting legal immigration, and permitting noncitizen legal permanent residents to make donations to political campaigns. At the aggregate level, ideology does not seem to make much difference in terms of policy support, especially on the general attitude toward affirmative action and the opinion toward providing language assistance toward the immigrant communities. However, both the very liberal and the very conservative respondents appear to provide stronger support for race-based affirmative action in hiring and promotion and for permitting permanent residents to make campaign donations than do those who place themselves in the middle of the ideological spectrum. A higher percentage of the very liberal than the very conservative would support race-based affirmative action in education and job training, while the proposal to limit legal immigration finds the strongest support among the very conservative and the weakest support among the very liberal.[4]

Political Interest

Research using the American National Election Studies (ANES) data series shows that the level of general interest in government and politics varies with political context, with political interest being higher in times of major social and political crises (Conway, 2000). From 1968 to 1976, between 33 and 38 percent of respondents indicated that they followed government and public affairs most of the time. In 2000, that level was 17 percent, while 13 percent indicated that they hardly followed political affairs. Among our survey's respondents, 24 percent of Asians indicate having very high interest, 37 percent indicate having moderate interest, 24 percent indicate having slight interest, and 13 percent indicate having no interest at all in politics and what goes on in government. Political interest is highest among South Asian Americans; 38 percent report being very interested and 34 percent report being somewhat interested. Less than two in ten Chinese Americans and about two in ten Vietnamese and Japanese Americans indicate having high political interest. More than four in ten Chinese and Korean Americans, nevertheless, indicate being somewhat interested. And, although about two in ten Filipino Americans and Vietnamese Americans express no interest at all, only four percent of Korean Americans report such a lack of interest in government and political affairs.

Whether or not one was born in the United States does not significantly impact the level of political interest, but the percentage of the very interested is higher among the foreign-born (26 percent) than the native-born (20 percent). The percentage of the very interested is higher among U.S. citizens (26 percent) than noncitizens (20 percent). However, U.S. citizens also register a higher level of apathy (15 percent) than noncitizens (11 percent). The relationship between family income and political interest is significant but weak. Those making $60,000 or more express the highest level of interest and lowest level of disinterest, but those making $30,000 or less do not necessarily score a lesser interest than those with mid-range incomes. Higher educational achievement, on the other hand, correlates strongly with higher levels of political interest.

Political Trust

Since the mid-1960s, national surveys have found a general decline in the levels of trust in the government in Washington among U.S. residents. A revival of trust occurred during the Reagan Administration but dissipated during the Clinton Administration (Conway, 2000). With incidents such as the Wen Ho Lee case and the general distrust among the American public toward "Big Government," Asian Americans would be hard pressed to place a high level of trust in U.S. national government officials. Asian Americans' levels of trust may also be affected by perceptions of government in the home country, with perceptions of ineptitude or corruption in home country government influencing attitudes toward U.S. officials at the national level.

Asian Americans' levels of trust in local government officials, however, may be a different matter. When respondents were queried about the extent to which they trust U.S. local government officials, close to four in ten indicate that local government officials could be trusted "just about always" (7 percent) or "most of the time" (30 percent); over half indicate that they can trust officials "only some of the time" (44 percent) or "none at all" (8 percent). Levels of trust vary among Asian American groups, with Koreans (43 percent), Filipinos (41 percent), and South Asians (41 percent) indicating higher levels of trust (just about always or most of the time) than members of other groups. These figures are lower than the 55 percent found among the total sample of the 1987 General Social Survey who indicated trust in local government officials all the time or most of the time. However, they are comparable to the percentages among African American respondents in the General Social Survey (6 percent all the time, 32 percent most of the time).

An interesting comparison is the extent to which Asian Americans born in Asia feel they can generally trust U.S. government officials compared to government officials in their country of origin. Immigrants were asked if they trust the U.S. government officials more, about the same, or less than government officials in the home country. Fifty-five percent indicate that they think they would trust the U.S. officials more, 26 percent indicate the same amount, and only 6 percent think they would trust the U.S. officials less. Almost 13 percent are not sure which government would be more trustworthy. Again, response patterns vary greatly by country of origin. The proportion of respondents within each immigrant group who report having more trust in U.S. officials than those in the home country ranges from 72 percent for Koreans, 67 percent for Vietnamese, and 60 percent for South Asians to 40 percent for Filipinos, 39 percent among Chinese, and 29 percent among Japanese immigrants.

Although ethnic origin is a significant factor shaping the level of political trust in local officials, nativity is not. Trust has some relationship to income in that lower income respondents report a higher level of trust ("just about always") as well as a higher level of mistrust ("none at all") than middle or higher income groups. Persons with no college education, compared to those who graduated from college or with higher degrees, also tend to report a higher level of trust and mistrust. Patterns of relative trust might be expected to vary with length of time lived in the United States, but it does not. However, trust does vary with citizenship status. Those immigrants who are U.S. citizens are more likely to trust the U.S. government more than their home country's government than are noncitizens who expect to become citizens. Noncitizens who do not expect to become citizens indicate equal levels of trust of the United States and home country governments.

Perceived Government Responsiveness

The study also measures perceptions of local government officials' responsiveness to citizen complaints. Survey participants were asked if a local public official would pay a lot of attention, some attention, very little attention, or no attention to a complaint. Nine percent think the local officials would pay a lot of attention and 33 percent think they would pay some attention. Perceptions of government responsiveness (paying a lot of attention or some attention) are highest among South Asian Americans (55 percent), Filipino Americans (54 percent), and Japanese Americans (43 percent). Less than one-third of Chinese and Korean Americans expect that local government officials would pay either a lot or some attention to their complaints.

Personal attributes such as citizenship status, nativity, education, and income have at most a weak relationship with respondents' perceived levels of government responsiveness. However, those who were born in Asia, did not attend college, and have a lower family income appear to have a higher tendency to perceive U.S. local government officials as unresponsive to their concerns and needs.

Perceived Influence on Government Decisions

When respondents were asked how much influence they think someone like themselves can have over local government decisions—a lot, some, very little, or none at all—only 6 percent respond "a lot" and 20 percent believe they can have some influence. Sixty-eight percent of respondents believe they have very little or no influence over local government decisions. Chinese Americans are least likely to believe they can have a lot or some influence (11 percent), with at least one-quarter of the respondents in other ethnic groups believing that they can have a lot or some influence over local government decisions. As high as 15 percent of Vietnamese, however, are not sure how to answer.

Asian Americans born in Asia are also asked if they feel they could generally influence decisions made by U.S. government officials more, about the same, or less than those made by government officials in their home country. Almost 40 percent say more, 24 percent say the same, and 17 percent say less, with 19 percent unsure of whether they would have more influence in the United States or the home country. Again, the responses vary greatly by country of origin, with 59 percent of the Koreans, 56 percent of the Vietnamese, 44 percent of the Filipinos, 38 percent of the South Asians, 32 percent of the Japanese, but only 19 percent of the Chinese saying they would have more influence over decisions made by U.S. officials. A majority of Asian-born Chinese indicate that they would have less influence over decisions made in the United States or that they are not sure in which country they would have more influence.

Unlike perceived government responsiveness, respondents' perceived level of personal influence over local government decisions is strongly related to personal attributes. In particular, citizens are much more efficacious about their ability to influence local government decisions than noncitizens. Those born in the United States, those having at least a college degree, and those having at least $60,000 in family income are more likely than others to report having at least some level of influence. Perceptions of influence over government do not vary with length of time lived in the United States. Immigrants who are citizens are more likely to perceive themselves as having more influence over the U.S. government than over home country government decisions. Those who do not expect to become citizens are least likely to indicate they have more influence over U.S. government decisions than over the home country government's decisions.

Summary Observations by Basic Sociodemographic Variables

Ethnic Group Origin. Do political beliefs and attitudes vary with objective ethnic identity as measured by the personal or family country of origin of the respondents? The answer is yes. Political ideology, interest, political trust, perceived political influence, and perceived government responsiveness all vary significantly by ethnic group origin. South Asians and Filipinos are more likely to call themselves liberal in political ideology; more Filipinos and Koreans than other Asians label themselves as conservative on the same scale. Political interest is higher among Japanese, Filipino, and South Asian Americans. Political trust is highest among Korean and South Asian Americans and lowest among Chinese and Japanese Americans. Given the history of the treatment of the latter two groups in the United States, their lower levels of political trust are not surprising. Other Asian ethnic groups might also see themselves as having experienced legal exclusion and similarly bad treatment. However, most are of recent immigrant background and may be less informed about their groups' respective histories of discrimination and exclusion.[5] Perceptions of political influence over local government decisions are significantly lower among Chinese Americans and highest among Filipino Americans and South Asian Americans. Korean Americans are least likely to perceive local government officials as responsive to their complaints. Those who are most likely to perceive local government officials as responsive are South Asian and Filipino Americans.

Citizenship Status. As might be expected, perceived influence on local government decisions varies with citizenship status, with citizens more likely to perceive themselves as having some influence. Noncitizens who expect to become citizens are less likely than citizens to think they have influence, and noncitizens who do not expect to become citizens are least likely to report that they have at least a moderate amount of influence. Citizens are also more likely to trust government and slightly more likely to be interested in government and politics. However, political ideology and perceived responsiveness of public officials does not vary with citizenship status.

Nativity and Immigration Generation. Do native-born and foreign-born Asian Americans differ significantly in their attitudes? The answer is no in terms of the levels of political interest and trust in government. In contrast, those who are native-born are more likely to perceive themselves as being somewhat conservative in political ideology and able to influence local government decisions, and to perceive local public officials as being responsive to complaints from citizens like themselves. Furthermore, those who are third generation or more in the United States are more likely to believe that they have influence over local government decisions and that public officials would be responsive to their complaints.

Education. Those with higher levels of education might be expected to have more interaction with government leaders and governmental regulatory activities beyond the usual street level bureaucracy (police, fire departments, motor vehicle administration, schools, and social welfare agencies). Does a higher level of educational attainment and the experiences and knowledge that usually accompany it impact political ideology, interest, and other political attitudes and beliefs? Higher levels of educational attainment are associated with more liberal thinking and higher levels of political interest. Eighty percent of those with a postgraduate degree express somewhat or very high levels of political interest. Perceptions of being able to influence local government decisions and of local public officials' responsiveness to complaints also increase with level of educational attainment. However, Asian Americans at each level of educational attainment are substantially more likely to expect public officials to be responsive to a complaint than they are to think that they can influence local government decisions.

Other Possible Correlates of Political Orientations

The extent and direction of political orientations may be influenced by other variables, such as sociopsychological engagement with one's own ethnic community, political, cultural, and social integration, racial interaction, and socialization context.

Sense of Linked Fate. The belief that one shares a linked fate with other members of one's own ethnic group and with other Asian Americans is associated with levels of political interest and perceived influence over local government decision making, but not with other political orientations examined in this chapter. Persons with a higher sense of linked fate also have higher levels of political interest and self-efficacy.

Ethnic News Attention. The attention paid to news about Asians in the United States and abroad and about what happens in Asia is related to political interest, but not to other political orientations. Political interest probably stimulates higher levels of attention to political and other news relating to Asian Americans and to events in Asia. In other words, political interest would lead to attention paid to the news, which would in turn lead to more interest, in a self-reinforcing cycle up to a certain maximum level of attention. How much attention is given to following the news would be a function of the time available and free from work, family, and other responsibilities.

Political Knowledge. Those respondents who rank higher in political awareness are significantly higher in their levels of political interest. Those who are low in political awareness are also substantially less likely to respond to the survey questions measuring political trust, responsiveness of local public officials to complaints, and belief in the ability of people like oneself to influence local government decisions.

Party Identification. We might expect those who identify more strongly with one of the political parties to have more positive or stronger political orientations. And indeed, those who are higher in strength of party identification score higher on all five political orientation measures. Furthermore, those who have been active on behalf of an Asian American candidate or an issue affecting Asian Americans also score higher on all five of the dependent variables.

Organizational Membership. Membership in social and political organizations might be expected to result in higher levels of politically relevant information and the transmission either through formal organizational activities or through informal social communications of information about government and politics and evaluative assessments of government policies, actions, and leaders. A number of scholars note the effects of social integration on both political orientations and political participation. Verba, Schlozman, and Brady (1995) argue that both information and politically relevant skills are learned through participation in community and religious organizations. Freedman (2000) views integration into community organizations as the key to successful mobilization of minority group members into politics.

Participants in our survey were asked if they are a member of any organization or if they take part in any activities that represent the interests or viewpoints of their ethnic group. Sixteen percent report membership or activity in an ethnic group of that type. Those who are members express significantly higher levels of liberal ideology, political interest, perceived influence over local government decisions, and responsiveness of local public officials to their views than do nonmembers.

Religiosity. Another measure of social integration is the frequency of attending religious services. Those who are more frequent attendees report higher levels of conservative ideology, political interest, and perceived influence over local government decisions, but not higher levels of political trust or perceived responsiveness of public officials.

Indicators of Socialization and Racial Interaction. Other measures of social integration include close friends of another race, living in an integrated neighborhood, a positive attitude toward interracial marriage, higher levels of use of English at home and at work, and a longer length of residence in the community. Living in a predominantly white neighborhood is associated with higher levels of political interest and perceived influence over local government decisions. More frequent use of English and having a close friend who is white are associated with higher levels of political interest, perceived responsiveness of public officials, and perceived influence over local government decisions. Those who are supportive of interracial marriage score higher on all of these dependent variables.

Experience of Discrimination. Discrimination against Asian Americans, both overt and subtle, continues to exist despite constitutional amendments, laws, and regulatory policies that seek to end formal practices of racial and ethnic discrimination, and despite campaigns to eliminate more subtle practices of discrimination. Perceptions of discrimination vary among our sample, as do the types of discrimination suffered. An index summing up the number of different types of discrimination reported by each member of the sample ranges from 0 to 7; the mean discrimination score is approximately 1.[6] Sixty-nine percent of those born in the United States and 62 percent of those born overseas claim that they have not experienced any of the seven types of discrimination listed in the survey instrument. However, reporting discrimination varies by citizenship status, with those who are not citizens and who do not expect to become citizens more frequently reporting that they have not been subjected to any of the seven types of discrimination.

How does experiencing discrimination affect one's political orientations? Those who do not report discrimination are more trusting of government officials and perceive public officials to be more responsive to complaints. Those who are victimized by a hate crime are more liberal in ideology. Those who report higher levels of discrimination also express higher levels of political interest.[7] However, they are not more likely to think that someone like themselves can influence a local government decision.

Length of U.S. Stay. Do political orientations of foreign-born Asian Americans vary with the length of time they have lived in the United States? Those who have lived a greater proportion of their lives in the United States are more likely to perceive themselves as able to influence decisions by local government officials. In contrast, neither ideology, trust, perceived responsiveness, nor political interest varies significantly with the amount of time spent in this country.

Place of Education. Learning about politics and government in the United States occurs in part through formal education and informal schooling at the elementary, middle school, high school, and college level. Those who received their education mainly outside the United States would receive less formal education and informal schooling in American political processes, and thus their patterns of political orientations might differ from those who obtained most of their formal education in the United States. However, political ideology, political trust, political interest, and perceived local government officials' responsiveness do not vary with place of education, but perceived ability to influence local government decisions does. Those who are educated primarily in the United States are more likely to believe that they can influence decisions made by local government officials.

Results of Multivariate Analyses

The previous discussion in this chapter focuses on simple bivariate relationships among variables. Which variables remain significant in accounting for patterns of Asian Americans' political attitudes and beliefs when the effects of other variables are controlled? To answer that question, we turn to the results of a series of multivariate analyses. The independent variables are rescaled to range between 0 and 1. The scores on each of the dependent variables range between 1 and 4. Ordinary least squares (OLS) regression is used as the method of analysis.[8]

The following sets of independent variables are used as predictors of Asian Americans' political orientations regarding their political ideology, political interest, trust in state and local government, perceived responsiveness of local public officials to citizen complaints, and perceived influence over local government decisions. The five indicators of respondents' ethnic or country of origin are Filipino, Japanese, Vietnamese, South Asian, and Korean, with the effects of membership in any of these groups being compared with the effects of being Chinese. Three measures of social-psychological engagement are used; these are common culture, panethnic linked fate, and attention to Asian American news. The measures of political engagement employed in the analyses are political knowledge, Democratic partisanship, Republican partisanship, liberal ideology, and citizenship status, with perceived political influence, political ideology, and political interest also used as predictors of other dependent variables. The five measures of civic participation, acculturation, and racial interaction are frequency of English language use, having experienced race- or ethnic-based discrimination, ethnic organization membership, participation in support of an Asian American candidate or cause, and frequency of attendance at religious services. Socialization and social connectedness are measured by educational attainment, family income, gender, employment, age, length of community residence, proportion of life lived in the United States, and place of education (whether the majority of education was received in the United States or in another country). For separate analyses of that part of the sample who are foreign born, independent variables also include four measures of homeland ties (current political activism in the home country, prior political activism, frequency of contact with the home country, and plan to return to live in the home country).[9]

Predicting Patterns of Political Ideology

Table 3.2 shows regression analysis predicting levels of political ideology, measured as support for liberalism. The results demonstrate that support varies by ethnic group, with South Asian, Japanese, or Vietnamese Americans predicted to have a higher level of political liberalism than their Chinese counterparts. Also, a significant predictor of support for a strong liberal ideology is paying more attention to news stories about Asia and Asian Americans. As expected, Democratic partisanship positively, and Republican partisanship negatively, predicts support for liberalism. Working for Asian American candidates or causes and having higher levels of education also predict higher levels of liberal self-identity. Frequency of attending religious services, on the other hand, has a weak and negative effect on the strength of liberal political ideology.

When the analysis is restricted to just those born outside the United States, few variables are statistically significant in accounting for placement on the liberal ideology index. Being South Asian (as opposed to the comparison category, Chinese) is significant, as is attention to ethnic news stories and participation in support of Asian American candidates or causes. Democratic partisanship is a significant and positive predictor, while Republican partisanship has significant and negative impact. No other predictors achieve statistical significance.[10]

Predicting Patterns of Political Interest

Table 3.3 shows that two measures of social-psychological engagement—perceptions of a common fate shared by Asian Americans and attention to Asian American news—contribute to explaining patterns of political interest. Also significant in predicting patterns of political interest are perceived influence on local government decisions, political knowledge, and Democratic partisanship. As expected, those who have been active in support of Asian American candidates or causes also have higher levels of political interest. Being Vietnamese or

Table 3.2 OLS Estimations of (Liberal) Political Ideology

	TOTAL SAMPLE			FOREIGN BORN		
	b	s.e.	t	b	s.e.	t
(Constant)	.696	.235	2.963	.646	.328	1.970
Ethnic Origin or *Primordial Ties (ref = Chinese)*						
Filipino	.194	.131	1.481	.245	.172	1.425
Japanese	.249^	.146	1.701	.383	.249	1.540
Korean	−.039	.113	−.342	−.032	.135	−.234
South Asian	.536**	.137	3.928	.531*	.169	3.142
Vietnamese	.220^	.133	1.650	.212	.185	1.146
Sociopsychological Engagement						
shared culture	.023	.036	.641	.024	.047	.517
panethnic linked fate	−.039	.032	−1.205	−.035	.042	−.830
attention to Asian American news	.188*	.098	1.919	.237^	.129	1.841
Political Engagement						
political knowledge	.121	.169	.716	.141	.216	.653
Democratic partisanship	.147**	.030	4.880	.127**	.040	3.174
Republican partisanship	−.145**	.041	−3.561	−.109*	.053	−2.066
citizenship status	−.068	.059	−1.147	−.091	.076	−1.202
Civic Participation, Acculturation, Racial Interaction						
religious attendance	−.039^	.023	−1.738	−.045	.030	−1.489
ethnic organization membership	.100	.091	1.089	.081	.122	.669
participation in Asian American causes	.079*	.037	2.120	.100^	.054	1.873
English language use	−.017	.060	−.281	−.022	.079	−.278
experience with discrimination	.024	.094	.255	−.042	.125	−.338
Socialization and Social Connectedness						
education	.051*	.025	2.038	.040	.033	1.204
family income	.018	.021	.852	.029	.027	1.047
age	−.003	.002	−1.268	−.001	.003	−.446
employed	.064	.072	.888	.081	.096	.841
proportion of life in U.S.	−.154	.145	−1.067	−.383	.269	−1.426
non-U.S. education	−.086	.086	−.990	−.089	.110	−.808
Homeland Ties						
active in homeland politics				−.072	.185	−.391
maintain homeland contact				−.002	.034	−.048
plan to return to Asia				.055	.187	.296
prior partisanship				−.026	.052	−.508
N	828			517		
F	6.47**			3.30**		
Adj. R-sq.	.132			.107		

Note: The dependent variable is a 4-point self-identification of political ideological scale where a score of 4 is very liberal, 3 is somewhat liberal, 2 is middle-of-the-road, and 1 is not liberal. b = unstandardized ordinary least squares (OLS) regression coefficient, s.e. = standard error.

^ $.05 < p \leq .10$ * $.005 < p \leq .05$ ** $p \leq .005$

Source: PNAAPS, 2000–2001.

Table 3.3 OLS Estimations of Political Interest

	TOTAL SAMPLE			FOREIGN BORN		
	b	s.e.	t	b	s.e.	t
(Constant)	1.017	.212	4.797	.985	.295	3.344
Ethnic Origin or *Primordial Ties (ref=Chinese)*						
Filipino	−.028	.114	−.246	−.240^	.145	−1.660
Japanese	−.015	.131	−.115	−.010	.221	−.044
Korean	.047	.095	.501	.021	.110	.188
South Asian	.214^	.121	1.759	.092	.147	.624
Vietnamese	.254*	.121	2.103	.181	.159	1.139
Sociopsychological Engagement						
shared culture	.000	.033	.002	.003	.041	.070
panethnic linked fate	.068*	.029	2.349	.043	.037	1.167
attention to Asian American news	.680**	.089	7.641	.733**	.115	6.367
Political Engagement						
political knowledge	.392*	.153	2.554	.115	.193	.597
political influence	.169**	.036	4.698	.144**	.046	3.110
Democratic partisanship	.086**	.028	3.119	.092*	.036	2.570
Republican partisanship	.030	.037	.812	.035	.046	.751
liberal ideology	.012	.032	.372	−.013	.040	−.318
citizenship status	−.036	.054	−.663	−.017	.067	−.254
Civic Participation, Acculturation, Racial Interaction						
ethnic organization membership	.027	.082	.325	.099	.108	.913
participation in Asian American causes	.064*	.032	2.000	.041	.046	.904
English language use	.081	.054	1.504	.161*	.069	2.319
experience with discrimination	.059	.084	.705	.141	.109	1.298
Socialization and Social Connectedness						
education	.053*	.023	2.305	.051^	.030	1.719
family income	−.041*	.019	−2.158	−.048^	.024	−2.016
age	.000	.002	.169	.001	.003	.407
employed	−.050	.065	−.775	−.038	.084	−.452
proportion of life in U.S.	−.089	.130	−.686	−.070	.237	−.295
non-U.S. education	−.138^	.078	−1.776	−.087	.096	−.910
Homeland Ties						
active in homeland politics				−.152	.164	−.930
maintain homeland contact				.005	.031	.166
plan to return to Asia				.033	.160	.207
prior partisanship				.020	.046	.436
N	810			507		
F	14.61**			6.87**		
Adj. R-sq.	.288			.245		

Note: The dependent variable is a 4-point scale measuring the degree of R's interest in politics or what's going on in government in general. Excluded variables are gender, religiosity, and length of community residence.
Source: PNAAPS, 2000–2001.

South Asian American also points to higher levels of political interest. Having a higher level of educational attainment also positively predicts level of political interest but, surprisingly, having higher levels of family income is a negative predictor of political interest, other conditions being equal. Having received a majority of one's education outside the United States is a negative predictor of political interest.

Examining the predictors of political interest among just the foreign-born sample, being Filipino American is a negative predictor of political interest. Only attention to Asian American news stories is a significant predictor among the social-psychological engagement variables. Also significant and positive predictors of political interest are perceived political influence, English language use, Democratic partisanship, participation in support of an Asian American cause or candidate, educational attainment, and family income, with higher levels of family income predicting lower levels of political interest. None of the indicators of homeland ties shows any independent impact.

Predicting Patterns of Political Trust in Local Public Officials

Table 3.4 examines predictors of political trust in the total sample. Being South Asian, Korean, or Vietnamese American is associated with more trust in U.S. local and state government officials to do the right thing. Among the measures of social-psychological engagement, the belief that Asian Americans share a common fate and attention to Asian American news stories are significant and positive predictors of trust. Perceived political influence positively impacts levels of political trust. Turning to the measures of acculturation/racial interaction, personally having experienced discrimination is a strong negative predictor of political trust patterns. None of the socialization context or social connectedness variables is significant in predicting political trust.

Among just the foreign-born portion of the sample, none of the ethnic origin variables is significant in predicting patterns of political trust. Perceptions of a common fate with other Asian Americans is associated positively with political trust, while personal experience of discrimination is associated negatively with political trust among immigrants to the United States. Perceived influence on local government decisions is a positive predictor, but, interestingly, Democratic partisanship is a negative predictor of trust. Only age is significant among the socialization variables, and only maintaining homeland contacts is significant among the homeland ties variables. Being older and maintaining more homeland contacts both predict more trust.

Predicting Local Public Officials' Perceived Responsiveness to Citizen Complaints

Turning to perceptions of local public officials' responsiveness to citizen complaints, Table 3.5 shows that only being of Korean ethnic origin, as compared to being Chinese, is a significant, although negative, predictor. Among the measures of political engagement, perceived political influence, Republican

Table 3.4 OLS Estimations of Political Trust in Local Officials

	TOTAL SAMPLE			FOREIGN BORN		
	b	s.e.	t	b	s.e.	t
(Constant)	1.778	.189	9.385	1.553	.266	5.838
Ethnic Origin or Primordial Ties (ref=Chinese)						
Filipino	.137	.100	1.368	.206	.128	1.611
Japanese	.014	.116	.122	−.090	.189	−.476
Korean	.167^	.087	1.916	.134	.101	1.326
South Asian	.204^	.109	1.873	.153	.132	1.165
Vietnamese	.189^	.111	1.691	.139	.146	.949
Socio psychological Engagement						
shared culture	−.007	.030	−.237	−.014	.038	−.371
panethnic linked fate	.047^	.027	1.755	.076*	.035	2.167
attention to Asian American news	.120^	.069	1.749	.100	.089	1.120
Political Engagement						
political influence	.143*	.033	4.373	.111*	.042	2.638
Democratic partisanship	−.018	.023	−.782	−.054^	.030	−1.794
liberal ideology	.017	.029	.601	.041	.037	1.096
Civic Participation, Acculturation, Racial Interaction						
participation in Asian American causes	−.028	.028	−.992	−.014	.041	−.333
English language use	−.027	.049	−.543	−.028	.065	−.441
experience with discrimination	−.274**	.077	−3.540	−.303**	.102	−2.988
Socialization and Social Connectedness						
education	−.004	.020	−.203	.018	.026	.674
age	.003	.002	1.522	.007**	.002	2.884
proportion of life in U.S.	.097	.112	.867	.079	.204	.386
non-U.S. education	−.025	.071	−.358	−.099	.087	−1.128
Homeland Ties						
active in homeland politics				−.050	.152	−.327
maintain homeland contact				.046^	.028	1.631
plan to return to asia				−.127	.144	−.881
prior partisanship				−.030	.042	−.717
N	759			475		
F	3.16**			2.21**		
Adj. R-sq	.049			.053		

Note: The dependent variable is a 4-point scale measuring R's frequency of trusting his or her U.S. local and state government officials to the do the right thing. Excluded variables are gender, family income, religiosity, ethnic organizational memership, Republican partisanship, and political knowledge.
Source: PNAAPS, 2000–2001.

Table 3.5 OLS Estimations of Perceived Local Government Responsiveness

	TOTAL SAMPLE			FOREIGN BORN		
	b	s.e.	t	b	s.e.	t
(Constant)	1.191	.226	5.278	1.181	.322	3.672
Ethnic Origin or *Primordial Ties (ref=Chinese)*						
Filipino	−.123	.127	−.972	−.054	.169	−.318
Japanese	−.162	.139	−1.167	−.514*	.230	−2.236
Korean	−.446**	.109	−4.080	−.383**	.132	−2.911
South Asian	−.132	.133	−.993	−.151	.168	−.900
Vietnamese	.002	.140	.014	−.044	.191	−.232
Sociopsychological Engagement						
shared culture	.037	.034	1.080	.023	.045	.511
panethnic linked fate	.056^	.032	1.783	.073^	.042	1.742
attention to Asian American news	.075	.079	.950	.038	.104	.362
Political Engagement						
political influence	.327**	.039	8.452	.321**	.050	6.388
Democratic partisanship	−.020	.030	−.661	−.021	.040	−.540
Republican partisanship	.065^	.040	1.637	.123*	.051	2.410
liberal ideology	.118**	.035	3.387	.150**	.045	3.319
Civic Participation, Acculturation, Racial Interaction						
religious attendance	.043*	.022	1.930	.046	.030	1.567
ethnic organisation membership	.206*	.086	2.390	.109	.116	.943
participation in Asian American causes	−.060^	.035	−1.707	−.054	.051	−1.066
English language use	.071	.059	1.200	.088	.080	1.100
experience with discrimination	−.293**	.092	−3.177	−.250*	.124	−2.008
Socialization and Social Connectedness						
education	.017	.023	.746	.025	.031	.800
age	−.001	.002	−.665	−.001	.003	−.455
proportion of life in U.S.	.079	.130	.604	−.075	.238	−.315
non-U.S. education	.135^	.083	1.622	.091	.105	.868
Homeland Ties						
active in homeland politics				.037	.182	.202
maintain homeland contact				.012	.034	.359
plan to return to Asia				−.053	.173	−.304
prior partisanship				−.022	.050	−.433
N	709			437		
F	8.35**			5.06**		
Adj. R-sq	.179			.183		

Note: The dependent variable is a 4-point scale measuring R's perception of U.S. local government officials' level of responsiveness to complaints.
Source: PNAAPS, 2000–2001.

partisanship, and liberal ideology all have a positive and significant impact on perceived local public officials' responsiveness to complaints.

Among the measures of civic participation, acculturation, and racial interaction, having personally experienced discrimination and being active in support of Asian American causes are significant but negative predictors of belief in government responsiveness. These patterns suggest a strong association between negative beliefs about government responsiveness and those experiences that are likely to contribute to a strong sense of group consciousness. Political action for community empowerment might be triggered by the perceived lack of responsiveness to Asian American concerns.

Among the measures of civic participation and acculturation, religious attendance and ethnic organization membership are positive predictors. Other conditions being equal, having obtained one's education outside the United States may also increase perceived level of local government responsiveness; it is the only significant predictor among the socialization and social connectedness variables.

Turning to the foreign-born segment of the sample, both Japanese Americans and Korean Americans are significantly less likely to perceive local government officials as responsive. Having a sense of panethnic shared fate, perceiving oneself as having influence over local government decisions, being more liberal, being a more partisan Republican—each predicts a higher level of perceived local government responsiveness. None of the socialization or homeland ties measures are significant in explaining perceptions of public officials' responsiveness to citizen complaints among the foreign-born.

Predicting Perceived Influence over Local Government Officials' Decisions

Table 3.6 shows that Filipino, Japanese, Vietnamese, and South Asian Americans are all significantly more likely to perceive themselves as having an influence on local government officials' decisions than are Chinese Americans. Also significant are political knowledge, political interest, liberal ideology, citizenship status, and belief in the linked fate of Asian Americans. Among the civic participation/acculturation/racial interaction measures, frequency of attendance at religious services and activism in support of Asian American causes are significant predictors. Among the socialization measures, being employed is a significant and positive predictor, in contrast to family income, which—although significant—has a negative effect on perceived influence.

Examining predictors of perceived influence over local government decisions among just the foreign born segment of the sample, being Filipino, Japanese, or South Asian American is, again, significant. Also significant are being a liberal in political ideology, being a U.S. citizen or expected citizen, and having greater levels of political knowledge and political interest.

More frequent attendance at religious services and participation in an ethnic organization are positive predictors of perceived influence on local government

Table 3.6 OLS Estimations of Perceived Influence over Local Government Decisions

	TOTAL SAMPLE			FOREIGN BORN		
	b	s.e.	t	b	s.e.	t
(Constant)	.799	.213	3.744	1.099	.293	3.753
Ethnic Origin or *Primordial Ties (ref=Chinese)*						
Filipino	.456**	.116	3.932	.496**	.149	3.336
Japanese	.285*	.129	2.209	.430*	.216	1.990
Korean	.126	.100	1.257	.179	.118	1.515
South Asian	.390**	.122	3.202	.361*	.147	2.448
Vietnamese	.247*	.121	2.038	.118	.160	.741
Sociopsychological Engagement						
shared culture	.032	.032	.999	.045	.041	1.093
panethnic linked fate	.057*	.029	1.983	.060	.037	1.607
attention to Asian American news	−.051	.091	−.561	−.177	.118	−1.500
Political Engagement						
political knowledge	.291*	.151	1.922	.498*	.189	2.629
political interest	.159**	.035	4.603	.136**	.045	3.066
Democratic partisanship	−.012	.027	−.449	−.021	.036	−.598
Republican partisanship	.036	.037	.986	.037	.046	.806
liberal ideology	.078*	.031	2.507	.086*	.039	2.186
citizenship status	.105*	.053	1.994	.117^	.066	1.778
Civic Participation, Acculturation, Racial Interaction						
religious attendance	.041*	.020	2.024	.183^	.106	1.729
ethnic organization membership	.127	.081	1.567	.044^	.026	1.675
participation in Asian American causes	.068*	.033	2.064	.055	.046	1.192
English language use	.051	.053	.966	.045	.069	.653
experience with discrimination	−.132	.083	−1.586	−.219*	.109	−2.014
Socialization and Social Connectedness						
education	.010	.023	.461	.015	.030	.507
family income	−.031^	.019	−1.630	−.038	.024	−1.596
age	−.002	.002	−1.083	−.005*	.003	−2.043
employed	.131*	.064	2.041	.065	.083	.782
proportion of life in U.S.	−.027	.128	−.209	−.109	.233	−.467
non-U.S. education	−.021	.077	−.271	−.086	.095	−.906
Homeland Ties						
active in homeland politics				.000	.161	.003
maintain homeland contact				.038	.030	1.269
plan to return to Asia				−.177	.160	−1.107
prior partisanship				.013	.047	.276
N	792			494		
F	7.04**			4.07**		
Adj. R-sq	.160			.153		

Note: The dependent variable is a 4-point scale measuring R's perception of the amount of influence he or she has over U.S. local government decisions.
Source: PNAAPS, 2000–2001.

decisions. These patterns point to the role of organizations as sources of information and agents of political mobilization.

Experiences of discrimination, however, negatively impact the level of perceived influence. Among the socialization variables, only age is significant. Being younger in age predicts a higher level of perceived influence. None of the measures of homeland ties are significant.

Discussion and Conclusion

This chapter opens with a question on the current shape of the political orientations of Asian Americans. The first two orientations examined are political ideology and interest in politics and government in general. Using a conventional scale of political ideological self-placement, respondents are found to be more liberal (36 percent) than conservative (22 percent), with one in ten not sure of how to place themselves along the liberal-conservatism continuum, and 32 percent placing themselves as middle of the road. At the bivariate level, although ideological orientation is a good predictor of political partisanship, it does not appear to have strong policy content. Measured by their general interest in politics and political matters, Asian Americans are not politically apathetic, with six in ten respondents indicating either very high or moderate high levels of political interest.

Next examined are Asian Americans' attitudes toward government. About eight in ten Asian Americans indicate that they trust local officials at least some of the time. Among immigrants, over half indicate that they would trust U.S. officials more than homeland officials. Those who are naturalized are more likely to indicate trust than are noncitizens. In terms of perceived government responsiveness, about four in ten Asians think that their complaints would receive a lot or some attention from local public officials, but an equal share of Asians believe they receive very little or no attention at all from local officials. When perceived influence over local government decisions is considered, only one-quarter of Asian Americans think that someone like them could have a lot or at least some influence over local government decisions. Among immigrants, four in ten expect to have more influence on local U.S. than homeland government decisions; others either don't see any difference, see less influence, or are uncertain about their relative influence over local government decisions.

Taken as a whole, respondents express a bipolar set of evaluations about their political beliefs and attitude toward government. Although a large majority express at least some interest in political matters and some trust in U.S. local government officials, they also express a high level of frustration about the lack of government responsiveness to citizen complaints and their lack of personal influence on local government decisions. Immigrants who were socialized in a different political system back in Asia, however, are generally more positive about their experiences with the U.S. government officials in terms of political trust and perceived influence.

Several theories guided the research reported here. Those theories include ethnic ties, sociopsychological and political engagement, social and cultural adaptation, socialization and social connectedness, and homeland ties among immigrants. Indicators of the concepts in those theories are the explanatory variables included in the multivariate equations. At the bivariate level, political orientations are associated with ethnic origin, nativity, citizenship, and education. They are also associated in various degrees and ways with other factors suggested by previous research. For example, more frequent attendees of religious services are found to hold higher levels of conservative ideology. Asian Americans who experienced discrimination are more liberal in ideology and report higher levels of political interest. However, they report lower levels of political trust and perceived government responsiveness. Those who score higher in political partisanship strength also score higher on all five political orientation measures, but place of education does not seem to matter except on perceived ability to influence local government decisions.

In the multivariate analyses that include the total sample, country of origin is a significant predictor in several of the equations, but which ethnic groups are significant varies across the dependent variables. This may reflect defining moments in each group's historical experience in the United States. Those defining moments become imbedded in the collective memory of group members and impact their attitudes and beliefs about government. In addition, among immigrants the effects would in part reflect differences in homeland experiences and political cultures.

One sociopsychological variable that is a significant predictor within the total sample for four dependent variables (political interest, political trust, perceived responsiveness of government, and perceived influence over government) is belief in a linked fate of Asian Americans. Perhaps those who think their fate is tied to a larger community are more likely to feel empowered with respect to their relationship to the government than those who are more individually oriented. A second sociopsychological measure, attentiveness to news stories about Asia and Asian Americans, is a significant predictor of ideology, interest, and trust. It may be that those who are exposed to political affairs through the media also have a stronger sense of understanding of the government. Greater understanding of the government may again lead to a sense of empowerment within the political system, which in turn may contribute to a more positive evaluation of the government in general.

Zaller argues that political knowledge is a necessary component in the development and holding of political attitudes. Other conditions being equal, the measure of political awareness is significant in predicting political interest and perceived influence on local government decisions.

Among the acculturation and racial interaction predictors included in the multivariate analyses of the total sample, English language usage is not a significant predictor of any of the dependent variables. However, English use is positively associated with political interest among the foreign-born, suggesting that those who are able to access a wider range of political information due to greater use of English find politics more interesting.

Personally experiencing discrimination is a negative predictor of political trust and perceived public officials' responsiveness in both the total sample and the foreign-born sample. It is also a negative predictor of perceived influence in the foreign-born sample. This suggests that Asian Americans who have experienced discrimination may see the government as failing to adequately address discrimination. Or, it is possible that those who have experienced discrimination express negative attitudes about government responsiveness because they feel marginalized by both American society and its associated government institutions.

Several measures of political engagement are significant predictors of perceived public officials' responsiveness to complaints and influence over local officials' decisions. Being ideologically liberal, being a citizen or expecting to become a citizen, and possessing greater political knowledge and political interest are all significant predictors of perceived influence. Political interest and liberalism are also significant predictors of perceived government responsiveness, as is Republican partisanship.

Few of the social background variables are significant predictors in any of the analyses. Educational attainment is significant in accounting for patterns of political ideology and political interest in the total sample, and also for political interest among the foreign-born. Family income is significant but has a negative effect on levels of political interest and perceived influence in the total sample and on political interest in the foreign-born sample. Among the foreign-born, those who are older are more trusting but they are less likely to perceive themselves as having influence over local government decisions. Those who received more of their education outside the United States tend to have lower levels of political interest but are more likely to believe that local public officials would be responsive to their complaints. Last but not least, almost none of the indicators of homeland ties have any independent impact on political orientations among the foreign-born. However, maintaining a higher level of homeland contacts does contribute to higher levels of political trust in local U.S. officials.

In sum, with the exception of homeland ties, each set of the theoretical frameworks helps estimate the strength of political beliefs and attitudes toward government among Asian Americans. In particular, primordial ties and sociopsychological engagement in the context of racial and ethnic community formation, political engagement in terms of attachment to U.S. mainstream political institutions, and indicators of adaptation stages concerning civic activism and experiences of racial discrimination are more consistently useful ones. However, the usefulness of each set varies by the orientation measure in question and by subgroups within the larger sample.

CHAPTER 4

Understanding the Contours, Sources, and Impacts of Political Partisanship

This chapter seeks to understand the roles of political parties in the political adaptation and behavior of Asian Americans. We investigate the shape, the sources, and possible consequences of political partisanship among Asian Americans. And we attempt to assess its effectiveness in structuring political attitudes and behavior as compared to other socialization agents or forces. After a general review of the unique characteristics of political partisanship in American politics, we examine the tenuous but critical relationship between Asian Americans and the major political parties. We then discuss theories and past research findings on the political partisanship of this immigrant-majority and nonwhite population. Because the proportion of Asian Americans who do not affiliate with a party may be large and because it has important implications for immigrant political socialization and mobilization, we give special consideration to the phenomenon of and reasons for nonidentification. We also pay close attention to the role of ethnicity and international migration-related factors, in addition to political and institutional factors, in structuring the direction and the intensity of partisanship among persons of diverse origins and destinies.

The Curious (and Die-Hard) Concept of Political Partisanship in the American Context

The two-party system, with nearly all levels of governments run by individuals who belong to either one of the two major political parties (even if the positions are officially declared as nonpartisan), is a unique feature of the American democracy. The two major American parties—in addition to the media and interest groups—serve as crucial linkage institutions that connect people to their government by helping recruit candidates for office, organize campaigns and the vote, mobilize participation and turnout, and discipline legislative and executive actions. Partisan loyalties are consistently found to influence (and be influenced by) political participation, issue beliefs, candidate choice, and policy preferences of mass publics in the United States (Green, Palmquist, and Schickler, 2002). Huntington (1968: 401) argues that parties are "capable of structuring the participation of new groups in politics." Similarly, Eldersveld and Walton (2000: 9), in their overview of American parties, claim that parties mobilize social interests in order to compete for power in the political system. In theory, parties have an incentive to bring new voters into the political system in order to secure electoral victory.

Unlike party membership in many other political systems, membership in American political parties is open, voluntary, and free. There are no membership dues or citizenship and other requirements for affiliation; neither is there a legally or morally sanctioned penalty provision for not joining a ruling political party. To self-identify with a major political party or any political party is not considered a necessary component of civic duties. American parties are also loosely organized and do not hold strong ideological positions on most issues (Zeigler, 1993). Yet, an average of nearly nine out of ten adults surveyed in the American National Election Studies (NES) since 1952 identify with a political party either as strong, weak, or leaning Democratic or Republican partisans (Keith et al., 1992; Abramson, Aldrich, and Rohde, 1998; Conway, 2000).[1] Despite widespread concerns over the rise of political independence, the weakening of major partisanship, and the general "decline of parties" as key players in national politics (Wattenberg, 1998), the impact of partisanship on voting behavior has actually increased in recent U.S. elections (Bartels, 2000). Even in the ballot initiative process, major party organizations are found to actively bolster voter turnout for their candidates, divide the opposition with "wedge" issues, and promote their own party's platform and ideology in a weak party state such as California (Smith and Tolbert, 2001).

Clearly, although political party identification is less stable than previously thought,[2] it remains a fundamental orientation for most Americans at the dawn of the twenty-first century. Given its centrality in American politics, how many Asian Americans identify with a major political party? Which party are they more likely to identify with and why? Why and with what political consequences? These are the major research questions we address in our study of Asian Americans. A focus on Asian Americans, a population representing one of the nation's fastest growing, nonwhite, relatively affluent, immigrant-dominant, and multiethnic groups, allows us to explore partisanship in the United States from a unique and increasingly relevant perspective. The population's distinct immigration patterns and varied arrival contexts suggest the possibility of both interracial differences between Asians and non-Asians and interethnic differences among Asian ethnic groups in political incorporation patterns.

Political Parties and Asian Americans

Although Asian Americans are less than one-twentieth of the U.S. population, the population's rate of growth, collective socioeconomic resources, and concentration in key electoral states should make them natural and prime targets for mobilization and inclusion by major political parties. Their affiliation may be particularly sought after in times of intense competition when each party is eager to expand its electoral base. However, in both historical and contemporary times, Asian Americans have not experienced an easy alliance with political parties. Historically, urban machines and party organizations, especially on the Democratic side, played an indispensable and active role turning white European immigrant men and women into citizens and voters (Anderson, 1979; Sterne, 2001).[3] Yet in the same period, racial animosity, fears of economic competition, and political calculations drove both the Democratic and Republican parties to actively campaign to exclude the Chinese from immigration and citizenship in the late-nineteenth century (Sandmeyer, 1973; Gyory, 1998). Similar concerns prompted party members in Congress to pass immigration restrictions on the Japanese, Koreans, Asian Indians, and Filipinos in the first three decades of the twentieth century (Kim, 1994, 1996).

Asian Americans continue to suffer from lack of attention from the two major parties in the contemporary era. First, the ascendance of the Asian American population during the past forty years has coincided with the disinclination of political parties to actively recruit nonwhite groups for fear of losing critical white moderates or swing voters (Frymer, 1999). Second, changes in the political environment such as the adoption of the secret ballot, the abandoning of the party patronage system, and the rise of candidate-centered voting all negatively affect parties' ability to mobilize and recruit support from new immigrant communities (Cain, 1991; Conway, 2001a). Third, when interparty competition is low, present-day party organizations may be indifferent or even hostile to immigrant mobilization for fear of their disrupting the existing power structure and coalition base (Erie, 1988; Jones-Correa, 1998; Rogers, 2000). In addition, parties practice selective recruitment. In their efforts to mobilize the most people with minimal resources, they target those who are the most likely voters (Rosenstone and Hansen, 1993). Groups such as Asian Americans that contain a large bloc of unlikely voters (such as noncitizen immigrants who do not necessarily speak English fluently) may be disproportionately affected by selective recruitment strategies. In fact, a study of voter turnout at the precinct level in Chicago finds that machine-style political organizations may suppress Asian turnout because of practices of selective mobilization and political favoritism (Pelissero, Krebs, and Jenkins, 2000). Finally, as illustrated by recent controversies over campaign finance violations involving Asian-born donors during the 1996 presidential election and over espionage charges against a naturalized nuclear scientist Dr. Wen Ho Lee, the stereotypical images of Asian Americans as perpetual outsiders with foreign attachments are reasons for parties to distance themselves from Asian Americans, especially when an internationalized context is evoked (Kim, 2000).

These political trends support the observations that mainstream American party organizations and machines are not critical sources of mobilization for the present-day's mostly nonwhite immigrants (Jones-Correa, 1998; Rogers, 2000; Gerstle and Mollenkopf, 2001; Wong, 2001). Instead, community-based candidate and other social organizations may be bearing much of the burden of incorporating immigrant minorities into the U.S. system. Still, it is often not easy to disentangle party influence from community organizational influence on political mobilization and the vote. Community elites are typically active in local party politics, especially on the Democratic side. Although there is no official record, it is safe to assume that most labor and civil rights elites active within the Asian American organizational network are liberals and Democratic Party supporters. Participation in (Democratic) party politics is often the first step for Asian American political elites to enter electoral politics (Lien, 2001b). In addition, Geron and Lai (2001), in their study of Asian American elected officials, report that the majority of respondents were Democrats. Moreover, ethnic community-based party organizations are instrumental in linking ethnic politics to mainstream politics and parties. By offering the training ground for the acquisition of resources necessary to undertake campaigns and voter mobilization strategies, these organizations often provide the institutional means through which activists translate their participation strategies from protests to electoral politics (Nakanishi, 1986; Wang, 1991; Wei, 1993; Lien, 1997; Lin, 1998). A case study of the West San Gabriel Valley Asian Pacific Democratic Club (founded in 1985–) highlights its linkage role in facilitating the transition of local politics from white domination to growing Asian American political power by instituting the networks, resources, and organizations needed to back issues and candidates and work toward political empowerment (Saito, 1998). Thus, as community civil rights organizations gain importance in mobilizing voting participation, it may not be surprising to find a majority Democratic orientation among Asian American voters.

In a nutshell, while major American parties had fairly successful records of incorporating "new" European immigrants between 1880 and 1920, they have not been active in bringing Asian immigrants into the party system. As was demonstrated by the parties' handling of the 1996 campaign finance controversies and the Wen Ho Lee case, whenever their interests were perceived to be at stake, the major parties have quickly abandoned the Asian American population. Nevertheless, despite tenuous outreach and even hostility to Asian Americans by the major parties, Asian Americans themselves cannot afford to neglect or abandon major parties. Not only does American government continue to be organized around the two-party system, but a party label is usually the best cue for both information-deficient and information-overloaded voters to make decisions in the electoral process. For nonwhite immigrant communities, partisan labels may be second only to race or ethnicity in structuring the vote (Hero, 1992; Hill, Moreno, and Cue, 2001).

Based on the above observations, we suspect that, in their eagerness to become politically incorporated, and to the extent that they can (have resources, connections, and interest) or know how (possess knowledge and language skills), Asian Americans may be expected to adopt a mainstream political partisanship.

In fact, even before they become citizens and are eligible to vote, some Asian American immigrants may develop identification with the Democratic or the Republican Party (Wong, 2000). However, for reasons explained below, their overall rates of major partisanship may be lower than average Americans and there may be significant interethnic differences in the adoption and the intensity of identification with major parties. In addition, for adult immigrants, their current partisanship may be shaped both by past partisanship and by current involvement with the homeland in Asia. More importantly, as is the case for other Americans, political partisanship may also be the core organizing orientation that helps structure voting participation, candidate choice, and issue positions for Asian Americans. Stronger partisanship predicts higher voting participation. Partisan identifiers are expected to yield greater support for the candidates and issue positions endorsed by their respective party than leaners or nonidentifiers. Nevertheless, compared to other agents or forces of political socialization, political partisanship and party mobilization may not always be the only or the most potent sources of influence on the political behavior of Asian Americans.

Past Research on the Acquisition and Direction of Asian American Partisanship

As a population that is predominantly foreign-born and that includes many recent arrivals, Asian Americans' identification with major political parties (as Democrat or Republican) can be conceived of as part of the process of adapting to American institutions, society, and culture. Their acquisition of political partisanship can be influenced by a complex set of factors related to individual acculturation, political socialization, experiences with the U.S. racial hierarchy, and ethnic identity, as well as the larger political context. Theories of the development of party identification also point to other factors such as childhood socialization (Campbell, Converse, Miller, and Stokes, 1960; Kraus and Davis, 1976; Atkin, 1981; Fiorina, 1981; Niemi and Jennings, 1991), age or length of exposure (Converse, 1969, 1976; Nie, Verba, and Kim, 1974; Niemi et al., 1985), length of stay for immigrants (Wong, 2000), and economic advancement (Cain, Kieweit, and Uhlaner, 1991; Uhlaner, 2000) as possible determinants of political orientations. In addition, in the current era of particularized campaign politics, the acquisition of political partisanship may be a function of the mobilization or activation of the targeted public (Schier, 2000; Conway, 2001b).

The Acquisition of Political Partisanship

Unlike the majority of the NES (National Election Survey) respondents whose political affiliation may be strongly influenced by that of their parents, the majority of Asian Americans do not automatically inherit U.S.-based partisan orientations. Because a large majority of present-day Asian Americans are either immigrants themselves or children of immigrants from non-English speaking and/or non-Western style democratic regimes, they are less likely to be familiar with or develop an affect for the two major parties in the United States (Nakanishi, 1991, 1998). For adult immigrants in particular, continued interest in homeland issues and the political efficacy and belief system developed under a different political culture may impede new political learning and the acquisition of new political partisanship (Gitelman, 1982; Finifter and Finifter, 1989). Furthermore, lack of English proficiency and exposure to the U.S. political system via schooling in the United States may also inhibit some Asian Americans' exposure to the U.S. political system and the development of subsequent U.S.-party orientations. Besides possible discrimination by the two major parties, the very fact that participation in political parties in an electoral democracy is voluntary may deter the acquisition of party identification in the United States among Asian Americans. Challenges to the acquisition of partisanship among Asian Americans may also be compounded by lack of vigorous party recruitment and outreach efforts for post-1965 immigrants and minorities due to reduced resources, role transformation, and strategic mobilization.

Given the above factors, it is not surprising that past research using data collected in the 1980s and 1990s shows a high overall level of nonpartisanship among Asian Americans. In the 1984 California Ethnicity Survey, 48 percent of citizen respondents of Asian descent are either nonpartisan or other partisan (Uhlaner, 2000).[4] Nevertheless, lack of political partisanship among Asians is neither a stable phenomenon nor a foregone conclusion, especially among voters. An examination of twelve national, state, and local surveys conducted in the 1990s that contain a hundred or more Asian respondents finds "none" or "other party" responses vary from 16 percent among voters in the 1998 California primary election to 44 percent among registered voters in the 1993–1994 Los Angeles Survey of Urban Inequality or LASUI (see Lien, 2001b, Table 4.2). As high as 50 percent of Asian adult respondents in the 1995 Race Poll do not usually think of themselves as either Democrat or Republican. In part because of small sample sizes, the figures among Asians fluctuate more than those found among whites, blacks, or Latinos. But, generally, the percentage of people who do not identify with a major party (other or no partisanship) among Asians is higher than that among whites, which is higher than that for Latinos or blacks in each of the surveys.

Across Asian ethnic groups, results from two Southern California surveys and six community exit polls conducted between 1992 and 1998 suggests that the extent of none or other partisanship among Asians may vary by region and ethnicity (see Lien 2001b, Table 5.6). Poll respondents in the San Francisco Bay area exit polls have the lowest percentage share of independence (12 to 16 percent); South Asian voters in the New York area and Japanese and Korean voters in Southern California also tend to have a lower share of independence than other

Asian groups in the region. Outside of the Bay area, generally a quarter or more of the Asian voters do not identify with either of the major parties; as many as half of the Chinese and Korean registered voters in the 1993–1994 LASUI survey did not report any partisan affiliation.

Direction of Partisanship

Among Asians who think of their politics in traditional partisan terms, the direction of their partisanship is certainly not cast in stone. This is in part due to the crosspressures experienced by Asians of various ethnicities. On one hand, having entered the United States mostly in the aftermath of the civil rights movement, Asian Americans may form an affiliation with the Democratic Party based on racial identity and discrimination experiences (Cain, Kiewiet, and Uhlaner, 1991). Aggressive voter education efforts by community civil rights organizations may orient new voters to be more sympathetic with Democratic issues and candidates. On the other hand, the political orientations of individuals who entered mostly after the passage of the 1965 Immigration Act may be influenced by the ideological predispositions of one's home country and ethnic culture—with Asian immigrants who flee communist or authoritarian regimes being more likely to identify as Republican. The economic advancement thesis also suggests that social mobility made by immigrants over time may push Asians toward the Republican camp.

Another source of controversy about the partisan orientation of Asian Americans results from biases in survey methods. Generally, the overall small-ness in population size, lack of ethnic concentration in certain neighborhoods, extreme dispersion in geographic region, and the lack of English fluency for the majority of the immigrant population have precluded their inclusion in nation-ally representative surveys. Unless special targeting efforts are made, few Asians are included even in California statewide or regional surveys. As a result, the majority of the evidence is drawn from limited and flawed data sources where variations in question wording and research methods often make comparisons difficult (Lien, 2001b).

Nonetheless, some patterns do emerge by reviewing a consortium of sur-veys. In Lien's (2001b) examination of twelve national, state, and local surveys conducted in the 1990s, the Democratic Party edge among Asians is not con-sistently evident until the 1998 election.[5] Political context or year of election matters because the partisan orientation of new Americans may be influenced by the party affiliation of the sitting president as well as the perceived effects of immigration and minority-related policies taken by the majority party in Congress. The occupancy of the White House by a Democratic president from 1992 to 2000 and the switch to a Republican-controlled Congress after the 1994 elections—which then passed welfare reforms to cut immigrant and minority benefits—may explain in part the dominance of Democratic identifiers among Asian American voters.

Besides election year context, the distribution of partisanship and influence of ethnicity among Asians may vary by political region. Lien's (2001b) analysis of community exit poll results by ethnicity finds Bay area voters to be much more liberal, with each ethnic group reporting a Democratic majority except the Vietnamese.[6] Although both Japanese and South Asian Americans are more Democratic than Republican in every region, the same cannot be said of other Asian groups. For example, Filipino voters in both Southern and Northern California are more Democratic than Republican, but not so if they live in New York City. Over time, a trend of conversion toward the Democratic Party seems to have taken place during and after the 1994 election most prominently among Korean, but also Chinese and Filipino, American voters.

Plan of Analysis and Key Measures

The above review provides important information needed to better understand the contours and sources of political partisanship found in the PNAAPS. We use a standard three-part question in the PNAAPS to query the contours of political partisanship among Asians. All respondents are asked, "Generally speaking, do you usually think of yourself as a Republican, a Democrat, an Independent, or of another political affiliation?" Those responding "Democrat" or "Republican" are asked, "Would you call yourself a strong Republican (Democrat)?" Those responding "Independent" are asked, "Do you think of yourself as closer to the Republican or Democratic Party?" From these questions, we create a nine-point scale of party identification, which includes a conventional seven-point scale ranging from "Strong Democrat" to "Strong Republican," with "(Pure) Independent" in the middle. In addition, we assign a true nonpartisan category for those who respond, "no, do not think in these terms" to the first question as well as a "not sure" category for those who are uncertain of how to answer the first question. In most analyses, for the sake of parsimony, we use a four-point scale of party identification by combining the strong and moderate partisans under "Democrat" and "Republican," the leaners and pure independents under "Independent," and the unaffiliated and the unsure under "non-identifier".[7]

To describe the contours of political partisanship among the total sample of and by individual Asian ethnic groups, we first report crosstabulation results using the nine-point partisanship scale for both all respondents and immigrant respondents (Table 4.1). We then report partisanship distribution by ethnic origin and resident region (metropolitan area) using the four-point scale for both all respondents and those who voted in the presidential election of 2000 (Table 4.2). To assess the relationships between the acquisition of political partisanship and possible correlates at the aggregate level, we report partisanship distribution along the four-point scale for sets of variables dealing with the socioeconomic status and social connectedness, international migration and socialization stages, minority group experiences, and the political and institutional connectedness of respondents (Tables 4.3a–4.3c). To explore the relationships between homeland connections and political resocialization at the aggregate level, we report the percentage distribution of immigrant-only measures along the four-point partisanship scale (Table 4.3d).

We assess the unique or independent influence of each of the variables on the acquisition of political partisanship while controlling for the effects of all other variables by conducting a series of multivariate regression analyses. In Table 4.4 we report multinomial regression results to predict the acquisition of political partisanship. The dependent variable is the four-point partisanship scale. The "nonidentifier" is assigned as the category of reference. This coding decision permits us to compare the variables of influence not only for choosing a party affiliation but also for the adoption of the partisanship concept itself among Asian Americans. We test the influence of sociodemographic background, socialization stages, and racial group concerns with a restricted set of variables (Table 4.4a). We then assess the relative efficacy of homeland ties in deciding the adoption and the acquisition of partisanship among Asia-born respondents (Table 4.5).

To measure the strength of major partisanship, we create a 5-point scale with a value of 4 assigned to strong Democrats or Republicans, a value of 3 to weak Democrats or Republicans, a value of 2 to leaning Democrats or Republicans, a value of 1 to pure Independents, and 0 to all others. We report the ordinary least squares-based (OLS) regression results in Table 4.6. OLS is a statistical procedure suitable for estimating effects on a continuous dependent variable. We test the unique contribution of a restricted and full set of variables as well as those applied only to Asia-born respondents.

Last, we examine the relationships between political partisanship and Asian Americans' candidate choice and policy preferences. For candidate choice, we report the percentage distribution of the 2000 presidential vote by partisanship and by ethnicity as well as the ethnic bloc vote potential among Asian Americans (Table 4.7). For policy preferences, we look at respondents' attitude toward three measures of affirmative action as well as propositions on bilingual services, immigration control, and limitations on campaign contributions. We then report multivariate regression results estimating the unique and relative impacts of major partisanship and party contact on the requisite political behavior domains under investigation (Table 4.8). A list of question wording and coding scheme for the measures used is reported in the appendix.

The Contours of Political Partisanship among PNAAPS Respondents

Distribution of Partisanship

Table 4.1 reports the percentage distribution of political partisanship among the PNAAPS respondents along a nine-point scale. The aggregate figures confirm the Democratic orientation among the majority of Asians identifying with the traditional party categories of Democratic, Republican, and Independent, as well as the substantial proportion of no-partisanship (both unaffiliated and

Table 4.1 Percentage Distribution of Partisanship by Ethnic Origin

	Row Total	STRONG D	WEAK D	LEANING D	INDEP	LEANING R	WEAK R	STRONG R	NO PARTY	NOT SURE
ALL ASIANS	1218(913)	13(12)	23(22)	4(3)	6(6)	3(3)	12(11)	4(5)	20(20)	16(18)
Chinese	308(279)	8(7)	24(25)	1(1)	1(*)	1(*)	7(7)	2(2)	33(33)	23(24)
Korean	168(157)	8(7)	35(36)	3(3)	8(8)	1(1)	20(19)	2(2)	8(9)	15(14)
Vietnamese	137(135)	4(4)	7(7)	1(0)	12(12)	1(1)	5(5)	11(11)	31(31)	27(27)
Japanese	198(41)	12(5)	28(22)	9(10)	8(15)	3(2)	11(10)	1(2)	18(12)	11(22)
Filipino	266(180)	22(22)	18(18)	6(6)	5(3)	3(4)	16(14)	7(8)	13(13)	11(22)
South Asian	141(121)	23(21)	21(22)	5(5)	10(12)	9(8)	11(11)	6(6)	6(7)	10(10)

Note: Entries in parentheses are figures among immigrants. D=Democrat, R=Republican, INDEP=Pure Independent. Some row totals do not equal to 100 percent because of rounding.

Source: PNAAPS 2000–2001.

undecided). In the 2000 presidential election, 4 in 10 PNAAPS respondents either identify with or lean toward the Democratic Party, 2 in 10 either identify with or lean toward the Republican Party, and over 3 in 10 either do not identify with any party or are not sure of which party to identify with. "Weak Democrat" has the single largest percentage share (23 percent), followed by "no party" (20 percent) and by the uncertain (16 percent); partisan leaners and "strong Republican" have the smallest percentage shares (3–4 percent). Compared to the percentage distribution of partisanship found among 2000 NES respondents,[8] Asian Americans are more skewed toward the Democratic Party but they identify much less with a third party[9] or lean toward a major party. Moreover, a much larger percentage of Asians have not adopted any partisan orientation ("do not think in these terms") or are uncertain of their partisanship.

Combining those who are Independent with nonidentifiers ("no party" or "not sure"), we see that 42 percent of the PNAAPS respondents (44 percent among immigrants) do not identify with or lean toward either of the major parties. Although this figure is at least twice the size of the combined figures for the pure Independents and the nonpartisans found in the NES data series, it is not too much different from that found among non-Hispanic whites in the 1984 California ethnicity study or the 1995 Race Poll (43 percent). In a study of party identification in Australia, 39 percent of the surveyed American migrants either do not identify with or know of an Australian party (Finifter and Finifter, 1989). However, given the multiple obstacles adult immigrants face in adopting a new political identity in a different political system, the authors conclude that since about 60 percent did identify with an Australian party; American migrants in Australia are in fact capable of new learning and adaptation to the new political environment. Because about six out of ten Asians in the survey (68 percent among those who voted) do, in fact, identify with or lean toward one of the major parties, we believe considerable political learning has also taken place among Asian Americans in their acquisition of mainstream partisanship. Moreover, like the American immigrants in Finifter and Finifter's study, the increasing Democratic Party orientation of Asian Americans in the second half of the 1990s shows that the majority of Asian immigrants may be aware, responsive, and capable of adaptation to the political conditions in the receiving nation. For example, they may respond to the Clinton Administration and perceived anti-immigrant legislative proposals and policies.

We do not believe that we can label all those Asians who fail to adopt major party identification as "Independent." Only 6 percent of the PNAAPS respondents are pure (nonleaning) independents, but 35 percent of all are either no-partisan or undecided. Neither can all the unaffiliated be characterized as "apolitical." Crosstabulation results show that over half of the no-partisan (55 percent) and the unsure (50 percent) are either very or somewhat interested in political matters, even though their interest level is lower than that found among the pure independents (62 percent), which in turn is lower than that found among partisans and leaners.[10] In addition, some respondents may be rejecting either of the two major parties for explicitly political reasons (for instance, they do not think that either major party represents immigrants or racial minorities well).

Table 4.1 also shows that each ethnic group has a distinct pattern in the acquisition, direction, and strength of partisanship. Both Chinese and Vietnamese respondents have much higher percentages of no-partisans and undecided respondents than other Asians, while both Koreans and South Asians have a very low percentage of nonidentification. Both Filipinos and South Asians have greater proportions of strong Democrats, while Koreans have the largest proportion of weak Democrats and weak Republicans. Compared to other Asian American groups, Japanese respondents have the largest share of leaning Democrats, South Asians have the largest share of leaning Republicans, and the Vietnamese have the largest share of pure Independents. The percentage distribution of partisanship and nonpartisanship among immigrants is generally very similar to that found among the whole sample. However, the percentages of Democratic partisans as well as no-partisans among Japanese immigrants are lower, while those of pure independents and the undecided are higher, than the entire Japanese sample. These results may be due to the fact that the Japanese sample contains a lower proportion of immigrants than any other Asian ethnic group in the study.

Collapsing the distribution of partisanship into a more manageable four-point scale, we show in Table 4.2 that the majority of Chinese and Vietnamese respondents are nonidentifiers and at least four in ten respondents in other Asian groups are Democratic identifiers. Table 4.2 also shows that different ethnic groups exhibit different partisan traits. Compared to other Asians, Vietnamese have the smallest proportion of Democratic identifiers (12 percent), Chinese have the smallest proportion of Independents (3 percent), Japanese have the smallest proportion of Republican identifiers (12 percent), and South Asians have the smallest proportion of nonidentifiers (16 percent). Among voters, South Asians have the largest proportion of Democrats (57 percent), Japanese have the largest proportion of Independents (22 percent), and Koreans have the largest proportion of Republicans (35 percent), while Vietnamese have the largest proportion of non-identifiers (56 percent). Korean American voters have the greatest share of Republican identifiers (35 percent) overall, but Vietnamese American voters are essentially equally divided between Republican (17 percent) and Democratic identifiers (15 percent). Many of the Vietnamese respondents may have arrived in the United States as refugees who had fled a communist regime. The Republican Party, the U.S. party traditionally associated with anti-communist policies, has also been well organized in areas with a high concentration of Vietnamese Americans where most high-profile community leaders are Republican. However, their racial minority status and

Table 4.2 Percentage Distribution of Partisanship by Ethnic Origin and Metropolitan Area

ALL ASIANS	Row Total 1218(537)	DEMOCRAT 36(41)	INDEPENDENT 13(12)	REPUBLICAN 16(20)	NONIDENTIFIER 35(27)
Chinese	308(126)	32(38)	3(2)	9(14)	56(47)
Korean	168(57)	43(47)	12(9)	22(35)	23(9)
Vietnamese	137(54)	12(15)	15(13)	16(17)	58(56)
Japanese	198(124)	40(42)	20(22)	12(16)	28(20)
Filipino	266(125)	40(46)	14(12)	23(25)	23(18)
South Asian	141(51)	44(57)	23(18)	16(20)	16(6)
Los Angeles	417(177)	33(39)	12(12)	20(25)	34(24)
New York	204(74)	41(47)	12(10)	17(23)	30(20)
San Francisco	200(91)	40(50)	11(6)	8(11)	42(34)
Honolulu	195(102)	32(35)	15(16)	10(16)	43(34)
Chicago	202(93)	35(39)	15(18)	20(22)	30(21)

Note: Entries in parentheses are figures among voters in Election 2000. "Independent" includes leaners. "Nonidentifier" refers to those who either do not identify themselves in partisan terms or are not sure of which party to identify with. Some row totals do not equal 100 percent because of rounding.

Source: PNAAPS 2000–2001.

socioeconomic and social issue concerns may push the community increasingly toward the Democratic camp.

Table 4.2 also shows that region may matter in understanding partisanship among Asians. Both New York and San Francisco have larger proportions of Democrats than other regions. Both Honolulu and Chicago have slightly larger proportions of Independents. Both Los Angeles and Chicago have larger proportions of Republicans. And both San Francisco and Honolulu have higher proportions of the unaffiliated/undecided than other regions. These patterns not only hold, but become more evident among voters.

Possible Influences on Partisanship

To understand what may influence Asian Americans' acquisition and direction of political partisanship at the aggregate level, we report the percentage distribution of possible correlates of partisanship identified in prior research. Primarily, they can be grouped into four sets of variables: sociodemographic background, immigration and adaptation, racial group concerns, and political and civic institutional ties. In addition, for immigrants only, we look at the relationship between partisanship and homeland connections.

Turning to the first set of variables in Table 4.3a, we see that about half of those who do not have a college education are nonidentifiers. Attending at least some college (rather than none) is associated with more Democratic and Independent identification. Those who have finished college are more likely to identify as Republican than those who have not, though Democratic identifiers dominate at all levels of education. If higher educational achievement correlates with the acquisition of *any* partisanship, higher income levels may be associated with the acquisition of major party identification, especially Democratic. About half of those who report having family income at or over $60,000 identify as Democrat, while only two in ten identify as Republican. This pattern appears to contradict the economic advancement hypothesis that associates income mobility with being Republican. However, respondents at higher income levels do tend to register higher percentage shares of Republican and Democratic identification than people at the lowest income. It should be noted that as high as a quarter of the respondents do not indicate an income level. Close to one-half of them are nonidentifiers, but a quarter of them identify as Democrat.

The relationship between age and partisanship among the Asian Americans surveyed is also somewhat counterintuitive. Both the very young (age 18–28) and very old (age 61–100) include larger proportions of Democrats than other age groups. The eldest group has the lowest share of Independents, but not the highest share of Republicans. Interestingly, it's the youngest age group that has the lowest percentage of nonidentifiers. Age group does not seem to be a good indicator of the acquisition nor the direction of partisanship. Neither is length of community residence, which does not have a statistically significant relationship to partisanship. Gender makes no difference in the percentage share of Democrats or Independents, but a higher percentage of male respondents are Republican and a higher percentage of female respondents are nonidentifiers. Similarly, a greater share of the employed than the unemployed are Republican and a smaller share of the employed than the unemployed are nonidentifiers.

According to past research, an immigrant's length of stay in the United States may be a better predictor of partisan acquisition than age (Wong, 2000). In the PNAAPS, those immigrants who have been in the States for 5 years or less have a much higher percentage of nonidentification (46 percent) than those who have been in the States for 22 or more years (27 percent). The percentage share of Republican identification increases with the length of U.S. stay, with 23 percent of those who reside in the States for 22 or more years identifying themselves as Republican, compared to the 9 percent among those whose live in the States for 5 years or less. The highest percentage of Democratic identification is found, however, among those who reside in the United States for 16 to 20 years and the highest percentage of Independent identification is found among those who have either the shortest or the longest U.S. stay.

Turning to indicators of immigration and adaptation, we find that the acquisition of partisanship and immigration generation may not be a linear one (Table 4.3b). As we might expect, respondents of the foreign-born generation have the highest percentage of nonidentification. However, somewhat unexpectedly, nonidentification does not decrease with generation. Those who are of the third or more generation have a higher percentage of nonidentification than respondents of the second generation. In addition, second generation respondents report greater levels of Democratic partisanship than those who are third generation or more. When we examine the next set of variables, we see that the acquisition of partisanship may be related to citizenship status—noncitizens who do not expect to become citizens have the highest shares of nonidentification and independence but lower proportions of major partisanship compared to citizens or those who expect to become citizens. Nativity may matter in that foreign-born citizens have a higher proportion of nonidentification and independence than native-born citizens.

The data are clear about the influence of educational context on the acquisition of any partisanship. Among those Asian Americans who have received the majority of their education outside of the United States, the percentage of identification with any U.S. party is lower and their percentage of nonidentification is higher than the percentages found among respondents who received education mainly in the United States. Language use may be associated with the acquisition of partisanship in that those respondents who mostly use a language other than English to communicate both at home and in business settings also have the lowest percentages of identification with the major or third party and the highest percentages of nonidentification, compared to those who either use both English and another language or only English at home or in business transactions. English-only users generally have higher percentages of

Table 4.3a Percentage Distribution of Sociodemography and Social Ties by Partisanship

	Row Total	DEMOCRAT	INDEPENDENT	REPUBLICAN	NONIDENTIFIER
Education					
no college	329	32	8	12	48
some college	223	39	14	13	34
college or more	596	37	16	19	28
Income Levels					
<30k	283	36	10	12	42
30–59k	349	36	15	18	32
60k+	281	47	12	20	21
not sure/refused	305	25	14	14	47
Age Groups (in years)					
18–28	235	43	17	12	28
29–37	213	26	16	18	39
38–47	222	40	10	15	36
48–60	214	31	14	22	32
61–100	200	42	8	14	36

(*cont.*)

Table 4.3a *(Continued)*

	Row Total	DEMOCRAT	INDEPENDENT	REPUBLICAN	NONIDENTIFIER
Length of Community Residence (in years) (p=.32)					
1–3	256	36	13	14	37
4–6	214	30	15	15	40
7–11	237	33	11	18	38
12–20	263	38	14	17	30
21 or more	188	43	10	15	32
Gender					
male	612	35	14	19	32
female	606	36	12	13	38
Employed					
no	447	34	12	13	41
yes	771	37	13	18	32

Source and Note: See Table 4.2. All the chi-square tests of difference are significant at $\alpha=.05$ or better, except where noted.

Table 4.3b Percentage Distribution of Immigration, Socialization, and Racial Group Concerns by Partisanship

	Row Total	DEMOCRAT	INDEPENDENT	REPUBLICAN	NONIDENTIFIER
Immigration Generation					
first	924	33%	12%	16%	39%
second	172	47	17	14	22
third or more	122	36	16	19	29
U.S. Citizenship					
none	116	22	16	11	51
expected	278	34	13	14	39
yes	824	38	12	18	32
U.S. born	284	43	16	16	26
foreign-born	540	36	10	19	35
Years of U.S. Stay (Immigrants only)					
5 or fewer	220	30	15	9	46
6–10	221	33	9	15	43
11–15	134	31	9	18	42
16–21	156	43	11	18	28
22 or more	165	35	15	23	27
Non-U.S. Education					
no	510	38	16	19	28
yes	708	34	11	14	41

(*cont.*)

Table 4.3b (Continued)

	Row Total	DEMOCRAT	INDEPENDENT	REPUBLICAN	NONIDENTIFIER
Home Language Use					
mostly non-English	579	31	10	12	47
mixed	298	36	15	22	26
mostly English	322	42	17	17	24
Business Language Use					
mostly non-English	158	31	4	9	56
mixed	150	29	9	10	52
mostly English	863	38	15	18	28
Racial Group Concerns					
Hate Crime Victims					
no	1032	35	13	16	37
yes	186	41	15	17	26
Experience of Ethnic Discrimination					
no	810	31	13	16	40
yes	408	44	13	16	27
Sense of Panethnic Linked Fate					
no	516	30	12	16	42
not much	107	35	13	15	37
some	356	41	15	16	28
a lot	132	47	11	19	23

Source and Note: See Table 4.2. All the chi-square tests of difference are significant at $\alpha = .05$ or better, except where noted.

partisanship than those who are not, except that mixed home-language users have a higher percentage of Republican identification.

Questions in the PNAAPS also permit the testing of minority status hypothesis. Past literature suggests that those who experience minority group-based discrimination may identify more with the Democratic than the Republican Party. They may have greater Democratic identification compared to those who did not experience such discrimination. Using respondents' reported incidence of hate crime victimization and personal experience of ethnic discrimination as measures of minority status, evidence at the aggregate level clearly supports such assertions. We also find that the percentage of nonidentification is lower among those who personally experienced discrimination. Moreover, Asians who have the least sense of linked fate (or those who are least likely to think that what happens to other groups of Asian Americans may affect his or her own life in the United States) tend to have the highest percentage of nonpartisanship. By contrast, those who have a stronger sense of linked fate tend to register a higher sense of both Democratic and, to a lesser extent, Republican identification.

The relationships between political partisanship and indicators of political and civic institutional connectedness are examined in Table 4.3c. Generally, higher degrees of political partisanship are expected from those who have greater degrees of connections with social networks and political institutions. Among PNAAPS respondents, we find that those who never attend religious services have the highest share of nonidentification, and those who frequented religious services on a weekly basis have the highest percentage of Republican identification. There is no clear pattern between Democratic or third-party identification and religious attendance, but those who attended religious services either least or most frequently have the lowest percentage of identification as Independent. Compared to those who are not, being a member of a community organization is associated with a higher percentage of both Democratic and Republican identification, and a lower percentage of nonidentification with any party. The same pattern is found among those mobilized by a political party or group. The percentage of major party identification is higher and nonidentification is lower among those contacted by one or more political parties.

The strength and direction of mainstream political ideology may be associated strongly with the acquisition and direction of partisanship. About half of those respondents who are either very or somewhat liberal in ideology identify themselves as Democrat. Comparatively, only about a quarter of those who are either somewhat or very conservative identify as Democratic. Across the five-point ideological scale, the percentage of identification with the Republican Party is highest among the very conservative. The percentage share of party identification either as Democrat, Independent, or Republican is lowest among those who are unsure of their ideology. As many as seven out of ten in this group indicate no identification with a party. In terms of political interest, Asians who are more interested in political matters register higher percentages of Democratic partisanship than those who have lower levels of interest. Conversely, people who are least interested in politics register the highest percentage of nonidentification. Those who are very interested in politics also have a somewhat higher percentage of identification as Independent or Republican than those who are not interested in politics at all. Finally, Asians who report a higher level of political knowledge (in this case, familiarity with the U.S. presidential election process) also register the highest percentage of political independence, and, in correspondence, the lowest percentage of nonidentification with any political party.

Table 4.3d reports the percentage distribution of six immigrant-only measures. Past research on political (re)socialization suggests that experiences acquired prior to emigration may impact the acquisition of partisanship in the host country. We find some evidence of support at the aggregate level. Respondents who belonged to a homeland political or party organization prior to emigration have a lower percentage share of any partisanship and a higher percentage share of nonidentification than those who did not have prior partisanship. Asian immigrants who trust U.S. officials more than homeland government officials and who feel more efficacious in influencing decisions made by officials in the United States than homeland officials are characterized by lower percentages of nonidentification and higher percentages of Republican and Independent identification, but not Democratic identification. However, we find no relationship between participation in homeland politics after emigration and the acquisition of U.S. partisanship. Neither is there a clear pattern to suggest that maintaining more frequent contacts with the homeland may impede the adoption of new partisanship. Finally, those who expect to return to Asia report a higher level of Republican identification and a lower level of nonidentification than those who do not.

Summary of Aggregate-Level Findings

In sum, the bulk of the evidence suggests that, at the aggregate level, the acquisition of political partisanship by Asian Americans may be significantly associated with almost all of the factors mentioned in prior research. In terms of socioeconomic status, when asked about their party identification, those who are better educated, have higher incomes, and who are employed are more likely to indicate traditional party identification (Democrat, Independent, or Republican) rather than answer "no party" or "not sure." Males are also less likely to be nonidentifiers than females. On the other hand, age and length of community residence are not strong predictors of acquiring partisanship.

As expected, those who are more integrated into dominant U.S. society are also more likely to have acquired mainstream partisan orientations. Those who are U.S.-born and those who are expecting to become or who are citizens are more likely to acquire partisanship than those who are foreign-born noncitizens. Similar to past research, those immigrants who have spent more years residing in the United States are more likely to acquire partisanship than recent arrivals.

Table 4.3c Percentage Distribution of Political and Civic Institutional Ties by Partisanship

	Row Total	DEMOCRAT	INDEPENDENT	REPUBLICAN	NONIDENTIFIER
Religious Attendance					
never	273	32	10	9	49
1–2/year	281	37	18	8	37
1–2/month	150	40	13	17	29
3–4/month	98	34	18	22	26
every week	355	37	10	25	28
Ethnic Community Organization Membership					
no	1037	34	13	15	38
yes	181	46	14	22	18
Party Contact					
no	724	31	13	14	42
yes	494	42	13	19	26
Political Ideology					
very liberal	101	48	12	11	30
somewhat liberal	338	48	12	13	26
middle	385	34	16	12	38
somewhat conservative	225	27	13	29	30
very conservative	45	24	18	33	24
not sure	120	14	6	10	70

(*cont.*)

Table 4.3c (*Continued*)

	Row Total	DEMOCRAT	INDEPENDENT	REPUBLICAN	NONIDENTIFIER
Political Interest					
not at all	160	26	11	16	47
slightly	292	29	13	16	42
somewhat	455	38	12	15	35
very interested	293	45	16	18	21
Familiarity with the Presidential Election Process					
not familiar/ns	254	22	11	10	57
somewhat familiar	656	37	13	16	34
very familiar	308	43	15	21	21

Source and Note: See Table 4.2. All the chi-square tests of difference are significant at $\alpha=.05$ or better, except where noted.

Table 4.3d Percentage Distribution of Homeland Ties by Political Partisanship among Immigrants

	Row Total	DEMOCRAT	INDEPENDENT	REPUBLICAN	NONIDENTIFIER
Prior Membership in Homeland Political or Party Organization (p=.09)					
no	838	34	12	16	38
yes	75	31	5	13	51
Trust More of U.S. Government Officials					
no	413	36	9	12	43
yes	500	32	14	19	35
Feel Having More Influence on Decisions Made by U.S. Officials					
no	554	34	10	12	43
yes	359	33	15	21	32
Participation in Homeland Politics in the U.S. (p=.99)					
no	860	34	12	16	39
yes	53	34	11	17	38
Frequency of Contact with Homeland People in the Past 12 Months (p=.07)					
none	128	30	15	21	34
once a year/less	82	33	7	15	45
once several month	145	34	11	12	43
once a month	154	32	11	18	39
2–3 times/month	174	44	10	17	29
once a week or more	230	29	14	14	43
Expect to Return to Home Country in Asia (p=.16)					
no	863	34	12	15	39
yes	50	32	14	26	28

Source and Note: See Table 4.2. All the chi-square tests of difference are significant at α=.05 or better except where noted.

A similar pattern is found among those who were educated in the United States compared to those who were educated abroad, and between those who speak English or some English versus those who speak none at all.

Racial group concerns is related to the acquisition of partisanship at the descriptive level. Those who have been the victims of a hate crime or have experienced racial discrimination are more likely to acquire partisanship. Similarly, those who have a strong sense of linked fate with other Asian Americans are more likely to acquire partisanship than those with a weaker sense.

Those with strong institutional ties to religious, community, and political party organizations are more likely to acquire partisanship than those who do not exhibit strong institutional connections. In terms of ideology and interest in politics, those who are unsure of their ideology, uninterested in politics, or unfamiliar with the political system are not likely to adopt a partisan identity.

This study reveals some interesting findings related to homeland ties and the acquisition of partisanship among Asian American immigrants, as well. Prior membership in a party or political organization in the country of origin seems to inhibit the development of new partisan ties in the United States. Current activity in politics in the country of origin or current contact with people in the country of origin does not appear to have any effect on the acquisition of U.S. partisanship. Somewhat surprisingly, lack of party identification is *more* widespread among those who do not expect to return to their country of origin versus those who do expect to return. Foreign policy concerns regarding the Asian homeland may reduce the level of nonidentification. Finally, those who trust and feel they have more influence on the government in the United States compared to the government in their country of origin are slightly more likely to acquire partisanship than those who do not.

Also, with some notable exceptions, the relationships of the variables examined above with partisan direction are similar to those we would expect. In particular, Republican partisanship becomes more prevalent as respondents move up the socioeconomic ladder. However, it is important to note that the percent of Democrats remains larger than the percent of Republicans across all education and income levels. Those who score higher on minority status variables are also more likely to be Democrats.[11] Republican identity increases with religiosity, though, again, Democrats outweigh Republicans at every level of religiosity. Community organization membership and party contact seem to reinforce identification with a major political party. Major party identification becomes more pronounced with both organizational membership and party contact. Among Asian Americans in our sample, both membership in a community organization and party contact appear to increase identification with a major party. Finally, it is interesting to observe that party contact appears to have no relationship to Independent identity.

Predicting the Acquisition of Political Partisanship among Asian Americans: Multinomial Regression Results

In order to understand if and how each of these variables can make a difference in predicting the adoption and direction of political partisanship while controlling simultaneously the impact of all others, we turn to the multinomial regression procedure for answers. Cell values in Table 4.4, 4.4a, and 4.5 are logistic coefficients (b) or log odds; standard errors (s.e.) are to the right. The "Democrat" columns report the log likelihood for respondents who prefer identification as a Democrat to no identification ("no party" or "not sure"). The "Independent" columns report the log likelihood for respondents who prefer identification as an Independent to no identification. The "Republican" columns report the log likelihood for respondents who prefer identification as a Republican to no identification. As in predicting identity choices, discussion of results and comparison of effect size here are facilitated by estimating the parameters with rescaled independent variables whose values are restricted to vary between 0 and 1.

To evaluate the validity of the various hypotheses discussed in past research, we use the following sets of explanatory factors that are key to a composite conceptual framework proposed in an earlier chapter: four measures of political engagement (ideology, interest, knowledge, and citizenship status), two measures of civic institutional ties (frequency of attending religious services and organizational membership), three measures of acculturation and racial group concerns (English language use, sense of panethnic linked fate, and experience of racial discrimination), four measures of socioeconomic status and social network (education, family income, gender, and employment status), and three measures of time-related experiences (physical age, length of community residence, and length of exposure to U.S. politics as a proportion of one's life).[12] To tap into the foreign policy hypothesis, we consider respondent's ethnic or home country of origin. In addition, we control for socialization context in terms of place of education and residence region.

Table 4.4 presents the multinomial logistic regression results predicting political partisanship. Other conditions being equal, Asians who are more liberal in political ideology have higher levels of interest in and knowledge of political matters, have a heightened sense of belonging to the panethnic Asian American community, are linked to a social network via being employed, have spent a greater share of political life in the U.S., and are residing in regions other than Honolulu are more likely to be Democrats than nonidentifiers. Compared to persons of Chinese descent, those of South Asian, Japanese, and Korean origins have a stronger likelihood, while those of Vietnamese descent have weaker likelihood, to possess Democratic partisanship over nonidentification. Relatively speaking, the acquisition of Democratic partisanship versus no partisan identity among Asians is not associated with indicators of institutional connections either through community organization membership or religious attendance.

Table 4.4 Multinomial Analysis Predicting Political Partisanship

	DEMOCRAT		INDEPENDENT		REPUBLICAN	
	b	s.e.	b	s.e.	b	s.e.
(Intercept)	−1.516	.471	−4.329	.730	−4.675	.641
political ideology (5=v. cons.)	−1.292**	.383	.432	.481	1.478**	.464
political interest	.599*	.307	.646	.399	−.139	.372
political knowledge	.838*	.411	.688	.552	1.406**	.506
ethnic organization membership	.430	.278	.084	.353	.576^	.327
religious attendance	.046	.250	−.371	.331	1.083**	.316
sense of linked fate	.598*	.246	.211	.324	.062	.308
experience with discrimination	.274	.269	.203	.364	−.025	.346
education	−.193	.348	.941*	.483	.551	.450
employed	.382*	.190	.143	.251	.838**	.256
age	.831^	.453	−.240	.628	1.357*	.597
proportion of U.S. life	.990**	.377	.485	.492	1.099*	.462
non-U.S. education	−.198	.243	−.367	.310	−.564*	.286
region (Honolulu)	−.632*	.276	−.445	.333	−1.218**	.379
Ethnic Origin (ref=Chinese)						
Filipino	.630^	.348	2.452**	.567	.112	.497
Japanese	1.046**	.313	2.691**	.541	1.253**	.403
Korean	1.064**	.306	2.249**	.557	1.196**	.392
South Asian	1.337**	.373	3.322**	569	1.680**	.466
Vietnamese	−.859*	.385	2.207**	.535	.568	.421

N=935
−2 Log Likelihood (Intercept only) = 2428.86
Model Chi-Sq=336.45
Nagelkerke R-sq=.327; McFadden=.139

Note: The dependent is a categorical variable with 4 possible responses. The reference category is the nonidentifiers (the unaffiliated and the undecided). The parameters are estimated using multinomial regression procedures with rescaled independent variables where scores are to vary only between 0 and 1. Excluded variables are family income, female, length of community residence, English language use, and citizenship status. b=unstandarized logistic coefficient, s.e.=standard error, **p≤.005, *p≤.05, ^p≤.10
Source: PNAAPS 2000–2001.

Neither personal experience with racial discrimination, nor higher socioeconomic attainment, nor receiving education mostly outside of the United States may independently structure Democratic partisanship. However, in nine out of ten instances, being older in age and of Filipino descent is associated with a higher likelihood of being Democrat.

Turning to the second column of data in Table 4.4, we see that having more education is associated with greater odds of adopting Independent identification over nonidentification. Being of any other major Asian ethnicity than the Chinese also predicts greater Independent identification. No other variables are significant enough to predict the adoption of this orientation over nonidentification. In contrast, as seen in the third column, having a more conservative political ideology, possessing greater political knowledge, having more social connections through attendance at religious services and being employed, and having greater exposure to U.S. life through age or length of U.S. stay, is associated with the acquisition of Republican partisanship over nonidentification, all else being equal. Relative to other factors, having a non-U.S. education and residing in Honolulu are negatively associated with the acquisition of Republican orientation. Once other factors are controlled, compared to persons of Chinese descent, those of South Asian, Japanese, and Korean origin, but not of Vietnamese or Filipino origin, are more likely to acquire Republican partisanship over nonidentification. Holding other factors constant, nine times out of ten, community organization membership is positively associated with Republican identification over nonidentification.

Together, political ideology, political knowledge, employment status, age, proportion of one's life spent in the United States, residence in Honolulu area, and ethnic origin are significantly related to the acquisition of major partisanship over nonidentification among Asians. Political interest and sense of linked fate alone are positively linked to the acquisition of Democratic partisanship versus nonidentification. Indicators of civic institutional connectedness such as community organizational membership, frequency of attending religious services, as well as non-U.S. educational context are positively associated with the acquisition of Republican partisanship over nonidentification. Education and ethnic origin alone are positively associated with the acquisition of political independence. The negative and distinct relationship between the Honolulu region and major partisanship is surprising, given the strength of the Democratic Party machine in Hawaii. We suspect that the lack of competitive elections in most of the offices in Hawaii may contribute to the negative party sign associated with the Honolulu region, when other conditions are controlled.[13]

Other conditions being equal, experience with racial discrimination is not associated with greater odds of acquiring Democratic partisanship, and higher socioeconomic status is not associated with greater odds of acquiring Republican partisanship as opposed to nonidentification. The lack of impact of these two variables seems to be counterintuitive and contradict aggregate-level results. In fact, variables that appear to structure the direction and the adoption of political partisanship at the aggregate level, such as family income, gender, English language use, length of community residence, or citizenship status are dropped from the final model because of their lack of independent effect. Their potential impact may be knocked out by the inclusion of variables more explicitly linked to the acquisition of political partisanship.

Estimating Effects with Restricted Models

To explore the utility of basic socioeconomic status, demographic background, adaptation stages, and minority experience in structuring partisanship, we conduct an analysis with a restricted model that contains only these variables. We find that better education is positively associated with the likelihood of identification as Independent or Republican. Having greater family income (or homeownership) or being female does not have a significant relationship to the acquisition of partisanship, however. Greater residential mobility or living fewer years in the surveyed community is positively associated with the likelihood of identification as Independent or Republican. However, different from the results in the full model, having spent more years in the U.S. as a proportion of one's life (100 percent for the native-born) is positively and significantly associated with identification as Independent. Having acquired or expecting to acquire U.S. citizenship is associated with a greater likelihood to identify as Republican. Importantly, respondents' preference for using English more than another language to communicate within and outside of the home, and for consuming more English- than ethnic-language media, is positively associated with their acquisition of major partisan identification over nonidentification. Furthermore, experience with racial discrimination is positively associated with Democratic identification. Nevertheless, results from the preceding table show that having a sense of a unified minority community (linked fate with other Asian Americans) is more important than experiencing discrimination in predicting the acquisition of Democratic partisanship. This exercise confirms both the value of basic sociodemographic and socialization factors as well as the need to look beyond these factors in understanding the acquisition of partisanship among the Asian American population.

Predicting the Acquisition of Political Partisanship among Immigrant Asian Americans

The analysis in Table 4.5 attempts to shed light on some of the hypotheses related to immigrant political resocialization discussed earlier. We intentionally avoid using some of the politically more relevant indicators in favor of a restricted set of variables dealing with basic sociodemographic background, immigrant adaptation, and ethnic experiences to uncover the possible influence of homeland ties. We use the variables reported in Table 4.3d as indicators of homeland influence.[14] The multinomial regression results generally identify few instances of homeland influence, suggesting that the acquisition of new partisanship is not as influenced by past as by present experiences. However, other conditions being equal, being active in homeland politics after emigration, as well the intent to eventually return to Asia, may be associated with greater Republican

Table 4.5 Multinomial Analysis Predicting Political Partisanship among Immigrants

	DEMOCRAT		INDEPENDENT		REPUBLICAN	
	b	s.e.	b	s.e.	b	s.e.
(Intercept)	−2.354	.528	−3.537	.906	−4.284	.722
active in homeland politics	.782	.517	.707	.661	1.091*	.567
maintain homeland contact	.249	.409	−.271	.546	−.725	.483
plan to return to Asia	.413	.516	.463	.610	1.197*	.549
prior partisanship	−.863^	.508	−1.214	.837	−.636	.593
more trust and influence in U.S.	−.325	.271	.614^	.364	.337	.326
education	.753^	.417	.758	.600	1.580**	.531
age	.017	.647	−2.820*	1.042	.357	.802
length in Community	−1.581	1.758	−4.419*	2.274	−3.309^	2.000
length in the U.S.	1.594	1.235	5.182**	1.588	2.877*	1.406
citizenship status	1.124**	.371	.120	.506	1.278*	.491
English language use	.500	.608	−.607	.863	1.084	.751
experience with discrimination	.642*	.313	.225	.440	.467	.391
Filipino	.164	.572	2.810**	.848	−.003	.811
Japanese	.894*	.359	2.814**	.724	1.138*	.455
Korean	1.400**	.321	2.626**	.687	1.605**	.420
South Asian	1.755**	.432	3.981**	.748	1.732**	.539
Vietnamese	−.568	.477	2.379**	.737	.715	.505

N=639
−2 Log Likelihood (Intercept only) = 1674.12
Model Chi-Sq=221.13
Nagelkerke R-sq=.315; McFadden=.132

Source and Note: See Table 4.4.

identification. Concerns about U.S. foreign policy dealing with the containment of Communism in Asia may help explain this phenomenon. Also, nine out of ten times, having prior partisanship in the homeland may impede the acquisition of Democratic partisanship in the host land. Having more trust in U.S. government officials than those in the homeland and feeling more efficacious about personal influence on decisions made by U.S. than homeland government officials are positively associated with the acquisition of political independence over nonidentification.

With this restricted, immigrant-only model, we are given another chance to understand the effects of sociodemographic and socialization variables. One of the interesting findings is the different impact of length of residence measured at the local and the national level. Namely, other conditions being equal, living in the same city or town for a longer period of time is associated with lower odds of being Independent; but, in nine out of ten instances, it is also negatively associated with Republican identification. In contrast to the effects of living in the same locality for a longer period of time, spending more years in the United States has the opposite effect—of being positively associated with the odds of identification as Independent or Republican. The other important finding is that, among the immigrant sample, better education may be positively but marginally associated with the odds of acquiring Democratic partisanship and substantially associated with the odds of acquiring Republican partisanship over nonidentification. Whereas patterns of language use may not matter, experience with discrimination is positively associated with identification as Democrat and being younger is positively associated with identification as Independent. Being or expecting to become a citizen is linked to a higher likelihood of acquiring both Democratic and Republican partisanship. In addition, compared to being Chinese, immigrants of South Asian, Korean, and Japanese origins are more likely to acquire a major or minor partisanship over nonidentification. Other conditions being equal, both Filipino and Vietnamese immigrants are also more likely than Chinese immigrants to identify as Independent over nonidentification.

Predicting the Strength of Political Partisanship among Asian Americans

To understand which factors may impact the strength of identification with mainstream parties among Asian Americans, a five-point scale of partisan strength is used as the dependent variable. The independent and control variables are the ones used in the preceding section to predict the acquisition of *any* partisanship. The results of three models are reported in Table 4.6. Model (I) tests the impacts of basic sociodemographic and socialization variables among all Asians; Model (II) tests the impact of the additions of political and institutional connectedness, socialization context, and ethnic origin among all respondents; Model (III) tests the impacts of homeland ties, in addition to basic sociodemographic, immigrant adaptation, and ethnicity variables, for Asia-born respondents.

When only sociodemographic and immigrant adaptation variables are in the model, the coefficients in Model (I) show that respondents who have better socioeconomic resources, more social connections, have adapted to the dominant society through citizenship and language use patterns, and have experienced racial or ethnic discrimination are more likely to possess stronger identification with mainstream American political parties. Specifically, those who are better educated, employed, older in age, citizens or expect to be citizens, who use mostly English to communicate within and outside of the home and in consuming media, and who report being a hate crime victim or personally experienced discrimination in the United States based on his or her ethnic background are more likely to be either strong Democrats or Republicans. Other conditions being equal, higher family income may correlate with stronger partisanship, but living longer in the community may be negatively associated with the intensity

Table 4.6 OLS Model Predicting Strength of Mainstream Partisanship

	(I)		(II)		(III)	
	b	s.e.	b	s.e.	b	s.e.
(Constant)	−.002	.259	.137	.330	−.453	.379
education	.084*	.038	−.001	.037	.090*	.047
family income	.062^	.033			.070^	.039
female	−.065	.097			−.146	.122
employed	.226*	.109	.291*	.107	.108	.138
age	.008*	.003	.006^	.003	.009	.005
length in community	−.009^	.005			−.010	.012
proportion of U.S. life	.097	.211	.381^	.219	.523	.442
citizenship status	.261**	.086	.207*	.089	.404**	.105
English language use	.263**	.073			.104	.113
experience with discrimination	.494**	.139	.163	.147	.342*	.173
sense of linked fate			.096*	.045		
political ideology			−.097*	.050		
political interest			.097^	.056		
political knowledge			.567*	.225		
ethnic organization membership			.264^	.140		
religious attendance			.075*	.035		
non-U.S. education			−.118	.131		
Honolulu			−.524**	.151		
Filipino			.780**	.173	.790**	.206
Japanese			.418*	.201	.050	.324
Korean			.544**	.174	.811**	.181
South Asian			.846**	.192	.968**	.222
Vietnamese			−.245	.188	−.066	.250
active in homeland politics					.335	.260
maintain homeland contact					.013	.049
plan to return to Asia					.505^	.264
prior partisanship					−.049	.072
more trust and influence in U.S.					−.147	.150
N	1021		935		639	
F	10.09**		11.10**		6.94**	
Adj-Rsq	.082		.170		.157	

Source and Note: See Table 4.4. The Dependent variable is measured with a 5-point scale of partisanship strength with a value of 4 assigned to strong Democrats or Republicans, a value of 3 to weak Democrats or Republicans, a value of 2 to leaning Democrats or Republicans, a value of 1 to pure Independent, and 0 for all others. Model (I) is a restricted model for all. Model (II) is a full model for all. Model (III) is for immigrants only. In Model (II), insignificant and excluded variables are family income, female, length in community, and English language use.

of identification with mainstream parties. In contrast, gender and the percentage of exposure to U.S. politics as a proportion of one's life are not statistically significant in predicting strength of partisanship.

When variables measuring political ties and involvement in civic institutions, sense of panethnic community, socialization context, and ethnic origins are included, the coefficients reported in Model (II) show that while employment and citizenship status remain significant, the impact of socioeconomic status, language use, and experience of discrimination disappear. Age and percentage of political exposure become marginally significant with the additional variables, however. Importantly, those who are ideologically more liberal, possess a greater level of political knowledge, attend religious services more frequently, and show a greater sense of shared fate with other Asian Americans are more likely to have a strong identification with the two major U.S. parties. On the other hand, once other variables are taken into account, those who live in Honolulu exhibit weaker partisan strength than those in other metropolitan areas. South Asian, Filipino, Korean, and Japanese Americans are more likely to identify strongly with a major U.S. party than Chinese or Vietnamese Americans. Nine times out of ten, having a stronger interest in political matters and being a member of a community organization may also correlate with a gain in the intensity of major party identification.

Among immigrants, the coefficients in Model (III) show that only education, citizenship status, experience with discrimination, and, to a lesser extent, family income are useful predictors of strength of party identification. Being South Asian, Korean, or Japanese also tends to be associated with greater identification with major parties as compared to being Chinese, Filipino, or Vietnamese. None of the indicators related to homeland ties, with the possible exception of the intent to return to Asia, may significantly impact the strength of mainstream partisanship. Moreover, plans to eventually return to Asia are associated with a stronger, rather than a weaker, identification with mainstream parties in more than 90 percent of cases. Although citizenship status is not a prerequisite of partisanship, the multivariate regression results show that the strength of mainstream partisanship is closely and independently related to citizenship status in the American context for Asian Americans. In fact, citizenship emerges as one of the strongest predictors of partisan strength among Asian Americans. The analysis also shows that ethnic origin is often among the most significant influences on the strength (as well as the direction) of partisanship among Asian Americans.

The Potential Consequences of Political Partisanship

Do the direction and the strength of identification with the two major parties affect the political behavior of Asian Americans? And how does the influence of partisanship compare to other agents or forces of political socialization? Party influence is assessed in terms of two behavioral domains: (1) Candidate choice in the 2000 U.S. presidential election and in a hypothetical contest between Asian and non-Asian candidates, and (2) opinion toward affirmative action as a principle and as a policy on giving preferences in hiring and promotion for Asians.[15] The independent influence of partisanship on these outcomes is compared to those of mobilization by parties and individuals through homeland contact and to membership in ethnic community organizations as well as to the level of activism in religious institutions.

Limited past research on Asian Americans suggests that, like other Americans, identification with the two major parties is among the top predictors of candidate choice and issue opinion among voters—even though their party loyalty levels are generally lower than blacks and Latinos and comparable to whites (Cho and Cain, 2001; Lien, 2001b). Past research on these three non-Asian groups suggests that contact or recruitment by a political party, group, or individuals may not only increase participation but also affect *attitudinal* involvement in the political system as well (Rosenstone and Hansen, 1980; Verba, Schlozman, and Brady, 1995; Leighley, 2001). Although we do not know of any survey-based research prior to this study that compares the efficacy of these forces of political learning among Asians, we suspect that because they are explicitly political in nature, party identification and politically relevant contacting by political parties, groups, or individuals may play a larger role in shaping the political opinion of Asian Americans than their involvement with civic institutions such as community-based and faith-based organizations. Furthermore, by becoming more integrated into the political system, as indicated by stronger identification with a major party and by being contacted by parties or individuals, Asian Americans may develop an opinion position that counters the assumed interests of a nonwhite, majority-immigrant community.

Distribution of Candidate Choice and Issue Position

Table 4.7 reports the percentage distribution of candidate choice by partisanship. Among 2000 presidential election voters, Democrats tended to support Gore and Republicans were more likely to support Bush. However, Gore received a higher degree of support from fellow partisans than Bush. Independent voters registered the highest percentage of support for third party candidates (6 percent), but a much higher percentage of them (25 percent) refused to indicate their vote choice. Perhaps more importantly, an overwhelming proportion of Asian American Independents (40 percent) and nonidentifiers (50 percent) threw their support behind Gore in 2000.

Due to the small sample sizes, one must use caution before drawing any conclusions based on the individual ethnic group samples. However, among the different Asian ethnic groups, it seems clear that the majority of those identifying with a major party voted for their party's candidate. For example, 95 percent of Korean American Democrats voted for Gore and 94 percent of Korean American

Republicans voted for Bush. South Asian Democrats reported the lowest percentage of support for Gore (72 percent) and South Asian Republicans reported the highest percentage of support for Bush (80 percent). Although six in ten Chinese nonidentifiers voted for Gore, the votes of nonpartisans appear up for grabs among Japanese and Filipino voters.

Table 4.7 also contains hints in terms of the comparative role of race/ethnicity and partisanship in structuring the vote. We ask respondents' preference for an Asian American than a non-Asian candidate in a hypothetical situation. About 64 percent Democrats, 60 percent nonidentifiers, and 58 percent Republicans indicated preference for an Asian American; the percentage is slightly lower among Independents (53 percent). When these respondents who indicated support for a coethnic candidate initially were confronted with a follow-up question about candidate quality, less than a quarter of partisans would vote for a fellow Asian if he or she were considered less qualified. Supporters of the two major parties did not differ much in their percentage of support, but nonidentifiers scored the highest percentage of unconditional support for the ethnic candidate. This finding suggests that there may be an inverse relationship between partisanship and ethnicity in ethnic voting among Asian Americans.[16]

The possible influence of partisanship on policy opinion is examined using several policy questions focusing on the general attitude toward affirmative action and support for *specific* affirmative action policies. Respondents were also asked of their opinions about government-sponsored bilingual services, limiting legal immigration and permitting noncitizen legal permanent residents to make donations to political campaigns (table not shown). At the aggregate level, partisanship does not make much difference in terms of policy support. The only exception is on opinions toward providing special preferences in hiring and promotion for Asian Americans. A higher percentage of Republican than Democratic identifiers express strong opinions toward that policy measure.

The relative influence of party contact and individual contact on the political orientations of Asian Americans is investigated with two questions. The question on party contact asks the PNAAPS respondents if they had received any letter, e-mail, or telephone call from a political party or candidate organization or other political group about a political campaign. Forty-one percent of respondents claim that they had been contacted during the past four years.[17] Sixty-one percent of respondents who answer yes to this question report that the Democrats had contacted them, 43 percent indicate that the Republicans had contacted them, and 21 percent are not sure which party had contacted them. The question on individual mobilization asks, "In the past four years, did someone you know try to request you to vote, or to contribute money to a political cause, or to engage in some other type of political activity?" About 20 percent of respondents report that they had been contacted by an individual, such as a boss, church leader, program director, or friend. On community organization membership, respondent were asked if they belong to any organization or take part

Table 4.7 Percentage Distribution of Candidate Choice by Partisanship

	DEMOCRAT	INDEPENDENT	REPUBLICAN	NO PARTY/NS
2000 Presidential Vote				
Gore	84%	40%	12%	50%
Bush	6	22	66	27
Nader/other	1	6	2	1
refused	8	25	16	16
Column N	221	65	107	144
Chinese				
Gore	88	50	18	59
Bush	6	50	65	20
Column N	48	2	17	59
Korean				
Gore	74	40	5	40
Bush	4	–	75	40
Column N	27	5	20	5
Vietnamese (p=.07)				
Gore	100	14	33	40
Bush	0	71	56	40
Column N	8	7	9	30
Japanese				
Gore	88	48	15	28
Bush	2	15	50	28
Column N	52	27	20	25

(*cont.*)

Table 4.7 (*Continued*)

	DEMOCRAT	INDEPENDENT	REPUBLICAN	NO PARTY/NS
Filipino				
Gore	86	40	10	46
Bush	9	13	71	36
Column N	57	15	31	22
South Asian				
Gore	72	33	0	–
Bush	14	33	80	–
Column N	29	7	10	3
Ethnic Vote (prefer an Asian American Candidate)				
Yes	64	53	58	60
....Even if less qualified				
yes	22	18	24	28
no	71	80	67	61
No	20	29	27	18
Not Sure	16	18	14	22
Column N	434	157	193	431

Source and Note: See Table 4.2. Percentage points in each column may not add up to 100 due to rounding error or omitted categories. All the chi-square tests of difference are significant at %=.05 or better except where noted.

133

in any activities that represent the interests and viewpoints of their coethnics or other Asians in America. Fifteen percent of respondents answer affirmatively. On faith-based participation, respondents were asked of their frequency of participation in religious services. More than one-third of the respondents (37 percent) report attending religious services weekly or nearly weekly. Another one-third (35 percent) report attending either once or twice a month or a few times a year. Close to a quarter of the respondents do not report any attendance at all.

A series of crosstabulation analyses permit identification of any significant relationship between the four measures of political and social connectedness and Asian Americans' candidate choice and issue position (table not shown). Among voters, those contacted by acquaintances had a lower percentage of support for Gore (49 percent) than those who were not (58 percent). Among all respondents, those contacted by parties are less willing to support an ethnic candidate (56 percent) than those who received no contact (63 percent). Among those who indicate support for a fellow Asian American candidate, unconditional support regardless of qualification is higher among those who did not receive party contact. Also, support for the general concept of affirmative action—policies that grant qualified individuals equal access to employment, education, business, and contracting opportunities—is lower among those contacted by parties but higher among those who more frequently attend religious services. A similar pattern applies to a proposed mandate for government to offer bilingual services to immigrant communities—support is lower among persons contacted by parties or groups but higher among those who frequented religious services. These aggregate level results suggest that major political parties as agents of socialization may play a more important but contrary and conservative role in structuring the direction of Asian American voting participation than individuals or civic institutions. Confirmation of this observation is provided by the multivariate results in which we control for possible confounding influences.

Estimating the Behavioral Impacts of Political Parties: Multivariate Results

How much does political party matter in structuring the political behavior of Asian Americans? The unique contributions of the strength of identification with the Democratic and the Republican Party respectively and of party contact and individual contact are assessed relative to other factors discussed in the previous models. Specifically, the effects of identification with major political parties and party contact are compared to those of political and institutional ties and of minority identity and experience in predicting candidate votes and policy preferences. Selected results are presented in Table 4.8.

In terms of candidate choice, strength of identification with a major U.S. party is the strongest predictor of voting for a major party presidential candidate, even though being Democrat and Republican exerts opposite effects. Contacting by parties does not but contacting by individuals does have a negative and significant relationship to the Gore vote. Controlling for other factors, those in Hawaii are less likely to vote for Gore than those in other metropolitan areas. Compared to Chinese respondents, those of Korean and South Asian descent are less likely to vote for Gore once other factors are taken into account. Net of all other factors, strong Republican identification is associated with lower support for Gore, while the exact opposite is true for Democratic identification.

Do the effects of partisanship extend beyond mainstream candidate choice among Asian Americans? Our findings show that preference of voting for an Asian American candidate regardless of qualification for the office is marginally increased with stronger Democratic identification. Being contacted by a political party, however, tends to have a negative relationship with voting for an Asian American candidate. In addition, as one might expect, having a strong sense of panethnic linked fate is positively associated with the likelihood of voting unconditionally for a political candidate of Asian descent. Other conditions being equal, residing in Honolulu is associated with a greater likelihood of voting for a fellow Asian American candidate. Similarly, compared to other ethnic groups, those who are Chinese are more likely to vote for an Asian candidate.

Regarding predictors of policy opinion among Asian Americans, we find no relationship between partisanship and support for affirmative action as a principle. Other conditions being equal, being contacted by a political party or group is associated with lower support. More frequent attendance of religious services, having a stronger sense of linked fate, or having less education is positively but marginally related to support for affirmative action as a principle. Party contact does not appear to be associated with support for bilingual services either. Possessing a stronger Republican identification may be associated with weaker support for bilingual services, but holding a more liberal ideology may be associated with stronger support for offering such services. Also, those who are educated mostly in the United States are less likely to support bilingual services. Compared to Chinese (the excluded category), Filipinos give stronger support to bilingual services; Japanese express lower support for both affirmative action as a principle and bilingual services; Koreans give more support for bilingual services; while Vietnamese have stronger support for both policy areas.

Clearly, these results show that the significance and degree of party influence depend on the type of political behavior and policy domains examined as well as on the measures of party influence. That is, partisanship, as a political attitude, is quite distinct from being contacted by a political party, even though the two are also intricately related to each other because of strategic mobilization practiced by parties. Generally, compared to other agents of socialization, identification with major parties is most influential in structuring Asian Americans' voting for a major party (and non-Asian) candidate. Greater identification with the Democratic Party is associated with a greater likelihood to support an Asian

Table 4.8 Logistic Regression Estimations of Candidate Choice and Policy Opinion

	GORE VOTE		ETHNIC VOTE		AFFIRMATIVE ACTION		BILINGUAL SERVICE	
	b1	s.e.	b2	s.e.	b1	s.e.	b2	s.e.
Republican partisanship	−2.415**	.644	.019	.052	.029	.303	−.181*	.075
Democratic partisanship	3.448**	.464	.062^	.038	.241	.218	.015	.056
contacted by party	.252	.327	−.202*	.092	−.369*	.173	.072	.134
contacted by individuals	−.845*	.352	−.105	.107	.242	.203	.089	.156
ethnic organization membership	.117	.384	.157	.115	.111	.216	−.100	.168
religious attendance	−.606	.410	.031	.028	.385^	.217	.058	.041
ideology (hi=conservative)	−.909	.612	.050	.042	−.394	.320	−.135*	.061
political interest	.553	.479	.001	.046	.229	.261	−.020	.067
political knowledge	−.722	.660	.099	.186	.561	.366	−.259	.271
panethnic linked fate	.402	.398	.082*	.037	.360^	.213	.025	.054
experience discrimination	−.153	.431	−.024	.120	.354	.229	.369*	.175
education	.680	.581	−.043	.030	−.521^	.314	−.003	.044
employed	−.132	.335	−.011	.087	.433*	.163	−.021	.127
age	−1.574^	.885	.000	.003	.918*	.393	−.001	.004
proportion of U.S. life	−.583	.713	−.160	.167	−.819*	.312	−.602*	.245
non-U.S. education	.170	.407	.337**	.106	−.181	.206	−.002	.155
Honolulu	−.857*	.413	−.319*	.123	.202	.234	.158	.180

(cont.)

Table 4.8 (*Continued*)

	GORE VOTE		ETHNIC VOTE		AFFIRMATIVE ACTION		BILINGUAL SERVICE	
	b1	s.e.	b2	s.e.	b1	s.e.	b2	s.e.
Filipino	-.694	.526	-.673**	.142	-.298	.266	.346^	.207
Japanese	-.398	.615	-.576**	.161	-.587*	.294	-.497*	.235
Korean	-1.487*	.597	-.418**	.141	.018	.275	.540*	.205
South Asian	-2.261**	.660	-.982**	.156	-.622*	.287	-.338	.227
Vietnamese	-.721	.533	-.336*	.153	1.443**	.387	.845**	.223
(Constant)	1.546	.885	1.946	.265	.437	.402	6.198	.387
N =	411		934		935		934	
−2 Log Likelihood=	344.31				1088.70			
Model Chi-Sq=	220.07				111.49			
Nagelkerke R-sq=	.555		.155		.155		.101	

Source and Note: See Table 4.4. The Affirmative Action model here estimates Asian Americans' attitude toward the general concept of affirmation action for the ethnic community. b1=unstandardized logistic coefficients or log odds, b2=unstandardized slope coefficients, s.e.= standard errors.

137

American candidate. Stronger identification with the Republican Party is associated with a weaker likelihood to support government-sponsored bilingual services. Being contacted by a political party or group is negatively associated with the likelihood of support for an ethnic candidate or affirmative action as a principle. Voters who are contacted by individuals are less likely to vote for Gore, other conditions being equal. Whereas membership in a community organization does not have any significant impact, having close contact with religious institutions is associated with a higher likelihood of supporting affirmative action. These results, while preliminary, offer rare insight into the importance of political partisanship and party contact, relative to other agents of socialization, in the political learning process for a nonwhite and majority immigrant community. They also pose a potential challenge to the formation and maintenance of the (pan)ethnic community as more members are becoming politically integrated into the American system through acquiring political partisanship and being targeted by political parties.

Conclusion

As one of the first comprehensive analyses of Asian Americans and the American party system, this study attempts to cover a lot of ground. The research reported in this chapter explores several important facets of the relationship between Asian American politics and the American party system, including the acquisition, direction, strength, and potential consequences of party identification among Asian Americans. Two findings on the contours of partisanship stand out. First, a large proportion of Asian Americans (more than one out of every three in the PNAAPS sample) do not identify with traditional party categories, either because they do not think in terms of conventional American parties or because they are unsure about their partisan identity. Second, an examination of the distribution of partisanship among different Asian American groups finds that, with the exception of the Vietnamese population, a decidedly Democratic partisan leaning characterizes the Asian Americans included in this study. The combination of these two characteristics clearly puts Asian Americans in the category of an emergent electorate.

We next turn to the acquisition of partisanship among Asian Americans. Research on Asian Americans, a population dominated by immigrants of different ethnic origins, represents an important opportunity to study the acquisition of partisanship in the United States. In particular, by studying Asian Americans, we are able to better understand the unique effects of ethnicity and political learning processes on the development of partisanship. We find that in order to understand the development of party identification among Asian Americans, ethnicity must be seriously taken into account. Different ethnic groups acquire partisanship at different rates. In particular, even when other factors are controlled, lack of party identification among Asian Americans appears to be driven by the Chinese and Vietnamese in our study. Key socialization variables outside of ethnicity and region that help explain the acquisition of partisanship among Asian Americans include employment, age, ideology, political knowledge, and the percent of one's life spent in the United States. The majority of these factors appear to be related to exposure to the American political system. As people become more familiar with American parties through exposure to the political system, they are also more likely to develop an American party identification.

In terms of partisan direction, identification with either of the two major parties can be commonly impacted by political ideology, political knowledge, employment status, age, proportion of life spent in the United States, region, and being Japanese, Korean, or South Asian American. However, significant differences exist, such as in the roles played by political interest, organizational membership, religious attendance, sense of linked fate, non-U.S. education, and being Filipino or Vietnamese American. Some of our research results provide strong support for traditional theories of partisanship. For example, religiosity is a strong predictor of Republican partisanship, while those who exhibit a strong sense of common fate with other Asian Americans are more likely to identify as Democrat. On the other hand, a focus on Asian Americans highlights the fact that traditional theories are not sufficient to explain partisanship among all ethnic and racial groups in the United States. We find, for instance, that greater levels of education are related to identification as an Independent; but greater family income, English-language use, and being native-born (as reflected in the proportion of life spent in the United States) also increase Independent identification when political and institutional connectedness and ethnicity are not controlled. The analysis comparing the restricted and the full model shows that the effects of language use, experience with discrimination, citizenship, and family income on major partisanship appear to have been channeled through indicators of political and civic institutional ties.

Do immigrants develop political orientations in ways that are similar to or different from the majority of Americans? Echoing the majority of discussions in the extant literature, among the Asian American immigrants in this study, those who are actively involved in politics regarding the country of origin or who have plans to return to their country of origin are more likely to acquire (Republican) partisanship. In nine out of ten times, prior partisanship in the home county interferes with the acquisition of Democratic partisanship; perceiving more government responsiveness and a greater ability to influence government in the United States than in the homeland encourages identification as Independent. However, maintaining contacts with the country of origin does not have an effect on the acquisition of partisanship generally.

The next step in the analysis examines variations in *strength* of identification with either of the two major parties among Asian Americans. A series of multivariate analyses reveals that citizens are more likely to be strong partisans. Furthermore, attitudinal and active ties to American politics and institutions affect major partisan strength. Those who are more interested in and knowledgeable about politics are more likely to identify strongly with a major U.S. party, as are those who attend religious services regularly. Though it is clear from the discussion above that civic and institutional ties are likely to affect strength of partisanship, this research also highlights the extent to which race continues to be a critical factor in the development of political attitudes. Among Asian Americans in this study, those who score higher on measures of minority status are likely to exhibit stronger party identification. Racial minority group identity may have a politicizing effect on Asian Americans. In addition, differences exist among Asian American ethnic groups in terms of strength of partisanship. Finally, those who have a strong connection to their country of origin through activity in homeland politics or the maintenance of contact with friends and family members in the country of origin are no less likely to develop strong party attachments than those who exhibit a weak link to the country of origin.

The final stage of the analysis investigates the potential effects or consequences of involvement with the U.S. party system on Asian Americans' political behavior and policy attitudes. Similar to the general population, partisanship is a strong predictor of presidential vote choice. Although Republican identifiers are less likely than nonidentifiers to support bilingual education programs, partisanship has virtually no relationship to attitudes toward affirmative action. Neither does party contact have any relationship to the presidential vote or a policy on bilingual services, but it may negatively impact support for ethnic candidates and for affirmative action in general. Furthermore, major political parties as agents of socialization play a more important but contrary and conservative role in structuring the direction of Asian American voting participation than individuals or civic institutions. This finding of the party influence as posing challenges to the panethnic minority community, while not completely surprising, is worth heeding by both party activists and scholars of minority political incorporation.

In conclusion, despite the fact that American parties have excluded Asian Americans historically and often maintained a distance from that population group in the contemporary period, elements of the party system occupy a central place in the lives of many Asian Americans. Although the acquisition of Democratic party identity and the strength of major partisanship may be positively related to the sense of linked group fate, those Asians who are becoming more involved with the major parties may also develop voting preference and policy positions antithetical to the maintenance of the nonwhite immigrant community. These results provide nuanced affirmation and important challenges to previous conceptions of the contours, formation, and impact of political partisanship. These findings may be qualified as preliminary, for we do not have the privilege of examining the full range of policy positions. However, this study reveals the ways in which the rapid rise of the Asian American population may affect the shape of the party system and trends in American partisanship in particular.

CHAPTER 5

Political Participation in Electoral and Nonelectoral Settings

As emphasized throughout this book, consideration of the political attitudes and behavior of ordinary Asian Americans is critical for understanding how the country's increasingly multiethnic population is incorporated into the U.S. political system. This chapter assesses the extent to which Asian Americans participate in American politics and important factors associated with their participation. The forms of political participation focused on in this chapter include registration, voting, and participation in political activities beyond voting, such as signing a petition, making a political donation, working with others on a community problem, and protesting. Attention to participation in electoral and nonelectoral activities allows one to contend with critical issues related to how Asian Americans contribute to the country's increasingly diverse political landscape.

In order to better understand the political involvement of Asian Americans in the United States, key themes in studies of political participation that focus on resources, engagement, and recruitment are examined (Verba, Schlozman, and Brady, 1995). However, because the contemporary Asian American population is dominated by nonwhite immigrants of multiple ethnic origins, explanations of political participation that relate specifically to racial group concerns, ethnicity, and factors related to international migration are also considered. As noted at the inception of this book, the formation of political attitudes and opinion among Asian Americans is conceptualized as a function of not only their personal socioeconomic status and demographic background, but also of their engagement with political, cultural, social, and other civic institutions in the United States. In addition, drawing on theories of panethnicity and transnationalism discussed earlier, the effects of minority-group consciousness and socialization contexts across national boundaries are considered. It is with this larger theoretical framework in mind that statistical analyses, literature, and results are considered.

Theories of Political Participation and the Asian American Population: Resources, Engagement, and Institutional Connections

Basic Socioeconomic Status

Studies of political participation emphasize the importance of basic socioeconomic status (i.e., income, education, and demographic characteristics related to resource accumulation) in determining whether or not individuals will participate in politics (Verba and Nie, 1972; Wolfinger and Rosenstone, 1980; Rosenstone and Hansen, 1993; Conway, 2000). More recent studies have attempted to refine the basic socioeconomic status model by focusing on specific resources, such as money and civic skills (Verba, Schlozman, and Brady, 1995; Leighley, 2001). Having more money, for example, leads to more input into the political system through campaign donations and giving to other political causes. Another important resource for understanding participation is formal education (Wolfinger and Rosenstone, 1980). Education is thought to facilitate participation because it fosters civic skills by helping people learn to organize or communicate in ways that make it easier to take part in politics (Verba, Schlozman, and Brady, 1995). Education may also lead to a greater understanding of political issues by helping people engage in complex political processes as well as by encouraging them to accept system-related democratic norms and practices (Junn, 1999).

Because the average median household incomes of Asian Americans are consistently higher than that of most Americans in recent decades (U.S. Census Bureau, 1999),[1] basic socioeconomic status theory predicts high overall rates of participation in voting and other political activities among Asian Americans. However, studies using the U.S. Census Bureau and other survey data find that voting-age Asian Americans register and vote at rates lower than their counterparts in all other major racial and ethnic groups (Uhlaner, Cain, and Kiewiet, 1989; Nakanishi, 1991; Lien 1994, 1997, 2001b; Cho, 1999; Junn, 1999; Uhlaner, 2000). This seeming paradox—high average socioeconomic status and low average rates of political participation—among Asian Americans leads researchers to suspect that education and family income may have less or a different impact on the participation of Asian Americans than on blacks, Latinos, and Anglos. They do not rule out the utility of socioeconomic indicators to understand the political behavior of Asian Americans, only that they may not be as important as some other factors examined in this chapter. In fact, Lien's (1998, 2000, 2001a, 2001b, 2003) research using census data that includes socioeconomic and demographic variables alone finds that education and family income have positive and strong effects on the voting registration and turnout of eligible U.S. adult Asians. How basic socioeconomic status compares to other variables, such as political interest and partisanship, in terms of political participation among Asian Americans is an important question for this study.

Although they are closely related, education and income are distinct from one another and their effects may vary across different *types* of participation among the general population. Participation studies conducted in the 1980s using the census data suggested that education was the primary component of socioeconomic status in terms of voting turnout (Wolfinger and Rosenstone, 1980). However, Verba, Schlozman and Brady (1995: 360) report that educational attainment is not a direct predictor of voting, rather it has an indirect effect on voting through political engagement. On the other hand, they show that family income has a direct, positive, and statistically significant effect on voting. In their study, both education and income are positively related to participation in activities beyond voting. In her analysis of participation among various Asian American ethnic groups using census data, Lien (2001b) finds that, other conditions being equal, it is educational attainment, but not having a higher income, that may increase the probability that registered Asian Americans voted between the November elections of 1994 and 1998. The distinct roles of income and education for Asian American participation are reported in the analyses below at both the aggregate and individual levels.

Political Engagement

Verba, Schlozman, and Brady contend that political participation depends upon resources *and* political engagement. Political engagement, or a psychological orientation toward politics, is measured conventionally by political interest, information, efficacy, and partisan intensity. These components of political engagement provide people with the "desire, knowledge, and self-assurance" to become politically active (1995: 354; for related arguments, see also Verba and Nie, 1972). They find that individual measures of political interest, knowledge, and efficacy predict both voting and participation in activities beyond voting that require time, such as working on a political campaign, contacting a public official, or working on a community problem (Verba, Schlozman, and Brady, 1995: 358; see also Campbell et al., 1960).[2]

Ideology is also included in the analysis below. Both partisan strength and ideology represent attitudinal engagement with the mainstream political system (recognition of the two major parties and identification along the traditional liberal-conservative spectrum). Research on Asian American political participation finds a positive relationship between the strength of partisanship and voting among citizens but not in activities beyond voting among all adults (Lien, 1994). One expects to see a similar pattern of relationship among the PNAAPS respondents.

Political Mobilization

Political scientists have long argued that parties and other organizations are important institutional sources of recruitment into politics. Being contacted by a political party or group is likely to increase voting and other types of participation for the American electorate in general (Dahl, 1961; Rosenstone and Hansen, 1993; Verba, Schlozman, and Brady, 1995; Conway, 2001b). In general though, research on racial minorities has emphasized low levels of party mobilization directed at minority groups, including blacks, Latinos, and Asian Americans (Hardy-Fanta, 1993; de la Garza, Menchaca, and DeSipio, 1994; Frymer, 1999; Wong, 2001). For example, data from the Citizen Participation Study, conducted in 1989 and 1990, show that while almost half of all non-Latino whites were asked to work on a campaign or make a campaign donation, only 27 percent of blacks and 14 percent of Latinos had similar mobilization experiences (Leighley, 2001). Despite the fact that they are not often targets of party mobilization, research shows that the effects of party mobilization on racial minorities' political participation can be quite dramatic. Leighley's (2001) analysis suggests that being mobilized is a significant and positive predictor of overall participation levels among both blacks and Latinos, even when socioeconomic resources, partisanship, and other potential influences on participation are taken into account.

Mobilization within Asian American communities has received little attention from scholars. Most studies devote their attention to the role of Asian American elected officials in generating interest and activity in elections (e.g., Nakanishi, 1996; Lai, 2000; Geron and Lai, 2001). One might expect that, consistent with studies of the general population and other racial minorities' political behavior, mobilization either by individual elites or groups will have a positive influence on the participation of Asian Americans.[3] In addition, because studies show that Asian Americans in Hawaii may register and vote at higher rates in the aggregate than Asians elsewhere because of the greater political empowerment and mobilization infrastructure in that state (Lien, 2001b), regional context is included as a control variable.

Affiliation with Civic Organizations

Involvement in institutions that are not explicitly political, such as churches and voluntary organizations, is thought to increase political activity among the general population (Verba, Schlozman, and Brady, 1995). Among the general population, church attendance is a leading indicator of voting participation across ethnic and racial groups (Ibid.; Houghland and Christenson, 1983; Alex-Assensoh, 2001; Jones-Correa and Leal, 2001). However, the effect of church attendance varies according to type of political activity. Studies find that church attendance does not appear to have a strong effect on political activities beyond voting, such as working on a campaign or contacting a public official (Houghland and Christenson, 1983; Verba, Schlozman, and Brady, 1995; Jones-Correa and Leal, 2001). Though scholars are devoting increasing attention to the role of religion and religious institutions in the lives of Asian Americans (e.g., Yoo, 1999; Min and Kim, 2002; Carnes and Yang, 2003; Iwamura and Spikard 2003), research that examines the link between religious activity and political participation among Asian Americans is scarce (but see Lien, 2003). Based on studies of other minority communities and research showing that religious institutions occupy a central place in many immigrants' lives, one would expect to find a strong relationship between church attendance and political involvement among Asian Americans.[4]

There is some evidence that involvement in civic associations outside of the church among Asian Americans is relatively low compared to other groups (Lien,

2001b; Stoll, 2001). Yet there is reason to believe that those Asian Americans who do participate in such organizations will be active in politics at higher rates than those who are not involved in voluntary associations. Scholars from de Tocqueville (1969) to Putnam (2000) suggest that civic associations support political life. Connections with community organizations may lead to increased political involvement because organizational involvement fosters civic skills (Verba, Schlozman, and Brady, 1995) and organizations constitute important spaces for the exchange of political cues and information (Rosenstone and Hansen, 1993). Similar to the church, nonreligious civic associations may be places where mobilization by community activists and leaders occurs (Schlozman, Verba, and Brady, 1999).

Membership in an organization or participation in activities that represent the interests and viewpoints of the respondent's ethnic group or other Asians in America may increase participation among the respondents in the study. Consistent with these studies, Wong (2001) argues that community-based and ethnic voluntary associations are likely to be among the primary sites where Asian American immigrants, in particular, learn about the political system and are exposed to opportunities for participation. Because activity in an Asian American or ethnic organization may provide opportunities for participation in American politics that are not available elsewhere (Wong, 2001), we suspect community-based organization membership will increase participation among Asian Americans.

Factors Related to International Migration, Racial Group Concerns, and Ethnicity

International Migration-Related Factors

Overall, one might expect that, because Asian Americans are a minority population dominated by nonwhite immigrants, their political behavior is likely to depend upon factors that have to do directly with international migration, race, and ethnicity. According to the March 2000 Current Population Survey, 64 percent of Asian Americans were immigrants in 2000 (Barnes and Bennett, 2002). Thus, it is important to take transnational processes into account when attempting to explain participation in politics among Asian Americans.

First, studies show that nativity is a strong determinant of political involvement among Asian Americans and Latinos. Although, at the aggregate level, Asian American immigrants are less likely to participate in American politics than the native-born generally (Ong and Nakanishi, 1996), participation rates among immigrants depend on the length of residence in the United States, language skills, and whether or not one is naturalized and registered (Cain, Kiewiet, and Uhlaner, 1991; Cho, 1999; Uhlaner and Garcia, 1999; Wong, 2000; Lien, 2001b). As Asian American immigrants spend more time in the United States, they are more likely to naturalize, register, and become voters (Ong and Nakanishi, 1996; Lien, 2000; Nakanishi, 2001). They are also more likely to develop partisan attitudes related to the American political system (Cain, Kiewiet, and Uhlaner, 1991; Wong, 2000; also see Chapter 4 in this book).[5]

In addition, at the aggregate level, researchers find a positive relationship between being a United States citizen and participation in American politics (Uhlaner, 1996; Montoya, 2002). Although noncitizens do take part in political activities in the United States (Uhlaner, Cain, and Kiewiet, 1989; Lien et al., 2001b; Wong, 2001), not having U.S. citizenship is a critical roadblock on the path to political participation for Asian Americans as a group (Lien et al., 2001). Lien (2001b) observes that in the 1990s, approximately half of the Asian American adult population was legally barred from voting due to lack of citizenship. In the face of stereotypes like the "model minority" that construct Asian Americans as politically apathetic, it is important to consider the role of eligibility requirements such as citizenship in shaping participation patterns. However, it is also important to note that while noncitizenship represents a major challenge to the political participation of Asian Americans, research shows that citizenship is not significant in predicting participation in activities other than voting, once other factors are taken into account (Lien, 1997).

DeSipio and Jerit (1998) assert that "while eligible immigrants and the recently naturalized often offer civic reasons to support their decisions to naturalize," the reasons for naturalization are also likely to be practical in nature (see also Pantoja, Ramirez, and Segura, 2001). For many Asian Americans, naturalization may represent a legal means to sponsor relatives from their countries of origin who wish to immigrate. Asian Americans might also naturalize in order to protect themselves from harsh laws aimed at those without legal documents. In contrast to these more practical considerations, some scholars contend that naturalization represents a sense of commitment to becoming full-fledged members of the United States. Based on this assumption, one might hypothesize that naturalization would be positively associated with more participation in primarily electoral political activities among immigrants (DeSipio, 1996: 196; Jones-Correa, 1998). Of course, caution must be used in drawing any conclusions about the causal relationship between citizenship and participation beyond voting that does not require citizenship That is, citizenship may engender more participation and political engagement or, conversely, political activity and engagement may lead to a greater likelihood of attaining citizenship.[6]

Having strong English-language skills and being educated in the United States are also hypothesized to affect political participation in the United States (Cho, 1999; Wong, 2001). Cho (1999) provides a thoughtful discussion of how political socialization is likely to be linked to English-language skills and the country where most education takes place among immigrants. English proficiency is likely to have a profound effect on immigrants' abilities to receive English-language political messages and information in the United States. In addition, those who are educated outside of the United States may be less likely to participate in activities that require socialization toward formal political institutions in the United States.

Several hypotheses are associated with another important aspect of international migration, the maintenance of transnational ties. On the one hand, one might expect that immigrants who are heavily involved in home country politics might be too preoccupied with politics outside of the United States to pay attention to American domestic politics (Harles, 1993; Portes and Rumbaut, 1996). On the other hand, those who are politically active in one context may continue to be politicized in other contexts as well (Wong, 2001). However, political activists are likely to be a minority in the immigrant community (as they are in any community). For the majority of immigrants, it may be that those who were inactive in the past become more active after migration through exposure to the more open United States political system. Some individuals might also become involved in the United States political system in order to bring about change in their ancestral countries of origin (Basch, Glick Schiller, and Blanc, 1994; Karpathakis, 1999; Smith, 2000; Lien, 2001b). We expect that connections to the homeland (especially those that are political in nature) and prior political party membership may exhibit a positive association with political participation within the U.S. context among Asian Americans.

Racial Group Concerns and Racial/Ethnic Identity

Lee (2000) reports that "contrary to popular beliefs of an overachieving, thriving Asian Pacific American 'model minority,' the levels of perceived discrimination reported by APAs is quite extensive" (115). Similar to other racial minority groups in the United States, Asian Americans indicate fairly high levels of perceived discrimination. Recent national survey data reveal that in 2001, 39 percent of Asian Americans compared to 40 percent of Latinos, 46 percent of African Americans, 39 percent of multiracial respondents, and 18 percent of whites report that they have experienced discrimination because of their racial or ethnic background.[7]

There are two competing hypotheses about how experience with racial discrimination will affect political participation. Experience with discrimination may lead individuals to become active in politics in order to challenge racial inequality (Uhlaner, 1991: 141). For example, Uhlaner (1991) finds that among racial minorities in California, even when other key variables are controlled, experience with discrimination leads to more participation in different types of political activities. Lien's (1997) research on Asian Americans in Southern California shows that, all else being equal, having experienced personal discrimination may increase participation in other activities beyond voting. However, victims of racial discrimination might also turn away from the political system, especially formal political participation, because they feel alienated from the political process (for related arguments, see Salamon and Van Evera, 1973; Henig and Gale, 1987). This study tests these competing predictions about the association between racial discrimination and political involvement.

Research on other communities suggests that those who have a strong pan–Asian American identity (i.e., "Asian American" as opposed to "American") might be more involved with politics because they are motivated by race-related concerns to participate in political activities that will benefit their community in the United States. Studies of African Americans, for example, have found that feelings of common fate contribute to the formation of group consciousness (Gurin, Hatchett, and Jackson, 1989). Lien's (1997) research on Asian Americans in Southern California finds that being concerned about group status may independently increase voting but not other types of participation, once other variables are controlled. This study will examine whether perceptions of linked fate among Asian Americans are related to participation in politics. We hypothesize that those who are more group-oriented in their outlook may be active in politics in order to advance group interests.

Activity and support for Asian American political causes and candidates also have to do with minority status and identity. In particular, membership in Asian American organizations or participation in activities that represent the interests and viewpoints of the respondent's ethnic group or other Asians in America is related to minority group consciousness and identity. Involvement in Asian American or ethnic organizations may be an expression of identity or a way of pursuing group-related interests (Wong, 2001).

Finally, the category of "Asian American" is made up of people of diverse origins. Indeed, one of the central challenges for Asian Americans in the United States has been the forging of a cohesive political community among people who are divided along ethnic lines that coincide and intersect with class, language, religious, generational, and regional divisions. Whether participation in politics varies by ethnic group, together with or independent of other factors, is investigated below.

Types of Political Participation

The types of political participation that are the focus in this chapter include registration, voting, and participation in political activities beyond voting. For voting behavior two measures are utilized, including a dummy variable (0-1) for vote turnout in 2000 among registered citizens and a dummy variable (0-1) for consistent vote turnout in both 1998 and 2000 among registered citizens. Participation beyond voting is captured by a scaled measure based on responses to a question asking about whether respondents had participated in a range of political activities in their communities during the past four years, including writing or phoning a government official, donating money to a campaign, signing a petition for a political cause, taking part in a protest or demonstration, and other types of activities. A complete list of question wording and variable coding is contained in the appendix of this book.

Factors Associated with Political Participation among Asian Americans

The discussion above points to socioeconomic status, political engagement, civic involvement, mobilization, racial group concerns, language use, migration-related issues, and ethnicity as variables potentially associated with Asian Americans' political participation. Also, level of education and family income are potential influences on Asian Americans' political participation.[8] Respondents were also asked whether most of their education took place in the United States or outside of the United States. This question allows one to distinguish between educational level and educational context. Variables related to political engagement include citizenship status (also a migration-related issue), measures of political interest, political knowledge, perceived political influence, strength of partisanship and ideology.

The PNAAPS allows us to investigate the importance of mobilization of Asian Americans by political parties, as opposed to by individuals, because it includes a question about whether respondents had received any letter, e-mail, or telephone call from a political party or candidate organization or other political group about a political campaign.[9] In addition, a measure of church attendance is included.

Variables related to racial minority status and minority group consciousness include perceptions of linked fate, membership in an Asian American organization, and experience with personal discrimination. In terms of variables that have to do with international migration, measures of English language-use, foreign-born status, length of residence, and participation in activities dealing with politics in the country of origin are included.

Finally, to account for differences in ethnic origin and region among the respondents, respondents are distinguished by country of origin. In addition, Honolulu is distinguished from other metropolitan areas because Hawaii is the only majority-Asian American state in the union. Because Asian American politics has developed differently on the islands compared to the continental United States, Hawaiian Asians may be exposed to a political environment that is not shared by Asians elsewhere. The study begins with a bivariate analysis based on these variables.

In order to test the separate effects of the variables described above when controlling for other possible influences, a series of multivariate analyses is conducted (Tables 5.6–5.8). In the additional multivariate analyses, length of time at current residence is included as an independent variable. Mobility may be a predictor of participation. In particular, those who are mobile may be less likely to participate in politics due to the disruption of ties to the local political system (for example, people must re-register at their new address). Putnam observes that residential stability is positively related to civic engagement at the individual level (2001: 205). Partisan strength and ideology are included under the category of political engagement. In addition to mobilization by a political party, a measure of mobilization by an individual, such as an employer or friend, is included. While the bivariate analyses include whether or not respondents belonged to a political party prior to migration to the United States, this variable was not included in the multivariate analysis shown below.[10] The voting models include whether or not respondents had taken part in an activity related to support for an Asian American cause or candidate. For ease of interpretation and comparison, independent variables were rescaled in maximum-likelihood procedures.[11]

The Extent of Asian American Political Participation

Figure 5.1 shows participation across a range of activities among Asian Americans using data from the PNAAPS. Data in the first set of bars

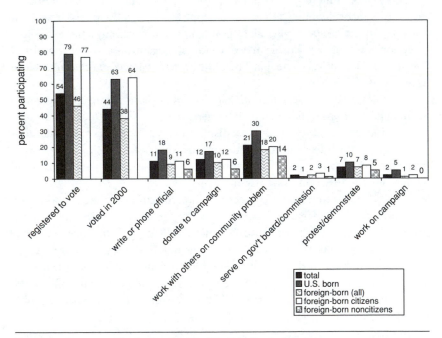

Fig. 5.1   Percentage Distribution of Political Participation by Nativity*
Note: The "foreign born (all)" category includes both citizens and noncitizens. However, only citizens are allowed legally to register and vote. Due to their ineligibility to register and vote, we exclude the "foreign born noncitizens" (last bar in each political activity group) from the analysis of voting registration and vote turnout in 2000.
Source: PNAAPS, 2000–2001.

illustrate that registering (54 percent) and voting (44 percent) are the most commonly reported types of political activity among Asian Americans.[12] Fewer Asian Americans participation in activities like working with others in the community to solve a problem (21 percent), donating to a campaign (12 percent), or writing or phoning a government official (11 percent). Still fewer participate through serving on a governmental board or commission (2 percent), protesting (7 percent), or working on a political campaign (2 percent).

Comparing the U.S.-born to the foreign-born samples, it is clear that in most cases those who were born in the United States are more likely to participate across all activities than those who are immigrants. For example, 79 percent of the U.S.-born sample claimed that they were registered to vote compared to just 46 percent of the foreign-born sample. Among the U.S.-born adults, 63 percent report voting in the 2000 election compared to 38 percent of the foreign-born adults. Similarly, 30 percent of the U.S.-born sample stated that they had worked with others in their community to solve a problem versus 18 percent of the immigrant sample. Also, more of the U.S.-born (18 percent) report writing or phoning a government official than immigrants (9 percent). However, differences between the U.S.-born and immigrants are less pronounced when one examines taking part in a protest (10 percent of U.S.-born versus 7 percent of immigrants).

Past research attributes low rates of voting participation among adult Asian Americans to structural barriers, including lack of availability of bilingual voter materials and eligibility requirements for voting (Kwoh and Hui, 1993; Lien, 2001b; Lien et al., 2001b; Nakanishi, 2001). The PNAAPS data support these findings. The picture of Asian American participation changes greatly depending on whether one assesses the population as a whole or concentrates on those who have met a key eligibility requirement for voting—acquiring citizenship. The first set of bars in Figure 5.1 shows that registration rate is 77 percent among foreign-born respondents who are naturalized citizens. Similarly, 64 percent of naturalized citizens claim to have voted in the November 2000 elections. These data reveal that Asian Americans who are naturalized citizens register and vote at rates that are virtually indistinguishable from their U.S.-born counterparts. Furthermore, though it remains true that Asian Americans demonstrate low rates of registering and voting overall, among Asian Americans who are citizens through either birth or naturalization, voting participation rates are comparable to the general American population. Though it is not reported in the tables, vote participation among registered Asian Americans in the PNAAPS study is 82 percent.[13] Although some might explain their low rates of participation by suggesting that Asian Americans are politically apathetic or more interested in politics in their countries of origin than in the United States, these data make it clear that it is critical to consider structural barriers, such as eligibility requirements, in order to fully understand participation patterns among Asian Americans.

Potential Influences of Socioeconomic Status, Political Engagement, and Civic Involvement

Table 5.1 shows the bivariate relationships between variables that have to do with socioeconomic status and resources and 1) voting registration, 2) voting turnout in 2000, and 3) participation in political activities beyond voting among eligible Asian Americans. The results suggest that, at the bivariate level, the relationship between age and participation through registration and voting is somewhat curvilinear. That is, consistent with the general population (Verba and Nie, 1972; Wolfinger and Rosenstone, 1980), the effects of age on registering to vote and voting in 2000 are greatest at the earlier stages of one's life, but are less profound among the oldest age groups. On the other hand, there does not appear to be a very strong relationship between age and participation in activities beyond voting.

For the most part, at the aggregate level, political participation is lower among the least educated and higher among the most educated. For example, while

Table 5.1 Percentage Distribution of Political Participation by Socioeconomic Status, Political Engagement, and Civic Involvement and Mobilization

	REGISTERED TO VOTE (AMONG CITIZENS)	VOTED IN 2000 (AMONG REGISTERED)	PARTICIPATED IN ACTIVITY BEYOND VOTING
Socioeconomic Status			
Age			
18–28	64	39	46
29–37	81	65	39
38–47	79	67	47
48–60	89	75	54
61–100	88	78	41
Education			
some or less	60	43	25
high school graduate	78	56	35
post-high school or some college	78	58	49
college graduate	83	73	45
some graduate school	87	75	59
postgraduate	90	82	63
Family Income		(p = .87)	
lower income (<30K)	75	83	34
higher income (>60K)	85	82	58
Gender	(p = .81)	(p = .48)	
female	80	64	39
male	80	66	50

(cont.)

Table 5.1 *(Continued)*

	REGISTERED TO VOTE (AMONG CITIZENS)	VOTED IN 2000 (AMONG REGISTERED)	PARTICIPATED IN ACTIVITY BEYOND VOTING
Political Engagement			
Political Interest			
not or slightly interested	71	70	32
somewhat or very interested	84	87	52
Political Knowledge			
knowledge score lowest on 7pt-scale	62	31	26
knowledge score highest on 7pt-scale	93	91	64
Citizenship			
citizen	NA	NA	51
not a citizen	NA	NA	32
Civic Involvement and Mobilization			
Membership in Ethnic Community Organization			
no	78	62	39
yes	90	81	73
Religious Attendance		(p = .09)	
twice a month or less	78	79	42
once per week or more	84	84	50
Mobilized by a Party			
no	67	49	32
yes	93	81	63

Note: Main entries are the percentages of participation within each cell. All the chi-square tests of difference are significant at p $\leq$.05 or less unless otherwise noted. See Appendix for pairwise Chi-Square tests for nonpairwise comparisons.
Source: PNAAPS, 2000–2001.

less than half of all registered voters with a high school degree or less turned out to vote in 2000, over two-thirds of those with some graduate school or a postgraduate degree turned out to vote in 2000. The relationship between income and political participation at the aggregate level varies according to activity. There is a positive association between income and registration among citizens, as well as between income and participation beyond voting. However, once they have overcome the registration requirement, those with lower incomes (83 percent) are just as likely as those with higher incomes (82 percent) to have turned out to vote in 2000.

For Asian Americans, a higher family (household) income may indicate that there are more workers in a family rather than a higher class status (Cheng and

Yang, 1996; U.S. Bureau of the Census, 1999). In addition, Asian Americans tend to be concentrated in urban, coastal areas characterized by higher costs of living than the national average, so higher incomes may partly reflect wages in these area, with a high cost of living rather than more resources (Ong and Hee, 1994). Ong and Hee show that though Asian Americans earn higher median incomes than non-Latino whites within the nation, within the high density Asian American cities of Los Angeles, San Francisco, Oakland, and New York City, Asian Americans earned less than whites. Thus, family income may not have the same relationship to voting among Asian Americans as among other populations.

The effects of gender among Asian Americans appear to be greatest in terms of activities beyond voting, rather than registering to vote or voting. The same or nearly the same percent of women and men registered to vote (among citizens) and voted in 2000 (among the registered). However, when it comes to participation in activities beyond voting, women appear less likely, at least at the bivariate level, to get involved in politics.

As predicted by Verba, Schlozman, and Brady's (1995) seminal study of civic involvement, political engagement appears to be a critical component of political participation among Asian Americans. Those who are more interested in politics and who demonstrate more political knowledge are much more likely to have registered to vote, voted in 2000, and participated in political activities beyond voting compared to those who did not.[14] In terms of registration, a gap of 13 percentage points separates those who claim that they are not interested in politics (71 percent) from those who claim that they are very interested in politics (84 percent). The percentage-point gap is even wider among those who voted in 2000 or had participated in an activity beyond voting. Some researchers suggest that citizenship is a reflection of political engagement, particularly engagement with mainstream politics in the United States (Jones-Correa, 1998). Indeed, those who were citizens by birth or through naturalization are more likely, at least at the bivariate level, to participate in activities beyond voting (32 percent of noncitizens claim to have participated in an activity beyond voting compared to 51 percent of those who are citizens).

Turning to the last rows in Table 5.1, one observes that civic involvement, a measure emphasized in most theories of political participation, is also associated positively with political participation, though the effect varies somewhat according to type of political participation. Specifically, those who are members of an Asian American organization are more likely to register to vote (90 percent) than those who are not members (78 percent), more likely to have voted in 2000 (81 percent) than those who are not members (62 percent), and more likely to have participated beyond voting (73 percent) compared to those who are not members (73 percent). These statistics show that Asian American organizations may serve as a conduit or provide opportunities for political involvement in Asian American communities.[15]

Other institutional sources also are associated with political participation among Asian Americans. Those who have been contacted by a political party or other political organization to participate are more likely to engage in every type of political activity. In fact, 9 out of every 10 Asian Americans citizens who have been contacted about participating in politics registered to vote. About 8 out of every 10 registered Asian Americans who had been contacted by a party or other political organization about participating in politics voted in 2000. One important issue to keep in mind in this case is the uncertain causal direction of the relationship between mobilization and participation. While it might be the case that mobilization precedes voter registration (and other types of participation), it may also be that those who are the most likely to participate are also the most likely to be targeted for mobilization by parties and other political groups (for discussion of this topic, see Rosenstone and Hansen, 1993; Verba, Schlozman, and Brady, 1995; Leighley, 2001).

Finally, consistent with past studies, those who frequently attend religious services appear more likely to register to vote (84 percent) compared to those who don't attend (78 percent) and more likely to have voted in 2000 (84 percent) compared to those who do not attend services frequently (79 percent, p=.09). Those who frequently attend religious services are also more likely to participate in activities beyond voting compared to those who attend religious services less frequently (42 percent and 50 percent participate in activities beyond voting, respectively).

Effects of Socioeconomic Status, Political Engagement, and Civic Involvement: Multivariate Results

Table 5.2 shows the regression of voter registration on socioeconomic status, political engagement, civic involvement and mobilization, and other relevant variables. Note that, once other variables are held constant, neither education nor income is associated positively with registration among eligible Asian Americans (citizens). In contrast, political interest appears to be associated positively with voter registration, and the relationship is statistically significant. The relationship between other measures of psychological political engagement and registration are not statistically significant.

Following past studies, a measure of mobilization (contact by a party or other organization) is included as an independent variable in this analysis. Indeed, party mobilization, through e-mail, phone, or letter, is one of the variables in the model that is associated most strongly with voter registration. Although one must exercise great caution in interpreting the effects of mobilization by individuals, parties, or community organizations on participation, there is some evidence from experimental field studies that contact may precede participation.[16] Unfortunately, our survey data do not allow us to distinguish between types of mobilization; it is not known if respondents were contacted more passively, through e-mail for instance, or through more active contacting, such as a phone

Table 5.2 Estimating Voter Registration among Eligible Asian Americans

INDEPENDENT VARIABLE	LOGISTIC ANALYSIS OF VOTE REGISTRATION AMONG CITIZENS (N = 598)	
	Regression Coefficient (b)	Standard Error
Socioeconomic Status		
education	0.24	0.48
income	0.29	0.48
Political Engagement		
political interest	0.94*	0.41
political knowledge	0.48	0.55
political influence	−0.30	0.46
strong partisan	0.37	0.32
ideology (high score = Conservative)	−0.56	0.49
Civic Involvement and Mobilization		
ethnic organization membership	0.29	0.41
religious attendance	0.43	0.35
participation in Asian American causes	0.03	0.18
mobilized by a party	1.25**	0.28
mobilized by individuals	−0.12	0.33
Acculturation/Racial Group Concerns		
English Language use	0.09	0.69
Panethnic linked fate	0.03	0.33
experience with discrimination	0.23	0.36
Region		
Honolulu	−0.17	0.33
Ethnic Group (reference group = Chinese)		
Japanese	0.34	0.59
Filipino	0.26	0.50
Korean	0.47	0.50
South Asian	0.41	0.56
Vietnamese	0.42	0.45
Immigrant Status		
foreign-born	−0.64^	0.35
(Constant)	−0.77	0.70

−2 Log-Likelihood (Intercept) = 489.36
Model Chi-Sq = 104.66
Nagerkerke R-sq = .26

Note: Control variables included in model but not shown in table are age, female, and length of time at current residence. The coefficient for age is positive and statistically significant. For this analysis as well as that contained in Tables 5.3 and 5.4, *direction* of partisan strength (Democrat or Republican) does not appear to be an important factor in the analysis. ^ p<.05 ≤.10   *.005<p ≤.05   **p ≤.005
Source: PNAAPS, 2000–2001.

call. Thus, while we are confident in reporting a strong association between mobilization and participation, we are also aware that we must be cautious in interpreting the causal direction of the relationship between mobilization and participation.

When logistic regression is employed in a multivariate analysis of vote turnout in 2000, the results suggest that, as one might expect from the bivariate analysis above, the most important variables associated with whether an Asian American registered citizen turned out to vote in 2000 are some of those highlighted in models of voting that include resources and engagement as key elements, such as higher levels of education, attending religious services, and political interest. However, contrary to the general model of voting, family income is related negatively to vote turnout in 2000. The full model and results are shown in Table 5.3.

Table 5.3 Estimating Voting Participation among Eligible Asian Americans

INDEPENDENT VARIABLES	LOGISTIC ANALYSIS OF VOTE TURNOUT IN 2000 N = 480		LOGISTIC ANALYSIS OF CONSISTENT VOTE TURNOUT (1998 AND 2000) N = 480	
Socioeconomic Status	b	s.e.	b	s.e.
education	2.39**	0.66	1.52**	0.48
income	−1.11^	0.63	−1.30*	0.48
Political Engagement				
political interest	1.07*	0.50	0.57	0.38
political knowledge	1.33^	0.71	0.90^	0.53
political influence	1.00^	0.58	−0.04	0.42
strong partisan	0.54	0.41	0.23	0.31
ideology (high score= conservative)	1.07^	0.61	−0.10	0.45
Civic Involvement and Mobilization				
ethnic organization membership	−0.07	0.42	−0.55^	0.30
religious attendance	1.41**	0.45	0.96**	0.33
participation in Asian American causes	0.09	0.19	0.36*	0.13
mobilized by a party	0.44	0.31	0.79**	0.26
mobilized by individuals	−0.08	0.36	0.16	0.26
Acculturation/Racial Group Concerns				
English language use	−0.43	0.82	−1.05	0.65
panethnic linked fate	−0.09	0.40	−0.25	0.31
experience with discrimination	−0.36	0.42	0.49	0.32

(cont.)

Table 5.3 *(Continued)*

INDEPENDENT VARIABLES	LOGISTIC ANALYSIS OF VOTE TURNOUT IN 2000 N = 480		LOGISTIC ANALYSIS OF CONSISTENT VOTE TURNOUT (1998 AND 2000) N = 480	
Region				
Honolulu	−0.30	0.40	0.20	0.33
Ethnic Group (reference group=Chinese)				
Japanese	−0.31	0.67	1.33*	0.56
Filipino	−0.61	0.61	0.77	0.48
Korean	−2.26**	0.59	−0.49	0.46
South Asian	0.98	0.92	0.57	0.54
Vietnamese	1.35^	0.81	0.59	0.51
Immigrant Status				
foreign-born	−0.28	0.42	−0.45	0.33
(Constant)	−1.98*	0.91	−2.95**	0.72
	−2 Log-Likelihood (Intercept)=342.11 Model Chi-Sq=118.22 Nagerkerke R-sq=.35		−2 Log-Likelihood (Intercept)=513.21 Model Chi-Sq=135.24 Nagerkerke R-sq=.33	

Note: Logistic Analysis Vote Turnout in 2000: 1=voted in 2000, 0=registered, but did not vote in 2000. *Logistic Analysis of Vote Turnout in 1998 and 2000:* 1=voted in 1998 and 2000, 0=registered, but did not vote in 1998 and 2000. Control variables included in model but not shown in table are age, female, and length of residence. The coefficient for age is positive and statistically significant in both models. Listwise deletion of missing cases was used in the analysis. When missing values are imputed using the mean for each variable the models are largely unchanged with the following exceptions: p-values decrease in most cases; for the analysis of turnout in 2000, the coefficient sizes associated with education and religious attendance are somewhat attenuated; for the analysis of turnout in 1998 and 2000 the coefficient size for education is somewhat attenuated. Across all variables, there were missing data for approximately 2 percent of cases. *Source:* PNAAPS, 2000–2001.

In addition, multivariate analysis of voting frequency, or consistent turnout habits, shows that education and attending religious services are frequently strong predictors of consistent voting participation. As predicted by models of vote turnout introduced by Rosenstone and Hansen (1993) and others, party mobilization appears to be associated strongly with vote turnout in 1998 and 2000. In addition, being active about Asian American causes is a strong, positive predictor of frequent voting habits. However, neither perceived political influence (efficacy), strength of political partisanship, ideology, or membership in an Asian American organization has the predicted effect among registered Asian Americans (see Table 5.3).

Multivariate analysis of participation beyond voting suggests significant differences from the results generated using the voting models (Table 5.4). For example, education is not significant in predicting participation beyond voting but family income is positive and the relationship is statistically significant. Compared to the singular act of voting, there may be higher costs, including time, associated with political activities beyond voting that are more easily absorbed among those with greater economic resources. Also, some factors that are statistically insignificant in terms their association with voting, such as membership in

Table 5.4 Estimating Participation Beyond Voting among Asian Americans

VARIABLE	TOTAL SAMPLE N = 849		IMMIGRANT SAMPLE N = 627	
Socioeconomic Status	b	s.e	b	s.e
education	0.03	0.03	0.03	0.03
family income	0.07*	0.03	0.08**	0.03
Political Engagement				
citizenship status	0.04	0.07	0.08	0.08
political interest	0.21**	0.05	0.18**	0.05
political knowledge	0.68**	0.19	0.41*	0.20
political influence	0.12*	0.05	0.14*	0.05
strong partisan	0.01	0.03	0.01	0.03
ideology (high score = Conservative)	0.00	0.03	0.00	0.03
Civic Involvement and Mobilization				
ethnic organization membership	0.66**	0.12	0.51**	0.13
religious attendance	0.02	0.03	0.03	0.03
mobilized by a party	0.18^	0.09	−0.02	0.10
mobilized by individuals	0.73**	0.11	0.57**	0.12
Acculturation/Racial Group Concerns				
English language use	0.00	0.08	0.00	0.08
panethnic linked fate	0.09*	0.04	0.11*	0.04
experience discrimination	0.36**	0.12	0.31*	0.13
Region				
Honolulu	0.30*	0.13	0.32^	0.17
Ethnic Group (reference group=Chinese)				
Japanese	0.09	0.20	−0.32	0.26
Filipino	0.17	0.17	0.08	0.18
Korean	−0.08	0.15	−0.09	0.14
South Asian	0.41*	0.18	0.30^	0.18
Vietnamese	0.58**	0.17	0.27^	0.16

(cont.)

Table 5.4   *(Continued)*

VARIABLE	TOTAL SAMPLE N = 849		IMMIGRANT SAMPLE N = 627	
International Migration-Related Variables	b	s.e	b	s.e
foreign-born	−0.40**	0.13	N.A.	N.A.
percent of life in the United States	N.A.	N.A.	−0.43	0.33
educated outside U.S.	−0.30**	0.11	−0.33**	0.11
active in homeland politics	N.A.	N.A.	1.24**	0.19
(Constant)	−0.91**	0.31	−1.21	0.31
	Adjusted R-Square=.37		**Adjusted R-Square=.34**	

Note: OLS Regression, Dependent Variable=Scale of Participation beyond Voting. Control variables included in model but not shown in table are age, female, and length of time at current residence. The coefficient for age is positive and statistically significant only for the foreign-born and that for length of residence at current address is positive and significant only for the full sample. Listwise deletion of missing cases was used in the analysis. However, when missing values are imputed using the mean for each variable the models are largely unchanged with the exception that in the model with the full sample, the size of the coefficient associated with education outside of the U.S. is attenuated, and for the foreign-born sample the size of the coefficients associated with the variable for family income, education outside of the U.S., and Honolulu residence are attenuated. In addition, p-values decrease in most cases. Across all variables, there were missing data for approximately 2 percent of cases.
Source: PNAAPS, 2000–2001.

an Asian American organization and mobilization by individuals, exhibit positive and statistically significant associations with participation other than voting. This finding is discussed in greater detail in the discussion below. Consistent with research on the general population, the association between participation beyond voting and attending religious services is not statistically significant.

Ethnic Group Differences

To what extent does political participation among Asian Americans vary according to ethnic group? The data in Table 5.5 include the relative frequency that each ethnic group in the study participates in a particular activity. Data for the groups as a whole are reported in order to convey the most general rates of participation across each ethnic group. In the sections that follow, frequencies are reported for members of each ethnic group that are *eligible* to participate. The first three columns in Table 5.5 include the rates of participation for each group as a whole. The last three columns contain the rates of participation for just the immigrant members of each group.

In terms of overall rates of participation, it is clear that Japanese Americans demonstrate the highest rates of registering to vote (75 percent) and voting

Table 5.5 Percentage Distribution of Political Participation by Ethnic Groups

	TOTAL REGISTERED	TOTAL VOTED IN 2000	TOTAL PARTICIPATED BEYOND VOTING	IMMIGRANTS REGISTERED	IMMIGRANTS VOTED IN 2000	IMMIGRANTS PARTICIPATED BEYOND VOTING
Chinese	49%	41%	35%	46%	39%	35%
Japanese	75	63	55	24	20	21
Korean	48	34	39	46	33	38
Vietnamese	43	39	33	44	40	34
Filipino	62	47	50	59	47	47
South Asian	39	36	57	34	73	54

Note: Distribution does not take into account eligibility requirements for registration or voting; see Table 4 for participation among eligible members of Asian ethnic groups.
Source: PNAAPS, 2000–2001.

(63 percent). Filipino Americans, in general, also demonstrate fairly high rates of registration (62 percent) and voting participation (47 percent). In comparison, the other ethnic groups in this study are characterized by much lower rates of registration and voting—less than half of Chinese, Korean, Vietnamese, or South Asians, were registered to vote. About 40 percent or less of each of these groups voted in 2000. While voting is usually considered the most common political activity (Verba, Schlozman, and Brady, 1995), it is interesting to note that among some groups, such as Korean Americans, Filipino Americans, and South Asians, rates of participation beyond voting exceed voting rates among voting-age adults.

Immigrant status, as highlighted throughout this book, is an important aspect of political participation among Asian Americans of every ethnic origin. While this topic is addressed later in the chapter, it is worth noting that some of the variation between ethnic groups' rates of participation may be due to immigrant status. Note that the gap in participation rates between Japanese Americans and other groups shrinks considerably once immigrant status is considered. In a bit of a twist from what one might expect, South Asian immigrants (73 percent) appear more likely to have voted in 2000 than the sample of South Asians as a whole (36 percent). Again, it is important to keep in mind that the data in Table 5.6 reflect overall rates of participation among each group. Next, participation rates among ethnic groups that take into account eligibility requirements are examined. Later in this chapter the extent to which the factors associated with participation vary according to ethnic group is discussed.

The first six rows of data in Table 5.6 show the rates of participation for each ethnic group included in the study. Registration rates include only those who are eligible to register (citizens), and voting rates include only those who are eligible to vote (registered citizens). Once eligibility is taken into account, one observes that well over 75 percent of all groups, with the exception of Vietnamese Americans (65 percent), report registering to vote. Japanese (88 percent) and Korean (87 percent) Americans register at the highest rates, followed by Filipino (79 percent), Chinese (78 percent), and South Asian (78 percent) Americans. Although Vietnamese American citizens appear to register at lower rates than other Asian American ethnic groups, the second column of numbers reveals that once registered, Vietnamese Americans turned out to vote in 2000 at some of the highest rates (92 percent) of any ethnic group except for South Asian Americans, who also voted at high rates once registered (93 percent). Over 80 percent of Chinese and Japanese Americans registered respondents claimed to have voted in 2000. Over two-thirds of registered Filipino Americans reported voting in 2000. Korean Americans who were registered to vote turned out in 2000 at the lowest rates (71 percent), according to the study results.

This finding on the lower propensity of Korean American voting participation is consistent with past research (Lien, 2001b: 186). Korean Americans are somewhat distinct from other Asian ethnic groups in terms of reasons for

Table 5.6 Percentage Distribution of Political Participation by Ethnic Origin, Racial Group Concerns, and International Migration-Related Variables

	REGISTERED TO VOTE (AMONG CITIZENS)	VOTED IN 2000 (AMONG REGISTERED)	PARTICIPATED IN ACTIVITY BEYOND VOTING
Ethnic Group Origin			
Chinese	78	84	35
Japanese	88	83	55
Korean	87	71	39
Filipino	79	76	50
Vietnamese	65	92	33
South Asian	78	93	57
Region	(p=.77)		
Honolulu	79	75	53
other metropolitan area	80	83	43
Acculturation/Racial Group Concerns			
English Language Use		(p=.48)	
English language use low^t	76	83	37
English language use high	82	80	52
Panethnic linked fate	(p=.74)	(p=.54)	
yes, a lot	80	84	64
no	79	81	42
Experience with Personal Discrimination		(p=.08)	
yes	86	84	55
no	77	78	38
International Migration-Related Variables			
Foreign-Born		(p=.33)	
yes	77	80	40
no	85	83	59
Years of U.S. Stay		(p=.10)	
1–5 years	NA*	NA*	32
6–10	66	86	35
11–17	78	86	39
18 or more	84	82	49
Educated Outside U.S.		(p=.12)	
yes	76	84	37
no	83	79	55
Active in Homeland Politics	(p=.41)	(p=.47)	
yes	83	88	78
no	77	82	37
Prior Partisanship	(p=.13)		
yes	56	92	67
no	45	82	47

Note: All the chi-square tests of difference are significant at p≤.05 unless otherwise noted.

*Entries in these cells are omitted because the residency rules for citizenship, a necessary requirement for registration, is generally (thought not always), five years. See Appendix for coding of language variable. Low score is lowest 7 categories on 13-pt scale; high score are highest 6 categories on 13-point scale.

Source: PNAAPS, 2000–2001.

migration to the United States (for family reunion) and beliefs about the importance of an ethnic enclave community (Lien, 2001b). In addition, they are more likely than other groups to report high levels of attendance at religious services and to indicate "church" as the primary site for their organizational participation (Lien, 2001b). Previous research on their political behavior in Southern California finds that these distinctions in participation between Korean Americans and other Asian ethnic groups in the United States can be accounted for by other factors in terms of their voting registration and turnout, but not participation beyond voting (Lien, 1997). In fact, additional multivariate analyses show that all else equal, Korean Americans were less likely to vote in 2000 than the comparison group, Chinese Americans (Table 5.3).

In general, past research shows that Japanese Americans tend to participate in both voting and political participation beyond voting at higher rates than other Asian ethnic groups (Lien et al., 2001a). However, further multivariate analysis shows that compared to their Chinese American counterparts, both Vietnamese and South Asian American respondents are more likely to participate in political activities beyond voting (additional regression analyses show that these groups also participate more than Japanese Americans). This result suggests that the propensity of Japanese Americans to participate in politics may be a function of their relatively high average scores in terms of education, socioeconomic resources, length of residence, citizenship rates, English language skills, and greater concentration in Hawaii. When these variables are held constant, the effect of being Japanese per se is no longer distinctive in terms of registration, voting in 2000, or participation beyond voting (Tables 5.3–5.4). However, Japanese Americans are more consistent in their voting habits than the reference group (Chinese Americans), even when other factors are controlled (Table 5.3).

Regional Differences: Hawaii vs. Others

The large population size and long historical presence of Asian Americans in Honolulu may lead to more participation there than in other cities, such as Chicago, where Asians are by no means dominant in terms of size, history, or political representation (Lai, 2000; Lien, 2001b). The majority of voters in Hawaii are Asian American. Geron and Lai (2001) report that in 1990 and 2000, Asian Americans comprised the majority population in all but two state election districts on the island and the majority of state legislators. Hawaii is the only state in the United States that contains majority Asian American congressional districts as well (Geron and Lai, 2001). Hawaii's Senators, Daniel Akaka and Daniel Inouye are Japanese American, and until her death in 2002, Representative Patsy Mink, also Japanese American, served for a combined twenty four years in the House of Representatives. Mink was the first Asian American woman elected to Congress. Table 5.7 shows that Asian American residents of Hawaii as a whole (not controlling for eligibility) generally do register, vote, and participate

Table 5.7 Percentage Distribution of Political Participation by Region

	REGISTERED	VOTED IN 2000	PARTICIPATED BEYOND VOTING
Honolulu	68%	52%	53%
Los Angeles	51	42	45
San Francisco	56	46	37
New York	43	36	39
Chicago	54	46	47

Note: Distribution does not take into account eligibility requirements for registration or voting; see Table 4 for participation among the eligible.
Source: PNAAPS, 2000–2001.

beyond voting at higher rates than their counterparts in other states. However, one sees in Table 5.6 that once eligibility requirements are taken into account, those in Hawaii do not appear to register or vote at higher rates than non-Hawaiians. Indeed, multivariate analysis confirms that once other factors are accounted for, Hawaiians are distinct from non-Hawaiians only when it comes to participating in activities beyond voting (see Table 5.4).

Racial Group Concerns

Table 5.6 also contains the bivariate analysis of participation and variables related to language and racial group concerns and consciousness, such as English language use, a strong feeling of linked fate with other Asian Americans, and experience with personal discrimination. While those (citizens) who use English often tend to register at rates that are slightly higher than those who do not, once registered, those who use English often vote at nearly identical rates as those who do not. In fact, though the difference is not statistically significant, those registered voters who do not use English often vote at slightly higher rates (83 percent) than those who use English more often (80 percent). In contrast, at the bivariate level, those who do not use English often are much less likely to take part in political activities beyond voting compared to those who use English frequently. However, further analysis shows that, once eligibility, socioeconomic status, and other variables are taken into account, English language use has virtually no direct effect on rates of participation among Asian Americans (Tables 5.3–5.4).

Moving down the rows in Table 5.6, one observes that the association between those variables related to racial group concerns and consciousness (perceived panethnic linked fate and experience with discrimination) and registering and voting are much weaker compared to their association with participation beyond voting. There is very little evidence of a strong relationship between having feelings of linked fate with other Asian Americans and registering to vote or voting in 2000. But perceptions of linked fate do appear to be strongly associated with participation in activities beyond voting. Only 37 percent of those who did not express strong feelings of linked fate participated in activities beyond voting compared to a majority, 52 percent, of those who did indicate strong perceptions of linked fate with other Asian Americans. Experience with discrimination also appears to be more strongly associated with participation beyond voting compared to registering or voting. Those who indicated that they had not encountered personal discrimination were much less likely to have participated beyond voting (38 percent) than those who did not feel they had experienced personal discrimination (55 percent). Further multivariate analyses shown in Tables 5.3–5.4 suggest that, other conditions being equal, feelings of linked fate with other Asian Americans and experience with discrimination have little independent effect on voting (see also Lien, 1997), but may exhibit a strong, positive association with involvement in politics outside of formal channels such as voting.[17]

International Migration

The PNAAPS data allow us to investigate the effects of several migration-related variables on political participation (bottom half of Table 5.6). Across political activities, the U.S. born participate more than the foreign born, but the association of foreign-born status with participation beyond voting is most notable in the last column, showing differences in participation beyond voting between immigrants and nonimmigrants. Forty percent of those who are immigrants reported that they had participated in a political activity beyond voting, while 59 percent of those who were born in the United States made the same claim, a gap of 19 percentage points. In contrast, the percent of Asian American immigrant voters (80 percent) was nearly identical to the percent of Asian American voters who were born in the United States (83 percent). Multivariate analysis (Table 5.2) shows that foreign-born status exhibits a marginally negative relationship with voter registration. In addition, further multivariate analyses confirm that even when other factors that might affect participation are considered, foreign-born status is a negative and statistically significant predictor of participation beyond voting, but not of voting (Tables 5.3 and 5.4). These results are consistent with past research on foreign-born status and voting among Asian Americans (Lien, 1997).

One might expect that participation in politics among immigrants would vary somewhat according to length of residence in the United States. As people spend more time in the United States and become more familiar with the political system, they are also likely to feel more comfortable participating in politics.[18] Length of residence might also be related to increased understanding of the political system and greater political interest. Among the foreign born in the PNAAPS sample, there is a modest and statistically significant correlation between measures of political knowledge and length of residence, but the correlation between length of residence and political interest is not statistically significant (not shown in tables). There appears to be some degree of association between length of residence and whether respondents register to vote or participate beyond voting (Table 5.6). However, once respondents overcome the hurdle of registration, length of residence does not seem to affect voting rates. Studies using census data have suggested the importance of length of residence on Asian American immigrants participation in politics (Ong and Nakanishi, 1996; Lien, 2000, 2001a) and these effects are likely to be related to the acquisition of language skills and immigrants becoming citizens over time (Wong, 2000). Additional multivariate analysis shows that once citizenship status and English language use are accounted for (in addition to civic participation, mobilization, and other variables), length of residence in the United States does not appear to have an independent effect on voting turnout in 2000 (not shown) or on participation beyond voting (Table 5.4) among Asian American immigrants. However, even when other factors are taken into account, there does seem to be a positive, statistically significant relationship between registering to vote and length of residence in the United States and consistent voting participation (table not shown).

Similar to immigration status, at the bivariate level, the effects of whether the majority of a respondent's education took place inside or outside of the United States depends to some degree upon type of political activity. Those who were educated outside of the United States were much less likely to report taking part in an activity beyond voting (37 percent) than those who received the majority of their education in the United States (55 percent) (Table 5.6). Those citizens who were educated outside of the United States were also slightly less likely (76 percent) than their U.S.-educated counterparts (83 percent) to have registered to vote. Surprisingly, among registered voters, those who were educated outside of the United States were more likely to have voted in 2000 than those who received most of their education in the United States.[19] These findings appear somewhat election-specific, however. When asked about their participation in the 1998 elections, *more* of those who were educated in the United States claimed to have voted than those who were not educated in the United States (results not shown in tables). In general, though clearly not in every case, those who were primarily educated outside of the United States participate at lower rates than those who were educated mainly in the United States. These findings suggest that place of education matters as much as degree of education in the United States. Consistent with Cho's (1999) hypothesis, the U.S.-born may experience political socialization through "different channels" than immigrants, and the education system may be one of the most important socialization environments.

The relationship between political participation and involvement in politics having to do with the country of origin is assessed at the bottom of Table 5.6. There appears to be a fairly consistent positive relationship between political activity in the country of origin and registering to vote, voting, and participation beyond voting. However, the relationship appears to be strongest in terms of political activity beyond voting. Additional multivariate analyses confirm that, all else being equal, those who are active in politics related to their country of origin are among the most likely to be involved in political activities beyond voting in their communities (Table 5.4).[20] Contrary to those who believe that strong ties to or involvement in the country of origin detract from political participation in the United States, this study suggests that Asian Americans who participate in activities that have to do with politics in their countries of origin also tend to get involved in political participation beyond voting in their communities in the United States. One explanation for this finding is that politically active people will participate in politics wherever the opportunity, or necessity, arises. Another explanation is that individuals get involved in politics in the United States in order to bring about change in their countries of origin. Some people may seek the help of their local U.S. representative in influencing U.S. foreign policy toward their country of origin, for example. In fact, previous analyses reveal that in separate analyses of three specific types of political participation (contacting a government official, working with others in one's community on a problem, and protesting), being active in country-of-origin politics is always a strong predictor of participation (Wong, Lien, and Conway, n.d.).[21]

Finally, the last two rows of data in Table 5.6 show that those respondents who were members of a political party prior to migrating to the United States appear more likely to participate in U.S. politics than those who were not political party members in their countries of origin. While this pattern is consistent at the bivariate level, once the other variables described above are included in a multivariate analysis, prior membership in a party does not appear to have a direct effect on whether or not Asian Americans participate in American politics (not shown in tables).

Conclusion

The results in this chapter suggest that the variables highlighted in models of participation that include resources, engagement, and institutional connections as critical components provide a useful start for understanding the participation of one of the fastest growing non-white minority groups in the United States—Asian Americans. The bivariate analysis shows that, consistent with past studies, age is associated positively with more participation in registration and voting except for among the very old. Education is associated generally with greater levels of participation across all the activities included in this study. Higher family income is associated with higher rates of voting registration among citizens as well as participation in activities beyond voting, but not in voting among the registered.

Variables related to political engagement are important to consider in Asian Americans' political participation, since those who are interested in or knowledgeable about politics also tend to participate more. Mobilization and institutional affiliation, another set of variables highlighted in general theories of participation, also appear to have a fairly consistent association with political participation in bivariate analyses. In addition, in the aggregate, more citizens than noncitizens are likely to participate in political activities beyond voting. However, further analyses show that once other factors are considered, such as socioeconomic status, political engagement, mobilization and minority status, citizens are no more likely to participate than noncitizens in activities beyond voting that do not *require* citizenship (Table 5.4). Because the direct effect of citizenship on participation beyond voting is altogether minimal, it is likely that citizenship in and of itself is a less important determinant of political participation beyond voting than other correlates of citizenship, such as political knowledge, political influence, and membership in an ethnic organization (correlations between citizenship and other variables of interest are shown in Table 5.8). One important implication of this argument is that citizenship drives alone are not likely to propel immigrants toward participation beyond voting. Perhaps more importantly, one should not assume that *lack* of citizenship implies lack of participation in nonelectoral settings.

At the multivariate level, consistent with studies of the general population, socioeconomic status, political engagement and church attendance emerge as important predictors of Asian American political involvement. Education matters more for voting than for registration or other types of political activity among Asian Americans, a result that is similar to Lien's earlier research (2001b). Family income, on the other hand, appears to matter more for activities other than voting than for registration or voting. In fact, when the effect is significant, greater family income is associated with a lower likelihood of voter turnout among the registered, a result that is different from past studies. The combined results from bivariate and multivariate analyses demonstrate a need for reconceptualizing the dominant and positive role of basic socioeconomic status in political participation for Asian Americans—a majority-immigrant and relatively affluent nonwhite population. They suggest the need to deconstruct the traditional role of basic socioeconomic status in predicting political participation for this particular population.

While the effects of individual variables measuring engagement with the political system are not as consistent with previous studies of the general population (Verba, Schlozman, and Brady, 1995), engagement, as indicated by either political interest or knowledge (or perceived influence over local government), predicts political participation through voting and participation beyond voting.[22] In contrast to past research on the larger population, in general, partisan strength and ideology do not have much influence on participation, voting or otherwise among Asian Americans.

In addition, as is the case for other racial groups (c.f. Houghland and Christenson, 1983; Wald, Owen, and Hill, 1988; Verba, Schlozman, and Brady,

Table 5.8 Factors Associated with Citizenship among Foreign Born: Correlation Coefficients

VARIABLE	CORRELATION WITH CITIZENSHIP (0–1, 0 = NOT A CITIZEN)
age	.23*
female	−.05
residential length	.41**
education	.00
family income	.08**
attendance at religious services	.09**
political interest	.03
political knowledge	.10**
political influence	.09**
strong partisan	.13**
ideology (high score = Conservative)	−.01
member of ethnic organization	.07**
mobilized by party	.28**
mobilized by individual	.16**
panethnic linked fate	.06
experienced personal discrimination	.06
language use (high score = mostly English)	.14*
Honolulu	.08*
Japanese	−.10*
Chinese	.01
Filipino	.14*
Korean	−.06*
South Asian	−.13*
Vietnamese	−.06*
percent of life in United States	.45*
educated outside United States	−.17**

Note: *$p \leq .05$ (one-tailed) **$p \leq .05$ (two-tailed)
Source: PNAAPS, 2000–2001.

1995; Harris, 1999), church attendance is found to be a critical determinant of voting, but not registration or participation beyond voting, among Asian Americans. In fact, it turns out to be one of the most critical determinants of voting, even when compared to other types of institutional affiliations, such as membership in an Asian American organization. We argue that attendance at religious services plays a role in the political participation of Judeo-Christian Asian Americans that is similar to its role other communities. However, because some Asian Americans are affiliated with non-Judeo Christian religions, such as Buddhism, for which attendance at services is not always an important part of religious practice, these findings are likely to be most relevant for those Asian Americans who affiliate with Judeo-Christian religions.

When one examines the multivariate results, it is clear that mobilization by the party (via e-mail, letter, or phone call) is associated more strongly with voter registration than other types of participation (even voting). Other types of mobilizing forces, such as contact by an individual to participate or membership in an ethnic community organization, do not appear to have any association with voter registration. Somewhat surprisingly, multivariate results show that neither membership in of an Asian American organization nor contact by a party or individual has any significant relationship with voting in 2000. However, when it comes to consistent voting habits, party mobilization is much more important as a factor in comparison to mobilization by an individual or membership in an Asian American organization. This finding provides evidence that parties target strategically habitual voters.

This analysis has some interesting implications for the relationship between Asian Americans and the American party system. As described above, the aspect of the party system that appears to matter most for Asian Americans' political participation is the mobilization effort made by the parties to get Asian Americans to register and turn out consistently. Psychological orientation toward either of the two parties, as indicated by strong partisanship, does not exhibit a strong association with any type of political participation examined here. Again, it is important to use caution when examining party contact or other sources of mobilization and political participation. More research, perhaps using an experimental design, is necessary before drawing firmer conclusions about the direction of relationship between party contact and involvement in political system.

Several other findings deserve comment. First, confirming the bivariate results, additional multivariate analyses suggest that being a member of an Asian American organization, having feelings of linked fate with others of the same racial background, and experiencing racial discrimination are positive and statistically significant predictors of political participation beyond voting, but not voting. In fact, membership in an Asian American organization exhibits one of the strongest associations with participation beyond voting. This suggests that experiences that may heighten one's racial or panethnic group consciousness can increase an immigrant-dominant population's participation in political activities that do not require citizenship and registration. In contrast, although a strong relationship between party contact and voter registration and consistent voting is revealed, the relationship between mobilization by a party and participation beyond voting is much weaker. Also, mobilization by an individual increases the likelihood of participation beyond voting.

In addition, results from this study suggest that it is important to consider the effects of ethnic group origin and racial group concerns on Asian Americans' political participation. In very general terms, Japanese Americans are more likely to participate in politics than other Asian American groups. Much of the dominance of Japanese Americans in the political sphere is related to the group's

Table 5.9 Political Participation and Associated Variables by Ethnic Group

		CHINESE	KOREAN	VIETNAMESE	JAPANESE	FILIPINO	S. ASIAN
Percent Voted in 2000 (among those registered)							
education	no college	**77**	**58**	93	**76**	**61**	100
	college	**91**	**78**	89	**88**	**92**	90
political interest	no or slightly interested	75	55	96	66	**64**	89
	somewhat or very interested	86	**76**	89	**94**	**85**	94
religious attendance	twice a month or less	83	70	90	80	63	88
	almost every week or more	89	69	100	92	83	96
member ethnic organization	no	83	70	91	**80**	74	88
	yes	100	78	100	**95**	82	100
mobilized, party	no	81	60	90	71	**63**	90
	yes	86	81	94	88	**85**	94
mobilized, individual	no	**80**	71	91	**78**	74	91
	yes	**97**	72	100	**94**	79	95
English language use	low	**85**	71	92	80	77	100
	high (mostly English)	**81**	73	90	83	75	91
panethnic linked fate	no, or doesn't affect much	82	73	90	81	78	94
	yes, affects a lot	**100**	72	100	83	68	93
experienced with discrimination	no	81	70	92	79	74	**83**
	yes	87	73	86	88	77	**100**
Participation beyond Voting							
education	no college	**27**	**25**	31	54	48	53
	college	**43**	**46**	36	60	55	61
citizen	no	**25**	**29**	34	16	**35**	49
	yes	**41**	**46**	33	31	**51**	61

(cont.)

Table 5.9   (Continued)

Participation beyond Voting		CHINESE	KOREAN	VIETNAMESE	JAPANESE	FILIPINO	S. ASIAN
political interest	no or slightly interested	24	22	24	41	37	41
	somewhat or very interested	40	44	41	64	63	63
religious attendance	twice a month or less	34	35	26	57	47	53
	almost every week or more	36	41	50	51	54	64
member of ethnic organization	no	34	33	29	50	46	50
	yes	63	100	80	70	65	79
mobilized, party	no	27	27	29	25	42	43
	yes	50	59	58	73	60	80
mobilized, individual	no	29	34	31	44	44	49
	yes	62	62	63	80	71	90
English language use	low	35	34	39	33	48	58
	high	43	50	30	58	51	60
panethnic linked fate	no, or no affect	33	34	29	56	50	54
	yes, affects a lot	54	63	57	75	65	75
experienced with discrimination	no	29	37	31	48	46	44
	yes	45	41	44	66	59	78
foreign born	no	38	46	NA	64	57	75
	yes	35	38	34	21	47	54
educated outside U.S.	yes	39	50	48	60	55	70
	no	34	35	26	29	46	49
politically active in country of origin	no	33	36	31	20	44	52
	yes	75	83	58	33	100	100

Note: Entries in bold show that Chi-Square tests of difference in participation between categories is statistically significant at p<.10 (two-tailed).
Source: PNAAPS, 2000–2001.

small proportion of immigrants and ability to meet the eligibility requirements for registering and voting. In addition, several factors may contribute to mobilization among Japanese Americans, including the movement for reparations for the internment of Japanese Americans during World War II and the historical prominence of Japanese American in the U.S. Congress.[23] The additional analysis in Table 5.9 shows how many of the variables discussed above are related to the participation of specific ethnic groups at the bivariate level. Note that, for the most part, the direction of the relationship (positive or negative) between the variables presented and political participation through either voting or participation beyond voting are in the same direction, regardless of ethnic group. When relationships run in the opposite direction than expected (e.g., a higher percent of South Asians who did *not* attend college voted in 2000 than the percent that did attend college), the differences are not statistically significant. However, there are variations in the *strength* of the association between particular variables and political participation that depend on ethnic group, at least at the bivariate level. For instance, the association between attendance at religious services and participation beyond voting appears to be greater among Vietnamese Americans than other ethnic groups. Also, foreign-born status seems to be more relevant for some groups' (Japanese, South Asians) participation beyond voting than for others. In contrast, the relationships between participation beyond voting and key variables such as political interest, membership in an ethnic organization, mobilization, activity in politics related to country of origin are remarkably consistent across ethnic groups.

Turning back to the general findings of the study, those in Honolulu participate in politics at higher levels than those in other states. However, multivariate analyses suggest that these regional distinctions partly can be explained away by other factors.

Among immigrant Asian Americans, involvement in politics dealing with the country of origin is associated with increased levels of participation in the host country, even when other variables are taken into account using multivariate techniques. This finding suggests that some Asian Americans who are active in home-country politics may be interested in politics in general and may want to seek the influence of the American public and U.S. policies toward their country of origin.

The significance of variables such as having feelings of linked fate and being involved in politics dealing with the country of origin suggests the necessity of paying greater attention to an array of factors having to do with racial group status and international migration when attempting to understand influences on the political participation of Asian Americans. The findings in this chapter show that Asian American political participation cannot be explained using any single model. Rather, it is best understood by drawing on traditional theories of political participation *as well as* those outlined in Chapter 1. For example, some aspects of political participation, such as participation outside of voting, involve time-related processes such as years spent in the United States, as acculturation theory predicts. Transnationalism, another theoretical framework this study relies on, also is relevant because connections with their countries of origin matter for Asian Americans' participation in a range of political activities. Finally, theories of panethnicity and racial formation help to explain the conditions under which a sense of panethnic fate and affiliations with community institutions are likely to be most important for political participation among Asian Americans.

CHAPTER 6

Where and When Does Gender Matter?

Are there gender differences in political attitudes and behavior among Asian Americans? In what ways do men and women of Asian descent differ and why? How significant is gender relative to other factors in predicting Asian American political attitudes and behavior? This chapter examines similarities and differences between Asian American men and women in the United States along a broad range of topics related to their political experiences explored in other chapters. They include socioeconomic status, socialization, ethnic identity, social and political connectedness, political orientation, political participation, candidate choice, and issue preference. Thus, this chapter's focus is on gender differences, not sexual differences, in political attitudes and behavior. Social scientists distinguish between "sex" and "gender." To quote Josephson and Tolleson-Rinehart. "Sex is the characteristics of the biological being; gender is the socially constructed aspect of self" (2000: 4).

In the following sections, theories on gender gaps derived mostly from studying mainstream whites are reviewed and their limitations in comprehending the Asian American situation are discussed. Next, descriptive statistics are used to identify and gauge the contours of gender gaps among the PNAAPS respondents in terms of factors that may impact the extent and direction of their political involvement. These factors include sociodemographic background, socialization stages and context, political and civic institutional ties, as well as indicators of Asian Americans' political attitudes and behavior (i.e., political orientations, participatory acts, candidate choice, issue concerns, and policy preferences). Gender differences are examined among nativity, ethnic origin, and citizenship groups. Then the relative significance of gender as a factor in understanding the political experience of Asian Americans is assessed using multivariate techniques by taking into account possible confounding factors that contribute to the observed gender gaps. To identify variables that help explain and distinguish the political attitudes and behavior of Asian American women from Asian American men, the results of separate multivariate analyses of the political orientations of men and of women are reported.

Theories about Gender Gaps: Why Should Gender Matter?

Several theories suggest that gender differences might exist. As Josephson and Tolleson-Rinehart point out, a substantial body of research demonstrates that "men and women come to political life with different kinds of information, experiences, and priorities" (2000: 3). Cultures create and maintain gender roles, which are expectations about how individuals should behave. Through a variety of socialization processes, individuals acquire knowledge of the gender role expectations appropriate to their culture. However, they may vary in the extent to which they act in accord with those gender role expectations. Furthermore, individuals who migrate from one country to another may experience conflicting gender role expectations in the multiple cultures they have experienced.

Although the founding principles of the United States include liberty, equality, and justice for all, women were banned from attending colleges until 1833, when Oberlin College began to admit women under a special program (Flexner, 1975). U.S. women's right to vote in all federal, state, and local government elections was not established until the Nineteenth Amendment to the U.S. Constitution was ratified in 1920. This came fifty years after the extension of voting and citizenship rights to former black male slaves via the Fourteenth and the Fifteenth Amendments. Women were not given an equal opportunity to education and to vote because they were believed to be "frail, frivolous, and less mentally capable than men" (Conway, Steuernagel, and Ahern, 1997: 10). The nation's conservative political, religious, and business leaders and organizers of corrupt local political party machines were fearful of women's potential influence on public policy that might pose threats to the status quo.

Despite the many changes in women's status in employment, education, and family life in the twentieth century, women continue to face different role expectations than men (Conway, Steuernagel, and Ahern, 1997: 21). Gender roles have implications for political attitudes and behavior and may result in differences in political orientations and participation in several ways. One is that boys and girls learn different orientations toward politics. Traditionally, as girls, women learned to shy away from public and political life and were told to focus on their responsibilities to home and family. They were less likely to develop an interest in politics and a sense of political efficacy than their male counterparts. They were less knowledgeable than men about the federal government and national politics. They were discouraged from engaging in political discussions and running for office because it was not deemed appropriate for women. Those who were politically active were often criticized for not spending enough time with their family. Although American women now vote in proportions equal to or greater than men, they are less likely to engage in political discussions and become politically active in areas other than voting.

In addition to differences in gender role expectations, another factor limiting women's full participation in the nation's politics is the disparity in opportunity structure created by the differential treatment of men and women in the framing and interpretation of laws, the regulations written to carry them out, and in the enforcement of both. While most overt forms of sex discrimination in employment, access to housing, and educational opportunities were made illegal in the United States under a number of laws enacted since the 1960s, subtle forms of discrimination still exist. Many women face additional constraints on their ability to participate politically because of situational factors, such as the demands of family life, and structural factors, such as lack of education, direct experience or mentoring, organization, and money. As a consequence of these factors, women are under-represented in certain occupations and in elective offices. For example, women are less likely than men to be members of the legal profession. Turning to elective offices, only 13.6 percent of the 108th U.S. Congress and only two of the nine U.S. Supreme Court justices were women in 2003. In that same year, women were less than one-quarter of all state legislators, and only six of the fifty governors were women.

Because of gender differences in socialization and opportunity structures, women have a different political profile than men. They are more compassionate on views toward the government's role in providing services and assistance to the less fortunate. This may refer to both the general principle and specific programs of affirmative action. They are more supportive of gun control and more opposed to the use of force to resolve conflicts. Women are more likely to identify with the Democratic Party and support its candidates. But few gender differences exist in other policy areas such as abortion or evaluations of government responsiveness and trustworthiness. As a group, women are less likely than men to consider themselves as politically effective and government as responsive to voters' concerns. Women also tend to have a lower sense of internal political efficacy and are more likely to consider politics as too complicated to understand (Conway, Steuernagel, and Ahern, 1997: 87–88).

A number of studies in the United States conclude that women are less interested than men in politics (Sapiro, 1983; Conway, Steuernagel, and Ahern, 1997; Bennett and Bennett, 1989; Verba, Burns, and Schlozman, 1997). Burns, Schlozman, and Verba (2001) attribute "gender differences in political interest and information to a genuine different in the taste for politics" (2001: 1070). Other explanations offered for women's lower levels of interest in politics include the socialization of women to believe that politics is a man's business, gendered patterns of education, women's more limited employment opportunities, gender differences in household responsibilities and in the time available to follow politics, and different patterns of media use. Furthermore, although the number of female elected officials who could serve as role models in local communities and the states is increasing, their number is still small and—with few exceptions, such as prominent U.S. senators or governors—their visibility to most of the public is limited.

In addition to having lower interest in politics, women tend to be less knowledgeable about politics and government than men and pay less attention to national politics (Verba, Burns, and Schlozman, 1997). Men have been found to be more knowledgeable about a number of different aspects of politics, including institutional structures, political processes, and current issues (Delli Carpini and Keller, 2000).

Gender Differences in Political Orientations among Asian Americans

While the modern women's movement undoubtedly changed social institutions and the views of a number of socializing agents, the effects of a changing culture may vary by race, ethnicity, nativity, and social class. Each ethnic group may differ in its culture and accompanying views on gender roles. For some women, race or ethnicity may be more important than gender. For others, concern over their economic situation may prevail over their political concerns. Persons born and raised outside of the United States may have different attitudes toward gender roles because of their socialization. However, their ability to adapt to the political culture of the new country may also be a function of the host country's attitudes toward them (Hoskin, 1989). Immigrants are more likely to attempt to unlearn their old political attitudes, a process known as desocialization, and learn new ones prevalent in the host society, a process known as resocialization, if the host country has a receptive policy.

Most of the observations on gender differences reported in the preceding section are based on studies of non-Hispanic whites. Asian American women may be similarly subjected to the biases in socialization and social structure in U.S. society, but their gendered experiences may be different from white women because of factors related to race, nativity, class, ethnicity and the interlocking nature of these systems of power. Like Asian men in America, Asian American women historically have been forced to confront a system permeated with pervasive and covert forms of racism, sexism, and colonization that limited their opportunities for social, economic, and political participation (Cheng and Bonacich, 1984; Mazumdar, 1989; Lowe, 1996; Espiritu, 1997). This common experience of racialization, of being treated as neither black or white, nor woman or man, but as the foreign "other," may help undermine the gender gaps among Asian Americans. Compared to white immigrant women, Asian immigrant women might have special socialization disadvantages in the United States because they mostly originated from cultures in which the proper roles and opportunities for women were especially restricted (Chow, 1987). They may also be less likely to be connected to U.S. social networks such as labor unions and church organizations (Ling, 1998). Being perceived as intricately connected to an "enemy" homeland in Asia may set apart the experience of U.S.-born Asian women from their white counterparts because of the loyalty question regarding Asians.

Like other women of color, Asian American women have often been relegated to a lower class status through exploitation, segregation, and subordination because of the interactive effect of racism and patriarchy in a competitive capitalist economy (Glenn, 1985). Nevertheless, among Asians, certain ethnic groups, such as Chinese-, Japanese-, and Korean-born women, may confront greater gender and generational hierarchies within their own households than other ethnic groups (Hune, 2000). Yet, for refugee groups such as the Vietnamese, women may be provided the circumstances to achieve gender equality because of their assuming greater economic responsibilities and decision-making power in family and community affairs in the new home country—even though they may simultaneously be ambivalent about departures from the traditional values of collectivism and cooperation (Kibria, 1990).

The multiple layers of racial, sexual, cultural, and class oppression confronting Asian American women may affect the construction of their social and ethnic identity as well as their political orientations and participation. The interactive effect of racism and patriarchy has often resulted in the subordination and exploitation of both Asian American women and men, with consequent economic deprivation of them. Not only may gender as a social marker be less significant for Asians than for whites, but the contours of gender gaps among Asians may be qualitatively different. Moreover, the significance and impact of gender may vary by ethnic group. Some may face more restrictions than others in economic and political opportunities and a more patriarchal culture. The timing and condition of immigration may affect the degree of familiarity with the American political system as well as the English language skills that facilitate acquiring information necessary for evaluating politics, policies, and politicians, and for political participation. The timing and conditions of immigration as well as cultural patterns may also impact women's opportunities for acquiring higher levels of education and subsequent employment opportunities.

A recent study of income data collected by the Current Population Survey among Asian Americans shows that, although both genders share the experience of receiving fewer dollars in return for their education and work in comparison to their white male counterparts, contemporary Asian American women are still not equal to Asian American men in educational achievement and earned income (Lien, 2001b). The issue of racial and gender discrimination is particularly severe for those Asians who never entered college. However, when social class is controlled, the common experience of racial exploitation may help forge a political outlook among Asians that downplays gender differences while not necessarily erasing interethnic differences (Lien, 1998).

To summarize, Asian American men and women may differ in their patterns of political participation because of unequal efforts by political elites to shape and activate their political attitudes and mobilize men and women to participate. Gender differences in political attitudes may also be fostered by different patterns of involvement in ethnic, social, religious, and political organizations and in the use of the mass media. In addition, employment and marital status may affect the formation of political ties. Married women who work outside the home usually assume a disproportionate share of household responsibilities. However, those who work outside the home may also be exposed to additional information about issues and candidates and to political mobilization efforts that do not reach those who are not employed. Groups' historical experiences in the United States, patterns of education and educational attainment, and members' degrees of group consciousness would be expected to affect their political orientations and behavior. Among immigrants, gender gaps may also exist because of differences in the timing of their arrival in the United States, English language fluency, and extent of opportunities for educational attainment afforded to women in the home country.

Identifying Gender Gaps in the Aggregate

The PNAAPS dataset permits us to present a first comprehensive overview of the contours of the gender gaps among Asian Americans. The sample consists of almost equal numbers of women and men, but it contains ethnic groups that vary significantly in the proportions that are foreign-born and female. The proportion of foreign-born women in each ethnic group is: Japanese, 22 percent; Filipino, 70 percent; South Asian, 75 percent; Korean, 91 percent; Chinese, 92 percent; and Vietnamese, 96 percent. The sample also varies in the proportion of each ethnic group that is female. As Table 6.1 illustrates, slightly more than one-third of the Vietnamese and 41 percent of the South Asian respondents are female, while the percentage female in the other four Asian American groups varied from 48 percent to 56 percent.

Sociodemographic Characteristics

Gender differences in political orientations and behavior could be attributed to differences between men and women in sociodemographic characteristics, such as patterns of educational attainment, language fluency, employment patterns, family income, and length of residence in the country. Alternatively, they could be a consequence of differences in the way the same levels of a variable interact with other characteristics to affect political orientations and behavior. We first examine the extent to which Asian American women and men differ in these sociodemographic characteristics.

Table 6.2a shows that Asian American men and women in the survey do not differ much in aspects of sociodemographic background except in patterns of employment. Men are more likely than women to be employed full time outside the home (54 percent of the men and 40 percent of the women). However, a slightly higher percentage of women are employed part time (11 percent of the

Table 6.1 Percentage Distribution of Gender within Each Ethnic Group

	CHINESE	KOREAN	VIETNAMESE	JAPANESE	FILIPINO	SOUTH ASIAN	ALL
Men	46%	44%	63%	44%	52%	59%	50%
Women	54	56	37	56	48	41	50
N	308	168	137	198	266	141	1218

Source: PNAAPS, 2000–2001.

Table 6.2a Percentage Distribution of Sociodemography and Social Ties by Gender

	MEN	WOMEN	ALL
Base N	612	606	1218
Education			
no college	26%	31%	29%
some college	20	19	19
college or more	54	50	52
Income Levels			
<30k	23	24	23
30–59k	30	28	29
60k+	25	21	23
not sure/refused	22	28	25
Age Groups (in Years)			
18–28	21	22	22
29–37	19	21	20
38–47	20	21	21
48–60	20	17	20
61–100	18	19	19
Length of Community Residence (in Years)			
1–3	22	23	22
4–6	19	18	19
7–11	19	22	21
12–20	24	21	23
21 or more	17	16	16
Marital Status			
married	63	63	63
single	29	26	27
other	8	11	10
*Employment Status**			
full time	54	40	47
part time	9	11	10
self employed	7	5	6
keeping house	1	14	8
attending school	8	9	9
retired	12	11	11

Source: PNAAPS, 2000–2001. *Chi-square test of difference is significant at $\alpha=.05$ or better.

women compared to 9 percent of the men). Slightly more men are self-employed (7 percent to 5 percent among women), and approximately equal proportions of men and women are retired (12 percent of the men and 11 percent of the women). A significant number are in school (8 percent of the men and 9 percent of the women), and 14 percent of the women are homemakers.

In the total sample, men and women do not differ significantly in a number of other sociodemographic characteristics. These include age distribution, marital status, and levels of family income. However, men and women born in the United States have higher family incomes than their immigrant counterparts. Neither do men and women differ significantly in levels of educational attainment, but women are less likely than men to have attained the highest levels of education (college graduate, postgraduate degree). Gender differences in educational attainment are largest among Chinese, Korean, and Filipino Americans and smallest among South Asian Americans.

Immigration, Socialization, and Minority Group Identity and Status

Men and women might be expected to differ in their political orientations because of differences in patterns of citizenship and immigrant status, proportion of their lives spent in the United States, and whether they were educated in the United States or in the home country. However, no significant differences on these characteristics exist between Asian American men and women who participated in the survey.

Language use patterns may play a critical role in the political integration of a group's members into the polity. Table 6.2b shows that more men than women report using English in business and financial transactions, with 77 percent of the men and 70 percent of the women using English. Seventeen percent of the women and 8 percent of the men report mostly using a language other than English. About half of both the men and women speak another language at home, 25 percent of the men and 29 percent of the women speak English, and the rest use both English and another language at home. When we control for nativity, women who immigrated to the United States are significantly less likely than U.S.-born women or foreign-born men to use English in business and financial transactions.

Turning to the language of media use, men and women are equally likely to report using ethnic media as a source of information, with one-third using it all the time or most of the time as their source of information. Following news stories about events affecting Asian Americans in the United States does not vary substantially by gender, with 55 percent of the men and 52 percent of the women consuming news stories on those topics. Fifty-eight percent of the men and 55 percent of the women follow news stories about events in Asia either fairly or very closely. Again, however, nativity affects patterns of news media use, with U.S.-born men and women significantly less likely to follow either news stories about Asian Americans or news stories about events in Asia.

Political attitudes and behavior could be affected by the ethnic self-identity individuals choose. Ethnic self-identification is subjective, reflecting cognitive, affective, and evaluative dimensions and attachments to both the home country and the United States. When asked to choose among the subjective identity alternatives of American, Asian American, Asian, ethnic group American, and

Table 6.2b Percentage Distribution of Immigration, Socialization, and Ethnic Group Identity and Concerns

	MEN	WOMEN	ALL
Immigration Generation			
first	78%	74%	76%
second	14	14	14
third or more	8	12	10
U.S. Citizenship	69	66	68
Expected Citizenship			
yes	70	73	72
no	24	19	21
not sure	6	8	7
Years of U.S. Stay (Immigrants Only)			
5 or fewer	23	26	25
6–10	23	26	25
11–15	15	15	15
16–21	18	16	17
22 or more	21	16	18
Non-U.S. Education	57	60	58
Home Language Use			
mostly non-English	49	48	48
mixed	26	24	25
mostly English	25	29	27
*Business Language Use**			
mostly non-English	10	17	14
mixed	12	13	13
mostly English	77	70	74
Use of Ethnic Media as Source of Entertainment, News, and Information (p=.07)			
all the time	11	15	13
most of the time	23	21	22
about the same amount	14	17	15
not very often	38	33	36
note at all	14	14	14
*Ethnic Self-Identification**			
American	13	12	12
Asian American	18	13	15
Asian	4	4	4
Ethnic American	36	32	34
Ethnic Asian	26	34	30
Racial Group Concerns			
hate crime victim	15	15	15
experience with ethnic discrimination	36	36	36
sense of linked fate to other Asians	56	51	54

Source and Note: See Table 6.2a.

ethnic group, gender differences in subjective identity are present. Men are more likely to choose American or Asian American, while women are more likely to identify with an ethnic group.

Patterns of political beliefs, attitudes, and participation may be affected by personal experiences of discrimination. Respondents to the survey were asked if they had ever experienced discrimination in the United States and the reasons and nature of discrimination. Equal percentages of men and women report being victimized by hate crimes (15 percent) and having experienced discrimination because of race or ethnicity (36 percent). When the specific nature of discrimination experienced by women and men is examined, again, no significant gender differences exist in the types to which they are subjected. Those most frequently reported by both men and women are discriminatory acts by strangers (20 percent of the men and women), by business (15 percent of the men and 17 percent of the women), and by either employers or fellow employees on the job (16 percent of the men and 14 percent of the women).

Does experiencing discrimination affect patterns of participation and political orientations? Experiencing discrimination could alienate individuals, reducing their levels of political participation. An alternative hypothesis is that discrimination would stimulate participation. Lien (1997) finds support for the stimulation hypothesis in predicting participation other than voting among Asian Americans in Southern California. Her finding is echoed in Wong (2003) in a study of Chinese Americans in the Los Angeles area. In this survey, both men and women who have experienced discrimination are slightly more likely to vote. Furthermore, for both men and women, those who report more types of discrimination under different situations also report performing more types of political activities. In addition, both men and women who have experienced discrimination have significantly higher levels of political interest. However, victims of discrimination do not differ from others in their levels of political trust, their perceptions of their influence over local government decisions, or the responsiveness of local public officials to complaints from citizens like them.

Men and women do not differ in other aspects listed in Table 6.2b. These include their patterns of belief in the linked fate of Asian Americans, immigrant generation, citizenship or expected citizenship rate, place of education, degree to which they use English in the home, or their length of residence in the United States.

Political and Civic Institutional Ties

Political participation is often the consequence of political mobilization efforts by political elites and ethnic group leaders (Rosenstone and Hansen, 1993; Verba, Schlozman, and Brady, 1995; Freedman, 2000; Schier, 2000; Burns, Schlozman, and Verba, 2001; Conway, 2001a, 2001b). Are Asian American men and women equally likely to be the targets of mobilization efforts by political parties or by individuals? Table 6.2c shows that 43 percent of the men and 38 percent of the

Table 6.2c   Percentage Distribution of Political and Civic Institutional Ties

	MEN	WOMEN	ALL
Political Mobilization			
contacted by political party or group	43	38	41
contacted by individuals*	23	16	19
Ethnic Organization Membership	15	15	15
Religious Attendance			
never	30	31	31
1–2/year	9	8	8
1–2/month	13	13	13
3–4/month	24	25	24
every week	24	23	24
*Political Interest**			
not at all	12	14	13
slightly	24	25	24
somewhat	36	40	38
very interested	29	20	24
*Familiarity with the Presidential Election Process**			
very familiar	34	17	25
somewhat familiar	51	57	54
not familiar	14	22	18
*Know Wen Ho Lee**	62	53	54
Know 80–20 Initiative	19	17	18
*Political Partisanship**			
Democrat	35	36	36
Independent	14	12	13
Republican	19	13	16
no/not sure	32	38	35

Source and Note: (See Table 6.2a).

women report being contacted by a political party in a political mobilization effort. Fewer men and women report being contacted by an individual than a party or group with a request to vote or contribute money or engage in some other form of political activity. However, again men are more frequently contacted, with 23 percent of the men and 16 percent of the women indicating they had been contacted by individuals in political mobilization efforts.

Men and women might differ in their membership in organizations that are explicitly oriented toward Asian American causes. However, that is not evident, as only 15 percent of both women and men report membership in at least one organization that has that agenda. They could differ in the number of organizations in which they are involved, but we have no measure of the number of ethnic-based organizations in which they are members. They might also differ in the intensity of their involvement. When asked how active they are as a member of an ethnic interest organization, more women members report that they are very active (34 percent to 27 percent for men) and more men members report that they are somewhat active (47 percent to 33 percent for women).

Participation in organizations, even if they do not have an explicitly political agenda, often results in increased levels of political information and political participation. For example, attendance at religious services and participation in activities associated with religious organizations provide mechanisms for the acquisition of politically relevant skills and acquiring politically relevant information (Verba, Schlozman, and Brady, 1995; Wald, 1997). However, Asian American men and women do not differ in the frequency of their attendance at religious services.

Both men and women who are members of ethnic-based organizations explicitly focused on supporting Asian American candidates and issues engage in more different types of political activities than do those who are not members of that type of organization. In contrast, among those who are not members of such organizations, men more frequently take part in political activities beyond voting.

Consistent with patterns found among whites, Asian American women and men differ in their levels of political interest, with a larger proportion of men than women reporting that they are very interested in what goes on in politics. Asian American men also have significantly higher levels of political knowledge than women by having a higher level of familiarity with the presidential election process and a greater likelihood of knowing who Wen Ho Lee is and how the federal government treated him.

Different from findings among whites, Asian American women are not more likely than Asian American men to identify with the Democratic Party. However, a higher percentage of men than women identify with the Republican Party and a higher percentage of women than men identify with none.

Political Orientations

Political ideology often serves as a guide to other beliefs and attitudes, such as those relating to political parties, candidates, and public policy issues. Do Asian American women tend to be more liberal in political ideology than Asian American men? Table 6.2d shows that, contrary to expectation, a slightly higher percentage of men are very liberal than women, with almost equal proportions of both genders placing themselves in the rest of the categories except "not sure." A much higher percentage of women than men are not certain of their ideological orientation.

Another important political orientation is trust in government. Survey participants were asked: "How much of the time do you think you can trust your local and state government officials to do what is right—just about always, most of the time, only some of the time, or none at all?" Men are more trusting than

Table 6.2d Percentage Distributions of Political Orientations by Gender

	MEN	WOMEN	ALL
*Political Ideology**			
very liberal	10%	7%	8%
somewhat liberal	28	28	28
middle	32	32	32
somewhat conservative	19	18	18
very conservative	5	3	4
not sure	7	13	10
Political Trust (p=.09)			
none at all	8	9	9
some of the time	47	53	50
most of the time	38	31	34
just about always	8	7	7
*Perceived Local Government Responsiveness**			
none at all	15	20	17
very little	31	35	33
some	43	35	39
a lot	12	10	11
Perceived Influence on Local Government Decisions			
none	26	33	29
little	45	42	44
some	22	19	21
a lot	6	6	6
*Trust U.S. Officials More** (among Immigrants)			
more	60	49	55
about the same	23	29	26
less	7	5	7
not sure	9	16	13
N	471	442	913
*Perceive More Influence on U.S. Officials** (among Immigrants)			
more	47	31	39
about the same	21	27	24
less	18	17	17
not sure	14	25	19
N	471	442	913

Source and Note: See Table 6.2a.

women, with 46 percent of the men and 38 percent of the women reporting that they trust their local and state governments just about always or most of the time, but that is still a minority of both men and women. Political trust is slightly higher among foreign-born men and women than among those born in the United States.

A keystone of democracy is that public officials are responsive to the public and that members of the public believe that they can influence the decisions of public officials. Men are more likely to perceive local public officials as responsive to their complaints. Fifty-five percent of the men and 45 percent of the women expect local officials to pay a lot of attention or some attention to their complaints. No significant difference exists between men and women in their perceived ability to influence the decisions of local public officials, with 29 percent of the men and 25 percent of the women believing they have a lot or a moderate amount of influence over local government decisions.

Differences in Political Orientations by Gender and Nativity

The results presented to this point generally have compared men and women without controlling for the effects of nativity. Approximately 78 percent of the men and 74 percent of the women in the sample are foreign-born. Are the differences that exist between men and women in their levels of political interest and their political attitudes and beliefs greater among the foreign-born or the U.S.-born? Foreign-born men are significantly more interested in politics than foreign-born women, while no significant difference exists between U.S.-born men and women in their levels of political interest. The reverse is true for perceptions of public officials' responsiveness to complaints, with greater differences occurring among the U.S.-born than among immigrants. Men born in the United States are significantly more likely to perceive public officials as responsive to complaints than are women born in the United States. No differences based on nativity exist in levels of political trust or perceptions of influence over local government decisions.

Differences in political orientations may result between women whose cultural and political socialization occurred completely in the United States and those who immigrated to the United States. However, no statistically significant differences exist between U.S.-born and foreign-born women in levels of political interest, political trust, perceived responsiveness of public officials, or perceived influence over local government decisions. In contrast, for two of those four political orientations, statistically significant differences do exist between men born in the United States and those who immigrated. Men born in the United States are significantly more likely than immigrant men to perceive local public officials as responsive to their complaints and themselves as able to influence local government decisions.

Immigrant men and women may also differ in their comparative evaluations of government in the United States and in their home country. Immigrants were asked if they generally trusted U.S. government officials more, about the same, or less than government officials in their home country. Sixty percent of the men and 49 percent of the women believe they can trust the U.S. government more. When asked if they think they can generally influence decisions made by U.S. government officials more, about the same, or less than those made by officials in the home country, 47 percent of the men and 31 percent of the women think they can have more influence over decisions made by the U.S. government.

Life Experiences and Differences among Women in Their Political Orientations

Life experiences contribute to explaining differences among women in their beliefs and attitudes. We might expect the patterns of political orientations of those who are members of organizations that focus on ethnic group issues and interests to differ from those who do not. And indeed, women who are members of ethnic interest groups do have higher levels of political interest and are more likely to perceive themselves as able to influence public officials' decisions. In contrast, they do not differ significantly from women who are not ethnic organization members in their levels of political trust or in their perceptions of the responsiveness of public officials to their complaints. Those who score higher on the index of personally experiencing discrimination are also higher in levels of political interest, but do not differ from other women in their levels of political trust, perceived influence over local government decisions, and the perceived responsiveness of local government officials to their complaints.

Women's levels of trust, perceived influence, political interest, and perceived public officials' responsiveness do not vary with differences in their citizenship status or length of time lived in the United States. However, women who are more attentive to the news have higher levels of political interest and are more likely to perceive themselves as being able to influence local government decisions. Women who are more frequent users of the English language have lower levels of political trust but score higher in perceived influence over local government decisions and the perceived responsiveness of local public officials to their complaints.

No significant differences in women's levels of political interest, trust, perceived responsiveness of public officials, and perceptions of influence over local government decisions occur with variations in women's ages, marital status, or frequency of attendance at religious services. However, women with higher levels of education and family income are more interested in politics and more likely to perceive themselves as having influence over local public officials' decisions. Those with higher levels of family income also are more trusting of public officials. Those who are employed outside the home are also more trusting of public officials and have higher levels of political interest.

Political Participation by Gender and by Citizenship

Is there a gender gap between Asian American men and women in their patterns of political participation? Examining voter registration and voter turnout among those who are citizens, four-fifths of both men and women are registered to vote. Based on self-reports of voter turnout by citizens, 64 percent of the women and 66 percent of the men voted in the 2000 presidential election. Neither are there gender differences in voting registration and participation in activities beyond voting. Differences do exist between U.S.-born and foreign-born citizens in their reported levels of voter registration, with 85 percent of U.S.-born men and 78 percent of the foreign-born men being registered. Among women, 85 percent of the U.S.-born and 76 percent of the foreign-born are registered to vote.

Those who are not citizens may participate in activities other than voting. Survey participants were queried about engaging in nine types of political activities other than voting during the past four years. Sixty-one percent of the women in the sample and 50 percent of the men report that they had not engaged in any type of political activity beyond voting in the prior four years. Twenty-four percent of the men and 20 percent of the women had been involved in at least one type, and 25 percent of the men and 18 percent of the women in at least two types of political activity beyond voting. Asian American men and women are not equally likely to participate in political activity that supports an Asian American candidate or issue concern. Men more frequently engage in that type of political activity, with 23 percent of the men and 17 percent of the women reporting activity in support of an Asian American candidate or issue during the previous four years.

Are there differences in the types of participation activities engaged in by men and women and by those who are citizens and those who are not? Table 6.2e shows that, although noncitizens do participate in a number of types of political activities other than voting, with one exception the proportion of noncitizens participating in any of the activities examined is lower than the proportion of

Table 6.2e Proportion Engaging in Participation Acts by Gender and by Citizenship

	NONCITIZENS			CITIZENS		
	MEN	WOMEN	GENDER DIFFERENCE SIGNIFICANT?	MEN	WOMEN	GENDER DIFFERENCE SIGNIFICANT?
write government official	7%	4%	no	14%	13%	no
contact editor	7	7	no	8	6	no
give money	8	5	no	18	11	yes
attend meeting, rally or fund-raiser	9	4	yes	21	15	yes
work with others to solve community problems	15	12	no	28	20	yes
sign petitions	8	9	no	21	18	no
serve on government board or commission	2	1	no	2	3	no
take part in protest or demonstration	5	4	no	10	7	yes
other activity	–	–	–	3	3	no

citizens participating. That one exception is women who are not citizens may write or talk to editors more frequently than women who are citizens. Among noncitizens, men report higher levels of political activity, except in signing petitions. Among citizens, men are also more politically active than women, except that a higher proportion of women report serving on a government board or commission. Noncitizen men are significantly more likely than noncitizen women to engage in four types of political activity. Among citizens, men are significantly more likely than women to engage in only one type of political activitiy.

Candidate Choice and Issue Concerns

Asian American men and women differ significantly in candidate support among those who voted in the 2000 presidential election (Table 6.2f). A higher proportion of women than men voted for the Democratic presidential candidate Albert Gore (60 percent versus 51 percent). Only 28 percent of the men and 23 percent of the women reported voting for Republican candidate George W. Bush.

Do Asian American men and women differ in their willingness to vote for an Asian American candidate even if they perceive the Asian American to be less qualified than a non-Asian American running for the same office? Only a small proportion respond positively and gender is not significant in willingness to make an ethnic-based vote choice. Fifteen percent of the women and 14 percent of the men indicate that they would vote for the Asian American even if the other candidate were more qualified.

Prior research demonstrates the existence of gender differences on a variety of issue attitudes among the mass public (Baxter and Lansing, 1975; Poole and Zeigler, 1985; Shapiro and Mahajam, 1986; Clark and Clark, 1996; Conway, Steuernagel, and Ahern, 1997). Women tend to be more liberal on social welfare policies, environmental issues, aid to the disadvantaged, education policy, and health issues. Women are more opposed to the use of force to solve either domestic or foreign policy problems. One explanation for such differences may be that men and women have different perceptions of what are the most important problems facing their families and their communities.

Respondents to the survey were asked what they considered the most important problem facing their ethnic group's people in the United States. One fifth of both men and women respondents did not answer the question. Those who did nominate a most important problem were asked if another problem were almost as important. Both responses, if two were given, are coded into the "most important problem" set of categories. Approximately equal proportions of men and women (slightly more than 10 percent) indicate that unemployment or inadequate job opportunities are an important problem and that racial and ethnic relations are also an important problem (12 percent). Also cited is a

Table 6.2f Percentage Distributions of Candidate Choice and Policy Preference by Gender

	MEN	WOMEN	ALL
2000 Presidential Vote (among Voters)*			
for Gore	51%	60%	55%
for Bush	28	23	26
N	281	256	537
Prefer Asian American Candidate			
yes	60	61	60
no	23	21	22
not sure	17	19	18
*Attitude toward Affirmative Action for Asian Americans**			
a good thing	64	62	63
a bad thing	7	5	6
no matter	19	18	19
not sure	9	14	11
*Providing Special Preferences in Hiring and Promotion for Asian Americans**			
strongly favor	16	14	15
favor	21	23	22
neither	22	21	22
oppose	23	23	23
strongly oppose	11	6	9
Not Sure	6	10	8
*Permitting Non-U.S. Citizens to Make Political Contributions**			
no opinion	15	18	17
strongly disagree	15	9	12
disagree	5	3	4
somewhat disagree	4	5	5
neither agree nor disagree	14	13	14
somewhat agree	13	14	13
agree	8	7	8
strongly agree	26	31	28
*Government Should Provide Bilingual Services**			
no opinion	5	7	6
strongly disagree	5	6	5
disagree	4	1	3
somewhat disagree	3	3	3
neither agree nor disagree	12	9	10
somewhat agree	12	12	12
agree	8	5	7
strongly agree	52	56	54

Source and Note: See Table 6.2a.

concern over loss of culture, which is viewed as a problem by 6 percent of the women and 8 percent of the men, and government insensitivity to the group's concerns or a lack of representation in government (7 percent of the men and 5 percent of the women). Discrimination is viewed as a problem by 5 percent of the men and 6 percent of the women.

Other differences in perceptions of several types of problems exist. These include personal inability to speak English well enough and acculturation issues (19 percent of the men and 24 percent of the women) and too much fighting within the ethnic community (6 percent of the men and 4 percent of the women). Although very few nominate pollution and overcrowding due to immigration as significant problems, women are significantly more likely to do so than men. Less than 5 percent nominate crime, drugs, education, affordable housing, moral decline, or family structure breakdown as community problems, and no significant differences exist among men or women in their concerns with these problems.

Attitude toward Affirmative Action and Other Policies

The survey includes several items focusing on affirmative action policies as they affect Asian Americans. Survey respondents were first provided with a definition of affirmative action, which is: "Affirmative action refers to any measure, policy, or law used to increase diversity or rectify discriminations that qualified individuals have equal access to employment, education, business, and contracting." Then they were asked: "Generally speaking, do you think affirmative action is a good thing or a bad thing for Asian Americans, or doesn't it affect Asian Americans much?" Among the men, 64 percent think affirmative action is a good thing for Asian Americans, 7 percent a bad thing, and 19 percent respond that it does not affect Asian Americans. Sixty-two percent of the women believe it is a good thing, 5 percent a bad thing, and 18 percent think that it does not affect Asian Americans. Nine percent of the men are not sure whether affirmative action is a good or bad policy, compared to 14 percent of the women.

When queried about specific affirmative action policies, the proportions of both men and women who think such policies are a good thing declines substantially. When asked if they support special preferences in hiring and promoting Asian Americans, 16 percent of the men and 14 percent of the women strongly favor the policy. Greater proportions of both men and women are opposed, with 23 percent of both women and men opposing the policy, and 11 percent of the men and 6 percent of the women strongly opposing it. Approximately one-fifth of both the men and women think it does not affect Asian Americans much, but more women than men are not sure how to answer the question. Support for affirmative action is higher when it deals with providing special assistance in education and job training for Asian Americans, but no gender differences are evident on this issue.

Gender differences do exist in Asian Americans' opinions toward two other policy areas. First, women are more likely to strongly agree and men are more likely to strongly disagree on permitting noncitizens to make political contributions in the United States. Second, although the majority of both men and women support demanding the U.S. government to provide public information and services important to the immigrant community in the immigrants' native languages as well as in English, a higher percentage of women than men strongly support such a policy.

Summary of Aggregate-Level Findings

The above discussion of gender differences in percentage terms helps identify areas where gender gaps may or may not be substantial. Primarily, Asian American men and women in the survey do not differ much in basic sociodemographic background, socialization context, adaptation experiences as cultural and racial minorities, participation in ethnic and church associations, and voting participation rates. However, a higher percentage of Asian American men than women identify themselves with U.S.-based (ethnic) labels. Compared to Asian American women, Asian American men receive more contacts from a political party, political groups, and individuals for a political cause, and they are more likely to be Republican. They show a higher level of political interest and knowledge, participate in more activities beyond voting, are more trusting in their local and state government officials, are more likely to perceive government as responsive to their needs, and feel more efficacious about their own influence over local government decisions. Asian American women are more likely than men to vote for a Democratic candidate, even though they are not more likely than men to identify with the Democratic Party. A higher percentage of women than men are uncertain of their political partisanship, ideology, and policy preferences, but women also take somewhat more compassionate policy positions that include greater support for noncitizens' right to participate in the political process via campaign donations and for the government to provide language services to immigrants. These findings suggest that, where gender matters in the aggregate, it plays a role among Asian Americans that bears similarity to the role gender plays in structuring the political attitudes and behavior of the white majority. Nevertheless, they also show that, in order to understand the role of gender for Asian Americans, it is often necessary to examine its intersections with nativity, ethnicity, and citizenship.

The Significance of Gender: Multivariate Results

How significant is gender as a factor in structuring the political attitudes and behavior of Asian Americans? Some of the observed gender gaps at the aggregate level may disappear after controlling for potential confounding factors. To understand the unique contribution of gender relative to other factors, a series of multivariate regression analyses are estimated that control for the following sets of variables (see the Appendix for question wording and coding): respondent's ethnicity or country of origin (Filipino, Korean, South Asian, Japanese, and Vietnamese, with the comparison being Chinese Americans); three measures of the sociopsychological bases of ethnic identity (belief in shared culture, sense of common or linked fate, and interest in ethnic news); respondent's level of political integration as indicated by his/her strength of identification with a mainstream political party and ideology, holding U.S. citizenship or having the expectation of acquiring citizen status, levels of activism in Asian American organizations and in religious or faith-based institutions, and level of participation in political campaigns involving Asian American candidates or issues; respondent's level of acculturation as indicated by his/her reliance on English to communicate at home, in business settings, and to receive information and entertainment from the mass media; four measures of everyday interracial interactions (attitude toward intermarriage, residence in a mostly white neighborhood, intimate friendships with whites, and experience with ethnic discrimination); and respondent's socialization in the United States (immigration generation, proportion of respondent's life in the United States, and whether his/her majority education was outside the United States). In addition, controls for sociodemographic background characteristics such as education, family income, gender, age, length of residence in a community, employment status, and marital status are included in the analyses.[1]

When gender is entered in multivariate regression models as one of the possible predictors of political attitudes and behavior, findings presented elsewhere in the book suggest that it is relatively insignificant as an independent factor in predicting patterns of political attitudes (political ideology, partisanship, political interest, political trust, perceived government responsiveness, perceived influence over local government decisions, and attitude toward affirmative action policies). Multivariate analyses also indicate that gender is not significant in explaining several types of political behavior (voting, registration, participation beyond voting, voting for presidential candidates, and voting for ethnic candidates).[2] In other words, whatever gender differences exist in the political experiences of Asian Americans may be mostly a function of their differences in ethnic origin, nativity, levels of sociopsychological and political attachment, degrees of cultural and social adaptation, and, to some extent, class.

In separate analyses of the political attitudes of men and women, some of these independent variables are significant in explaining both men's and women's political orientations as measured by political interest, trust, perceived influence over local government decisions, and perceived responsiveness of local government officials. The variables that contribute to explaining levels of political interest among both men and women include a sense of linked fate with other Asian Americans, following news stories about Asian Americans, following news stories about events in Asia, strength of party identification, level of educational attainment, and participation in support of Asian American issues or candidates.[3] However, while several variables explain patterns of political trust among men and among women, only one variable contributes to explaining trust patterns of both men and women. That one variable is experiencing discrimination. Greater commonality of significant explanatory variables exists in accounting for patterns of perceived influence over local government decisions. Significant in explaining both men and women's perceptions are being Filipino American, South Asian American, or Vietnamese American, believing Asian Americans share a linked fate, following news stories about Asian Americans and about events in Asia, strength of party identification, participation in support of Asian American issues or candidates, and level of educational attainment. Only two variables—being Korean American and experiencing discrimination—contribute to explaining both women's and men's perceived responsiveness of local government officials to complaints.

After controlling for other factors, gender remains significant in predicting respondents' ethnic self-identification and the likelihood of being contacted by individuals in political mobilization efforts. Specifically, other conditions being equal, Asian American women are less likely than Asian American men to adopt a panethnic self-identification as "Asian American" (or other U.S.-based identities as "American" or "ethnic American").[4] Asian American women are also less likely than Asian American men to become targets of political mobilization by individuals they know. What explains the continuing significance of gender in ethnic identity formation and in political mobilization by individuals?

In the balance of this chapter, the sources of gender differences—in making ethnic identity choices, adopting panethnic identity, and in political contacting by individuals—are examined by comparing the relative efficacy of the same variables in the female-only and male-only subsamples. Multinomial regression, a statistical procedure introduced in Chapter 2, is used to estimate ethnic self-identity choices among Asian American women (Table 6.3a) and among Asian American men (Table 6.3b). Logistic regression, a statistical procedure appropriate for analyzing dependent variables that have only two values, is used to estimate the acquisition of panethnicity and the likelihood of individual mobilization. In Tables 6.4 and 6.5, the first set of columns report results assessing the relative significance of gender within the full sample, the second and third set of columns report results of the same variables within respondents of each gender.

Making Ethnic Identity Choices

How different are Asian American women from Asian American men in the predictors of their ethnic self-identity choices? Results in Table 6.3a and 6.3b show that, for both women and men, the ethnic-origin measures are significant

Table 6.3a Predicting Ethnic Identity Choices among Asian American Women

	AMERICAN		ASIAN AMERICAN		ETHNIC AMERICAN	
	b	s.e.	b	s.e.	b	s.e.
Ethnic Origin (ref=Chinese, Korean, Vietnamese)						
Filipino	2.148*	.951	.423	.514	.598	.398
Japanese	1.929^	1.111	.341	.757	.140	.625
South Asian	3.506**	1.032	2.220**	.649	.701	.599
Political Integration and Civic Participation						
Republican partisanship	1.495^	.828	1.348*	.589	.936^	.509
liberal ideology	−.648	.698	−1.042^	.572	−.845^	.445
citizenship status	2.686*	1.281	1.967**	.614	2.161**	.447
ethnic organization membership	−.430	.609	−.988^	.587	.304	.429
participation in Asian America causes	2.462	2.287	4.458*	1.895	2.172	1.705
Acculturation/Racial Interaction						
English language use	1.806	1.609	1.461	.954	.486	.711
support intermarriage	.514	.805	.004	.606	−.284	.457
white close friends	.532	.468	.214	.391	.810*	.299
experience with discrimination	−1.162^	.640	−.133	.488	−.622^	.383
Socialization and Social Connectedness						
education	1.227	1.006	.158	.706	.259	.537
age	3.666**	1.222	2.859**	.972	1.766*	.744
married	−.638	.469	−.106	.385	−.242	.297
employed	.155	.486	.875*	.384	.054	.274
immigration generation	1.467**	.469	.697	.427	.653^	.387
non-U.S. education	−2.047**	.715	−.925*	.451	−.827*	.364
(Intercept)	−9.186	1.796	−5.091	1.026	−2.709	.784

N=462
−2 Log Likelihood (Intercept only)=1180.55
Model Chi-Sq=306.48
Nagelkerke R-sq=.526; McFadden=.260

Note: The dependent is a categorical variable with four possible responses. The reference category is R's self-identity as "ethnic Asian." The parameters are estimated using multinomial regression procedures with rescaled independent variables where scores are to vary only between 0 and 1. Excluded variables are family income, length of community residence, white neighborhood, religiosity, democratic partisanship, and sociopsychological indicators. b=unstandarized logistic coefficient, s.e.=standard error, ^ .05 < p ≤.10 *.005 < p ≤.05 ** p ≤.005
Source: PNAAPS, 2000–2001.

Table 6.3b Predicting Ethnic Identity Choices among Asian American Men

	AMERICAN		ASIAN AMERICAN		ETHNIC AMERICAN	
	b	s.e.	b	s.e.	b	s.e.
Ethnic Origin or Primordial Ties (ref=Chinese, Korean, and Vietnamese)						
Filipino	1.986*	.739	.212	.458	.119	.399
Japanese	3.158**	.952	−.123	.757	−.031	.686
South Asian	2.979**	.810	1.736**	.532	1.220*	.486
Political Integration and Civic Participation						
Republican partisanship	1.624*	.698	−.439	.564	.004	.472
liberal ideology	.138	.666	.197	.472	−.085	.412
citizenship status	2.227*	.957	1.821**	.527	2.052**	.440
ethnic organization membership	−1.741*	.646	.258	.413	−.094	.373
participation in Asian American causes	2.589	1.771	1.430	1.344	.920	1.208
Acculturation/Racial Interaction						
English language use	3.215*	1.318	.509	.845	.477	.731
support intermarriage	1.179^	.716	1.086*	.517	.990*	.453
white close friends	−.274	.430	.068	.320	.098	.278
experience with discrimination	−.254	.595	−.284	.451	−.063	.388
Socialization and Social Connectedness						
education	−.091	.867	−.750	.580	.456	.499
age	3.599*	1.265	3.253**	.978	2.984**	.885
married	.769	.528	−.760*	.388	−.328	.347
employed	1.019*	.513	.759*	.385	.553^	.337
immigration generation	1.082*	.512	1.090*	.479	.924*	.457
non-U.S. education	−1.723*	.527	−1.142**	.390	−1.061**	.348
(Intercept)	−9.841	1.624	−3.923	.973	−3.765	.869

N=503
−2 Log Likelihood (Intercept only)=1326.24
Model Chi-Sq=303.19
Nagelkerke R-sq=.488; McFadden=.229

Source and Note: See Table 6.3a.

in explaining choosing "American" over "ethnic Asian" as their preferred ethnic identity. Ethnic origin is not useful in accounting for the choice of "Asian American" or "ethnic American" over "ethnic Asian," except that both South Asian men and women are more likely to self-identify as "Asian American" than are men and women of other ethnic origin groups. Among men, South Asians are also more likely to self-identify as "ethnic American" than other ethnic groups.

Several measures of political integration and civic participation are significant in accounting for patterns of ethnic self-identification. Stronger identification with the Republican Party is associated with the likelihood of "American" identification for both men and women, but it is only associated with the likelihood of "Asian American" and "ethnic American" identification among women. The strength of holding a liberal ideology negatively impacts the panethnic and ethnic American identification among women; it does not affect their "American" identification or any U.S.-based identification among men. For both men and women, having acquired or expecting to acquire U.S. citizenship is associated with the likelihood of identification with any of the U.S.-based identity modes. Women's membership in an ethnic organization may deter the formation of their panethnic identification; for men, it has greater effect on deterring the formation of their "American" identification. More participation for Asian American causes does not significantly impact the direction of ethnic self-identification for both men and women, but it has a positive effect on panethnic self-identification among women.

Turning to measures of acculturation and racial interaction, more use of English language is associated with identification as "American" among men. Support for racial/ethnic intermarriage is significant in explaining the likelihood of choosing any of the three U.S.-based identity modes among men but none of the three among women. Conversely, women who have close friends who are white are more likely to identify as "ethnic American" rather than "ethnic Asian," but having close friends who are white isn't significant in explaining ethnic identification patterns among men. Also, although having experienced racial/ethnic discrimination may not significantly impact self-identification among Asian American men, it may significantly deter women's choice in self-identifying as "ethnic American" and possibly as "American."

Among the socialization and social connectedness variables, age and immigration generation are positive predictors of the three identity modes for both men and women, while education is not a significant predictor of any identity mode for either men or women. Obtaining one's education outside the United States predicts negatively to all three identity modes among both men and women. Being employed is positively associated with men's probability of identification with all three identity modes, but it only increases women's chances of identification as "Asian American" over "ethnic Asian." Being married (over 90 percent to another Asian) may deter identification as "Asian American" among men, but marriage does not affect women's ethnic identity choices.

Adopting Panethnicity

In Table 6.4, predictors for selecting "Asian American" as a subjective identity for men, for women, and for all, either as a first preference or as a forced choice after the panethnic probe, (see Chapter 2 for description) are presented. The first column reports results for the full sample. Compared to gender, only a respondent's citizenship status may be more useful to predict an Asian American's

Table 6.4 Predicting the Adoption of Panethnic Self-Identification by Gender

	ALL		WOMEN		MEN	
	b	**s.e.**	**b**	**s.e.**	**b**	**s.e.**
Ethnic Origin (ref=Chinese)						
Filipino	.559*	.286	.713^	.410	.443	.431
Japanese	−.030	.356	.249	.505	−.224	.540
Korean	−.166	.239	−.113	.339	−.275	.364
South Asian	.463	.306	1.082*	.493	.147	.421
Vietnamese	.436	.311	.928^	.511	.055	.418
Sociopsychological Engagement						
shared culture	.566*	.256	−.096	.381	1.167**	.364
linked fate	.417*	.206	.654*	.297	.131	.306
ethnic news interest	.704*	.289	1.177*	.425	.468	.421
Political Integration and Civic Participation						
democratic partisanship	.469*	.207	.321	.298	.668*	.305
liberal ideology	−.571*	.249	−.566	.378	−.554	.348
citizenship status	.746**	.255	1.121**	.384	.633^	.370
participation in Asian American causes	1.816*	.779	−.095	1.074	3.487*	1.300
Acculturation/Racial Interaction						
English language use	.165	.418	.623	.603	−.339	.637
support Intermarriage	.391	.268	−.106	.394	.809*	.390
white close friends	.192	.163	−.144	.240	.605*	.242
experience with discrimination	−.003	.220	.181	.308	−.164	.326
Socialization and Social Connectedness						
education	−.185	.297	.011	.462	−.303	.416
age	−.390	.406	−.572	.592	−.034	.603
employed	.097	.165	.189	.230	.072	.256
immigration generation	−.008	.167	−.150	.229	.014	.263
non-U.S. education	−.223	.194	−.673*	.299	.072	.269
female	−.690**	.150				
(Constant)	−.870	.483	−1.519	.668	−1.009	.714
N	910		429		481	
−2 Log Likelihood	1106.34		532.08		539.44	
Model Chi-sq(22,21)	114.38		62.25		59.13	
Negelkerke R-sq	.160		.180		.162	

Source and Note: See Table 6.3a. The dependent variable is a dichotomous variable indicating the presence of R's self-identification as Asian American both as a primary and secondary preference. The parameters are estimated using logistic regression procedures with rescaled independent variables where scores are to vary only between 0 and 1. Excluded variables are Republican partisanship, family income, length of community residence, and marital status.

likelihood to self-identify with the panethnic "Asian American" label. Indicators of ethnic culture; sense of shared culture and linked fate; interest in ethnic news, political partisanship, and ideology; and political activism for ethnic causes are comparatively less useful than gender in predicting the adoption of panethnic identification. Each of the above, however, is more useful than measures of cultural and social integration or indicators of socialization and social connectedness in predicting panethnicity.

Comparing the results for women and men in Table 6.4, women of South Asian, Vietnamese, and Filipino origins may be more likely to adopt panethnic identification than Chinese American women. Ethnic origin is not a significant predictor of panethnicity among Asian American men. Neither are indicators of sociopsychological engagement equally useful, with perception of shared culture the only useful predictor for men and the only useless predictor for women. Among measures of political integration and participation, democratic partisanship and political activism for ethnic causes are useful for predicting greater panethnicity for men but not for women, while citizenship status is a stronger predictor for women than for men. Among indicators of cultural and social adaptation, men who support intermarriage and have close friends who are white may be significantly more likely than other men to adopt panethnicity. The same is not true among women. Women who received their education mostly outside United States are significantly less likely to adopt panethnicity, but place of education is not significant for men. However, for both women and men, variables such as political ideology, English language use, experiences of discrimination, and basic sociodemographic background are insignificant in predicting the adoption of panethnicity among Asian Americans.

Political Mobilization by Individuals

Table 6.5 predicts the chance for Asian Americans as a whole and for men or women respectively to become targets of individual political mobilization efforts. Among the logistic coefficients for the full sample (the "all" column), gender is a significant predictor of individual mobilization, as are education, citizenship status, ethnic organization membership, having close friends who are white, and being Vietnamese. Comparing the results for women and men in the same table, no differences exist between Chinese women and other women and only a marginal difference exists between Chinese men and Vietnamese men, but not other groups of men, in their likelihood of being contacted by individual activists. Possessing U.S. citizenship or expecting citizenship may significantly increase men's likelihood of receiving individual mobilization efforts, but citizenship status only has a marginal effect on women. Having close friends who are white increases the likelihood of men receiving mobilization contacts from individuals, but that variable is not significant in explaining political

Table 6.5b Estimating Gender Differences in Political Mobilization by Individuals

	ALL		WOMEN		MEN	
	b	s.e.	b	s.e.	b	s.e.
Ethnic Origin (ref=Chinese)						
Filipino	−.146	.339	−.409	.541	−.089	.447
Japanese	−.191	.398	−.796	.639	.272	.520
Korean	−.060	.334	−.232	.499	−.082	.457
South Asian	−.224	.360	−.628	.606	−.095	.465
Vietnamese	−.954*	.446	−.891	.831	−.963ˆ	.544
Political and Social Integration						
citizenship status	1.338**	.364	.871ˆ	.538	1.718**	.501
ethnic organization membership	1.078**	.209	1.275**	.336	1.078**	.281
religious attendance	−.189	.252	−.417	.398	.028	.340
English language use	.609	.504	.379	.751	.860	.694
white neighborhood	−.193	.205	−.295	.327	−.141	.271
white close friends	.563**	.180	.235	.288	.825**	.242
Socialization and Social Connectedness						
education	1.634**	.395	2.164**	.667	1.475**	.506
age	.331	.506	.285	.762	.797	.709
family income	.431	.370	.545	.578	.193	.495
employed	.110	.208	−.165	.303	.515ˆ	.305
married	.042	.203	.171	.308	−.161	.283
immigration generation	.128	.172	.474ˆ	.257	−.129	.240
female	−.494**	.177				
(Constant)	−4.485	.514	−4.765	.746	−5.052	.732
N	1013		490		523	
−2 Log Likelihood	861.50		368.86		479.90	
Model Chi-sq(18,17)	142.26		57.35		88.28	
Negelkerke R-sq	.208		.190		.234	

Source and Note: See Table 6.4. The dependent variable is a dichotomous variable indicating R has been contacted by an acquaintance to vote, donate money to a political cause, or participate in other political activities.

mobilization contacts directed at women. In at least nine out of ten times, men who are employed and women who have longer family histories in the United States tend to be contacted more frequently. For both men and women, their likelihood of individual contact may increase with ethnic-organization affiliation and better education, with education having a stronger effect on women. For both genders, their chance of mobilization contact by individuals may not be significantly impacted by their frequency of attending religious services, English language use at home or in business settings, residing in a white neighborhood, or age, income, and marital status.

Conclusion

This chapter reviews the theoretical and empirical perspectives of the relationships between gender and political opinion. Limited past research has reported few gender differences in the political attitudes and behavior of Asian Americans. Utilizing a new dataset that surveys the political and social experiences of Asian American adults of multiple ethnicities, native tongues, and residential regions, the contours and impacts of gender on political orientations and behavior of Asian Americans has been examined in this chapter. At the aggregate level, although Asian American men and women do not differ in many aspects of social attributes, socialization experiences, and voting participation, they do differ in political orientations and other attitudes and behavior (e.g., political interest and knowledge, political trust, personal efficacy, perceived government responsiveness, presidential vote, party and individual mobilization, and participation beyond voting). Women have lower levels of political awareness than men and are less likely to trust local government or perceive government as responsive to complaints from people like them. Political mobilizing agents—both political parties and individuals—are less likely to contact women than men. Women tend to engage in fewer kinds of different political activities, they less are likely to be active in an organization that supports Asian American candidates or issues, and they are less likely to be active in support of Asian American causes. Some problems perceived as important by men are not perceived as important by women and vice versa. Moreover, the patterns of the gender gaps in political participation and political attitudes often become more evident when factors such as nativity, citizenship, and ethnicity are taken into account.

It is apparent that Asian American men and women differ in some aspects of their political attitudes and behaviors. However, gender issues at the aggregate level may not remain issues at the individual level when confounding factors contributing to the observed percentage differences between men and women are controlled. Indeed, the research reported here demonstrates that for some variables of interest, gender is a relatively insignificant predictor of Asian American political attitudes and behaviors. The two exceptions are in explaining patterns of ethnic self-identification and the chance of being contacted by individuals for political mobilization. Other conditions being equal, Asian American women are less likely than Asian American men to adopt the panethnic self-identification of "Asian American" and less likely to become targets of political mobilization by individuals they know. Comparing multivariate regression results analyzing the effects of all the explanatory variables together on these two cases, the relative significance of gender varies according to the behavioral domain investigated. Gender plays a greater role in impacting a respondent's likelihood of adopting a panethnic identity than of being contacted by individuals for the purpose of political mobilization.

Importantly, some variables are not equally useful in explaining the patterns of men's and women's political attitudes and behavior. When the predictors of the dependent variables are examined in separate equations for men and women, it is quite evident that the same independent variables may have very different effects in accounting for the dependent variables. The evidence presented in the multivariate tables suggests that separate explanations must be sought to understand the patterns of political orientations and behaviors among Asian American men and women. Seeking different explanations is especially necessary regarding the impact of ethnic culture, citizenship status, educational context, and social networks.

CHAPTER 7

Conclusions and Implications

This book represents an attempt to provide a comprehensive, systematic study of Asian American political attitudes and behavior by using a unique data set, the PNAAPS. In this chapter, we first review key findings from each main chapter. The efficacy of the conceptual frameworks introduced in Chapter 1 is then appraised in light of these findings toward the twin purposes of understanding the political experiences of Asian Americans as well as the larger issues of race, ethnicity, international migration, and political incorporation in American politics and behavior. In the final section, we discuss the implications of our findings for community empowerment and for building political coalitions across race, ethnicity, nativity, class, and gender.

The Contours and Sources of Asian American Public Opinion: Main Chapter Findings

This section reports key findings from the PNAAPS participants concerning the opinion patterns and factors that may be associated with the formation of political attitudes and behavior examined in Chapters 2 through 6. In many cases, the findings detailed below call for more elucidation than we are able to provide in this book. We hope that this overview raises new questions and offers possible directions for future research. We anticipate that the summary of findings described below signifies an important starting point of an investigation into the political attitudes and behavior of Asian Americans.

Ethnic Identity

Ethnic self-identity among Asian Americans in the PNAAPS survey is multi-layered and prone to be influenced by the characteristics of the survey (such as question wording) and social context in which the survey is administered. It also varies greatly by respondents' ethnic origin. Most of the respondents prefer to identify themselves in ethnic-specific terms, with the percentage of ethnic American identifiers slightly higher than that of Asian ethnic identifiers. A relatively small proportion of respondents would identity themselves first and foremost as "Asian American," but the majority are able to identify with this panethnic term after given a forced choice.[1]

How Asian Americans choose their ethnic self-identity is influenced by their ethnic origin, prior socialization, and social connectedness. Filipinos, Japanese, and South Asians, compared to Chinese, are more likely to identify as

"American." Persons of South Asian descent, more than of other Asian descents, are also more likely to identify themselves as "Asian American" and "ethnic American." Reasons that account for these differences among ethnic groups may originate in the historical and cultural formation of each ethnic group on both sides of the Pacific, and to sort these out is an important task for future research. Those who were educated outside of the United States and are female are less likely to indicate U.S.-based identities. An increase in age has the opposite effect. We speculate that length of exposure to the U.S. system and socialization context, such as attending school outside of the United States, may account for some of these findings.

We find that there may be an inverse relationship between educational attainment and identification with the panethnic mode. For the total sample—which is majority immigrant—those with more education are less likely to adopt a panethnic self-identity as an initial choice. Among the foreign-born, these findings imply that education alone (mostly outside of the U.S. context) is not an adequate measure of acculturation. That is, education is not positively associated with the U.S.-based panethnic identity mode among the foreign-born. Among the U.S.-born, those with more education are also less likely to adopt panethnicity as a forced choice. While educational institutions, especially colleges and universities, are often considered a primary site for the development of individual identity, one should not assume that more education, in and of itself, leads to panethnic identity in particular.

Ethnic self-identification is also associated with the degree of cultural, social, and political integration among Asian Americans. Being or expecting to become a citizen and exhibiting supportive attitudes toward intermarriage are associated with a higher likelihood of self-identification with each of the U.S.-based identities, but they are not associated with the acquisition and intensity of panethnicity. It might be that the process of becoming American by citizenship leads to stronger identification with the American, Asian American, or ethnic American labels. Or, perhaps those with stronger U.S.-based identities are more interested in becoming U.S. citizens. For persons of Asian descent who come mostly from homogeneous societies, having an open attitude toward intermarriage may indicate a willingness to move beyond primordial ethnic boundaries toward an acceptance of a more inclusive panethnic form of identity. Stronger identification as Democrat is associated positively with the acquisition and strength of panethnic self-identity among immigrant respondents. Stronger identification as Republican, participation in Asian American causes, and employment are associated positively with the adoption of "American" and "Asian American" identities (compared to identity as an ethnic Asian), but membership in an ethnic organization has the opposite effect.[2] These results indicate that political and economic integration may facilitate the adoption of U.S.-based identities among Asian Americans.

Experiencing discrimination because of ethnic background is associated negatively with the adoption of any of the U.S.-based identity modes, but positively with the adoption of panethnicity as a forced choice among the U.S.-born. Affiliation with an ethnic organization or experience with discrimination are both likely to maintain ethnic-specific or race-based boundaries among Asian Americans—perhaps preventing the formation of U.S.-based identities for the majority-immigrant respondents. However, experience with discrimination might also make some Asian Americans, in this case the U.S.-born, aware of the need to coalesce as a panethnic community in some circumstances. The complex nature of identity is revealed in these findings.

Indicators of sociopsychological attachment to the ethnic community are only marginally useful in understanding ethnic identity preferences, but they are very useful in predicting the acquisition and the strength of self-identification with the panethnic "Asian American" label as a forced choice. Perceiving a shared culture among Asians is the only significant predictor of ethnic choices and it is associated positively with self-identification as "Asian American" over "ethnic Asian." Perceiving a shared culture and a panethnic linked fate as well as paying attention to Asian American news generally is related positively to the adoption and intensity of panethnic identification. Thus, beliefs among respondents that Asian Americans share some commonalities in terms of culture, fate, and community events (news) are likely reflected in their self-identification. On the other hand, indicators of acculturation and social–structural adaptation as well as of socialization and social ties appear to be less useful in understanding the adoption and intensity of panethnic self-identity.

Among immigrants, prior party membership and participation in the homeland is negatively associated with the acquisition and the intensity of a new ethnic identity (panethnicity), but feeling more efficacious about one's influence on government decisions in the United States than in the homeland is positively associated with the adoption of panethnicity. Neither frequency of contact with the homeland, participation in homeland politics in the United States, nor a plan to return to Asia has any independent impact on the adoption of panethnic self-identity.

The findings reviewed above illustrate the complicated nature of ethnic identity and its relationship with factors that contribute to ethnic identity formation among Asian Americans. The findings point to the need to revise the extant literature, which is mostly informed by observing attitudes and behavior of the U.S.-born. The results also suggest that it would be a mistake to assume that ethnic-specific identities and panethnic identities are necessarily mutually exclusive, or that one mode is more critical for political participation and empowerment among Asian Americans than another. Rather, it is important to consider the extent to which ethnic-specific and panethnic identity exist simultaneously, each with the potential to serve as a resource for the development of political attitudes and participation in the United States.[3]

Political Orientations

Asian Americans who took part in the PNAAPS survey are more liberal than conservative in political ideology. Factors that predict stronger liberal ideology are ethnic origin (being South Asian, Japanese, or Vietnamese), paying greater attention to news regarding Asians and Asian Americans, working for Asian American candidates or causes, Democratic partisanship, and educational achievement. Within the Asian American community as a whole, however, there are signs that ideological development is an on-going process—one in ten indicate that they are unsure of how to place themselves along the liberal-conservative scale.

Asian Americans demonstrate a high level of trust in local government officials in the United States, but low efficacy in their ability to influence local government decisions. About 8 in 10 respondents indicate that they feel they can trust local officials at least some of the time, but close to 7 in 10 do not think they have at lot or at least some influence on local government decisions. That so many Asian Americans feel disempowered when it comes to political decision-making may reflect the marginalization of Asian Americans by government institutions. A greater effort by local governments to reach out to the Asian American community through bilingual channels and active representation might address the lack of democratic inclusion that these findings seem to point toward. Such efforts are critical, because those who exhibit low levels of efficacy are in many cases also less likely to participate. Hence, lack of efficacy might lead to low levels of political participation, which in turn reinforces feelings of marginalization. Asian Americans are split on their ability to get local public officials to respond to their complaints. Immigrants, however, are generally more positive about their experiences with the U.S. government in terms of political trust and perceived ability to influence political decisions than in their home countries in Asia.

Most Asian Americans indicate that they are interested in politics. A majority of respondents report having either very high or moderate interest in political affairs. Political interest depends on ethnic origin (with South Asian, Japanese, or Vietnamese respondents being distinct from their Chinese counterparts) and is positively associated with paying greater attention to news regarding Asians and Asian Americans, working for Asian American candidates or causes, Democratic partisanship, and higher educational achievement. In addition, perception of a common or linked fate among Asian Americans, political knowledge, and perceived influence on government are also linked to more political interest. These findings indicate a cluster of attributes that characterize the politically interested among Asian Americans. For example, those that are more interested in politics are also the most likely to acquire knowledge about politics, watch news about Asian Americans, and be active in their panethnic communities. They are educated and exhibit feelings of political efficacy, as well. However, higher family income and education outside of the United States are negatively associated with interest in politics and governmental matters. The latter relationship may have to do with the non-U.S. political socialization context, while the relationship between income and interest may appear to perpetuate the "puzzle" over the effect of income observed, once again, by comparing Asian Americans to the mostly U.S.-born population. As with the case of education, greater income achievement among contemporary Asian Americans—who are mostly middle-class, adult immigrants—cannot be readily interpreted as indicators of economic or social incorporation.

Experience with racial discrimination is associated strongly and negatively with trust in government. It may be that Asian Americans who experience racism in the United States feel that government officials cannot be trusted if they are part of a political system that allows for such negative experiences. It may also be the case that those who trust government officials the least are most likely to report racial discrimination, perhaps because they are more critical of the political and social system in the United States in general.

Experience with racial discrimination is also negatively associated with evaluations of government responsiveness, as is involvement in campaigns for ethnic candidates and causes. One possible explanation for the negative relationship of the latter may be that persons who are dissatisfied with the governmental status quo seek solutions within the community by working for ethnic candidates and issues. Factors that have a positive and independent association with perceived government responsiveness are perceived ability to influence the government, liberal ideology, Republican partisanship, participation in religious services, membership in ethnic organizations, and a non-U.S. education. Clearly, these results, especially the somewhat contradictory findings having to do with liberal ideology and Republican partisanship, deserve further investigation in the future.

In addition, we find that Korean Americans are less likely than their Chinese American counterparts to express confidence in American government responsiveness. We can only speculate about the reasons for these ethnic differences. One explanation might be that, among some people in the Korean community, the official government response was seen as inadequate when Korean-owned shops in Los Angeles were damaged during the unrest of 1992.

Factors that are associated with a greater belief in one's ability to influence the government are ethnic origin (being Filipino, South Asian, Japanese, and Vietnamese), belief in a panethnic linked fate, political interest and knowledge, liberal ideology, being or expecting to be a citizen, religious activism, participation for ethnic candidates or causes, and being employed. In 90 percent of cases, having a higher income is negatively associated with evaluations of political influence. Despite the cliché that money is power, money does not seem to buy feelings of greater political power for Asian Americans in this study.

Among immigrants who took the survey, homeland ties have little influence on their political orientations. Their ethnic origin makes little difference in predicting levels of political interest and trust, but being Japanese or Korean is associated with more negative evaluations of government responsiveness and Filipinos, Japanese, and South Asians are more likely to have positive attitudes about their political influence. Among Asian Americans in the survey, an experiences with racial discrimination is associated with less political trust, fewer evaluations of government responsiveness, and less perceived ability to influence government decisions. Their sense of a common fate with other Asian Americans is positively associated with their sense of political trust and government responsiveness. Their Democratic partisanship is positively associated with liberal ideology and political interest, but negatively associated with political trust. Their Republican partisanship is associated positively with perceived government responsiveness and negatively associated with liberal ideology. Being older is associated with greater political trust but lower perceived influence.

Political Partisanship

Despite past discrimination and continuing marginalization by American political parties, every two in three Asian Americans in the survey report identification with traditional partisan labels either as partisans or Independents who lean toward one of the two major parties. As partisans, they are decidedly more Democratic (36 percent) than Republican (16 percent) in political partisanship, except for the Vietnamese. However, more than one in ten (13 percent) prefer to identify with a third party. Different ethnic groups acquire partisanship at different rates. Furthermore, nonpartisanship is lowest among Filipinos and South Asians and highest among the Chinese and the Vietnamese.

At the aggregate level, partisanship correlates with better education, higher income, employment, being male, (but not age or length of time spent in a community), greater integration into the U.S. society (by being U.S.-born, U.S.-educated, a citizen or expecting to become citizen, or more years lived in the United States), experiences with discrimination, having a stronger sense of linked fate, stronger civic institutional ties, and greater political interest and knowledge. Once possible intervening factors are accounted for using multivariate techniques, some of these variables—such as family income, gender, English language use, length of community residence, citizenship status, and experience of racial discrimination—are no longer significant in predicting partisanship.

As people become more familiar with American parties through exposure to the political system (e.g., ideological strength, political knowledge, employment, age, percent of one's life spent in the United States), they are also more likely to develop an American party identification. Other conditions being equal, political interest and a sense of linked fate alone are more useful to predict the acquisition of Democratic partisanship. Indicators of civic institutional connectedness such as community organizational membership, frequency of attending religious services, and educational context are more useful in predicting the acquisition of Republican partisanship. Education and ethnic origin alone are useful for predicting an Independent political status.

Among the Asian American immigrants in the survey, maintaining contacts with the country of origin does not affect the acquisition of partisanship. However, those who are involved currently in politics regarding the country of origin or who have plans to return to their country of origin are more likely to report (Republican) partisanship. In nine out of ten instances, prior partisanship in the home county is negatively associated with the acquisition of Democratic partisanship; perceiving greater government responsiveness and a greater ability to influence government in the United States than in the homeland is associated with third-party identification. Perhaps prior partisan attachments interfere with the development of new partisanship in the United States. Among homeland ties, only the plan to return may predict the strength of mainstream partisanship.

Partisanship is a strong predictor of U.S. presidential vote choice, but, somewhat surprisingly, it has virtually no relationship to attitudes toward affirmative action policies. Republican identifiers are less likely than nonidentifiers to support bilingual education programs. Contact by a political party or group is negatively associated with support for an ethnic candidate or for affirmative action as a principle. These findings show that the significance and degree of party influence depend on the type of political behavior and policy domains examined, as well as on the measures of party influence used. They also show that elements of the two-party system occupy a central place in the lives of many Asian Americans. However, those who are more attached to or contacted by the two major parties may sometimes develop voting preferences and policy positions that are antithetical to the main interests of the nonwhite, majority-immigrant community.

Political Participation

Although just over 4 in 10 Asian Americans in the survey report voting in 2000, over 8 in 10 who have overcome the hurdles of citizenship and registration showed up at the polls. Participation rates vary according to ethnic group and type of political activity. For example, Japanese Americans demonstrate the highest rates of registering to vote and voting. Filipino Americans, in general, follow closely behind in terms of registration and voting participation. In comparison, the other ethnic groups in this study are characterized by much lower rates of registration and voting. Participation rates in activities beyond voting are highest among South Asians and lowest among the Vietnamese.

Consistent with past studies, variables related to socioeconomic status are independently significant for predicting the political participation of Asian Americans. Although education matters more for voting than for registration or other types of political activities, family income matters more for activities other than voting than for registration or voting. Moreover, greater family income is associated with lower, rather than higher, turnout among the registered. The combined results from both bivariate and multivariate analyses demonstrate a need for reconceptualizing the dominant and positive role of the basic socioeconomic status in the political participation of a nonwhite, predominantly foreign-born, and relatively affluent population such as Asian Americans.

Multivariate analyses show that being a member of an Asian American organization, having feelings of linked fate with others of the same racial background, and experiences with racial discrimination are positive and statistically significant predictors of political participation beyond voting, but not voting. Church attendance is strongly associated with voting, but not with registration or participation beyond voting. Indicators of political engagement (political interest, knowledge, and influence) positively influence both voting in 2000 and participation in other political activities. In contrast to past research on the larger population, in general, partisan strength and ideology do not have much influence on political participation, voting or otherwise. Mobilization by a political party through contact predicts more registration, more consistent turnout, and more participation beyond voting in the total sample. Political mobilization by an individual predicts participation beyond voting and registration in both the total and the immigrant-only sample. Those who are educated outside of the United States are less likely to participate beyond voting, but those immigrants who are active in politics related to their country of origin are more likely to be involved in activities beyond voting in the United States, as well.

Gender Gaps

Gender gaps among Asian Americans are more evident in political attitudes and behavior compared to many aspects of social attributes and socialization experiences. Like the majority of other American women, Asian American women have lower levels of political awareness than men and are less likely to trust local government or perceive government as responsive to complaints from people like them. They are less likely to be targets of political mobilization, be active in an organization that supports Asian American candidates or issues, or be active in support of Asian American causes. They tend to engage in fewer kinds of diverse political activities. However, Asian American women who crossed the barriers of citizenship and voting registration requirements do not differ from Asian American men in voting participation rates.

Among survey respondents, gender in and by itself is a relatively insignificant independent predictor of Asian American political attitudes and behavior. While gender matters at the aggregate level, it mostly disappears at the individual level when confounding factors contributing to the observed percentage differences between men and women are controlled. However, Asian

American women in the survey remain less likely than Asian American men to adopt a panethnic self-identification as "Asian American" and to become targets of political mobilization by individuals they know, even after controlling for possible confounding factors of gender gaps. Moreover, more often than not, the same variables may not be equally useful to explain the patterns of men's and women's political attitudes and behavior. The multivariate results suggest that separate explanations must be sought to understand the sources of ethnic self-identification choices, panethnic identification, and political contacts by individuals among Asian American men and women.

Implications for Conceptual Frameworks on Immigrant Adaptation and Political Incorporation

Chapter 1 makes the argument that the Asian American population, because of its nonwhite, ethnically diverse, relatively affluent, and predominantly immigrant characteristics, presents an ideal opportunity for researchers to explore and validate theories on immigrant adaptation and political incorporation developed by observing the behavior of mostly white European immigrants and, to a much lesser extent, native nonwhite groups. Four leading conceptual frameworks are reviewed: assimilation/acculturation, segmented assimilation, transnationalism, and racial formation/panethnicization. Based on preliminary findings of the PNAAPS, the adequacy of each framework in and of itself to comprehend the Asian American experience is called into question. A composite conceptual model that incorporates key features of the major frameworks is proposed to appraise the independent contribution and relative efficacy of components in each conceptual approach. Survey findings presented in Chapters 2 through 6 and reviewed in the preceding section of this chapter confirm that the experiences of Asian Americans present important challenges to any single theoretical framework for understanding political incorporation in the American context for this fast-growing population. Below we elaborate on that thesis by focusing on selected variables used in the multivariate analyses presented in the previous chapters. We demonstrate the need to reconsider current conceptualizations of the relationships among immigration, acculturation, integration, ethnic and political identity formation, and political participation.

English Language Use and Length of Stay

This assimilation/acculturation framework assigns a central role for English language acquisition, length of U.S. stay, socioeconomic status mobility, and social–structural integration to facilitate identity formation and political incorporation. This approach receives at best partial support from analyzing the opinion patterns of Asian Americans in the survey at the individual level. True, other conditions being equal, those who use English more to communicate at home, in business settings, and in consuming media and who are more supportive of intermarriage, are employed, and have spent a higher percentage of life in the United States prefer to identify themselves as "American" rather than "ethnic Asian." However, greater use of English does not contribute to the adoption of other U.S.-based self-identities nor panethnicity as a forced choice. Neither is it useful to predict political beliefs and attitudes toward government, except in increasing political interest among the foreign-born. More English use may be associated with higher levels of political participation and political partisanship, but only in models where political and civic institutional ties are not controlled. The significance of English language use, as well as family income, gender, and length of time spent in a community, disappears when variables more directly linked to political behavior are considered.

People who have spent more time in the United States (rather than in a particular community) are more likely to identify as "American" and to adopt major partisanship. Among immigrants, living for a longer period of time in the United States encourages identification as both Republican and Independent. However, other conditions being equal, neither the sheer length of time spent in the United States nor percentage of one's life spent in the United States predicts political orientations or participation.

Citizenship Status

Becoming a citizen is one of the first and direct indicators of political incorporation. It is important to note that the effects of citizenship manifest themselves most clearly in terms of opportunities to participate in formal political processes. The critical difference between U.S. citizens and noncitizens is that noncitizens are legally barred from voting registration and, thus, from voting. Possessing U.S. citizenship may strongly influence other domains of political behavior such as identity formation and political orientations, as well. Among Asian Americans in the survey, those who are citizens or expect to soon become citizens are more likely than noncitizens to identify with a U.S.-based identity mode rather than an "ethnic Asian" mode. Possessing U.S. citizenship or expecting citizenship is associated positively with the strength of mainstream partisanship for either the total or the foreign-born sample and the adoption of mainstream partisanship among immigrants. Citizens are also more likely to perceive that they have an influence over local government decisions than noncitizens. Citizenship status, however, does not independently impact the direction or strength of other political orientations. Neither does it significantly increase participation beyond voting or self-identification with panethnicity as a forced choice. The control of confounding factors leading to the acquisition of U.S. citizenship eliminates its direct significance in explaining political behavior in these instances. These inconsistent findings challenge prevailing assumptions about the central and indispensable role of U.S. citizenship in political participation and immigrant incorporation. Rather, greater emphasis may need to be placed on the antecedents of citizenship acquisition.

Education and Income

Among Asian Americans in the survey, more education predicts more voting among the eligible, and higher family income predicts more participation beyond voting. However, neither is significant in predicting voting registration among citizens, and more income is actually associated with less voting once possible confounding factors are controlled. Both education and income increase the strength of mainstream partisanship. Education is associated with greater identification with the two mainstream American political parties among immigrants, but with greater identification as politically Independent in the total sample. Unlike education, family income does not impact political partisanship or ethnic identity choices. Yet, more education does not facilitate self-identification as "American." Further, the relationship between education and panethnic self-identity is a negative one and it differs by nativity. Asian Americans as a whole and U.S.-born Asians with more education are less likely to consider themselves "Asian American" than their less educated counterparts. Education is associated with increased—but more family income with decreased—political interest in both the total and the foreign-born samples. Education increases the strength of identification with the liberal ideology, but only in the total sample. Neither education nor family income has any independent impact on evaluations of government.

The inconsistent and even puzzling findings in the roles of education and income—and, by the same token, language acquisition, length of exposure to the U.S. system, and citizenship status—in predicting patterns of political adaptation and incorporation of Asian Americans provide evidence to question the utility of the straight-line assimilation theory. They point to the need to focus on factors that may be more central to the daily experiences of Asian Americans. In addition, the relationship between educational and socioenomic achievement among Asians as a whole is likely to be weaker than that observed among the general U.S. population. The overpresentation of the foreign-educated professionals, the "astronaut" families, the glass ceiling phenomenon, the (perceived) language and cultural barriers, and other employment-related issues are some of the reasons that account for the greater disparity between educational attainment and income earnings among Asians. A discussion of the unique roles of educational context, homeland ties, and racial discrimination is in order.

Non-U.S. Education

More than being foreign-born, receiving an education mostly outside of the United States significantly discourages self-identification as a hyphenated or unhyphenated American. It also decreases the intensity of panethnic identification as a forced choice. Respondents with a non-U.S. education are less likely to be interested in politics and governmental matters, and they are less likely to participate in political activities beyond voting. Other conditions being equal, a non-U.S. education significantly decreases identification with the Republican

Party, but not necessarily with the Democratic Party or a third party. Neither does it impact *strength* of identification with major parties. A non-U.S. education does not independently affect patterns of political ideology or evaluations of trust and influence. However, respondents educated mostly outside of the United States are more likely to perceive U.S. local government officials as responsive to their complaints. They are also more likely to support voting for an ethnic candidate. Thus, place of education matters, but not at all times and in all aspects of political attitudes and behavior examined in this study.

Homeland Ties

A related concern to an immigrant community's likelihood to become politically incorporated is the immigrants' degree of involvement with people and government of the home country. Proponents of transnationalism would predict that the influence is very significant; the assimilation/acculturation perspective would predict that the influence is significant *and* negative. Among the immigrant portion of the PNAAPS, the impact of homeland ties is not always evident. When an impact does emerge, however, it is far from consistently negative. Although prior partisanship interferes with the adoption and the intensity of identification with the panethnic identity as well as the acquisition of Democratic partisanship, activism in homeland politics in the United States increases the likelihood of Republican identification as well as participation in activities beyond voting. Moreover, a plan to return to one's homeland is associated positively with identification as Republican over other parties, and the strength of identification with mainstream parties. Finally, having more positive evaluations of the U.S. government than the homeland government as well as perceiving one's greater ability to influence government in the United States is associated positively with the likelihood of panethnic identification as "Asian American" and identification as partisan Independent. It is important to note, however, that the influence of homeland ties is usually nonexistent when ethnic origin and political engagement in the United States is controlled.

Racial Discrimination

A defining difference between the classic assimilation and segmented assimilation theory is the latter's acknowledgement of the persistent barriers of racial discrimination and other factors in the U.S. economic and social structure impeding the social and political advancement of immigrants and their descendents. Whereas discrimination is considered overall a negative force for the foreign-born, the theory of reactive ethnicity (discussed in Chapter 2) posits that racial discrimination is a positive force in mobilizing group consciousness and political participation for the U.S.-born. This idea is confirmed in analysis of the PNAAPS data. Experience with racial discrimination or hate crime victimization is associated with a lower likelihood of adopting U.S.-based identities over ethnic Asian identity among the majority-immigrant sample. However, it exhibits a positive relationship with the adoption of panethnic self-identity for the U.S.-born sample. Experiencing discrimination in the United States may undermine Asian Americans' trust in U.S. government and evaluations of government responsiveness. It might also impair immigrants' perceived ability to influence U.S. government decisions. Experience with discrimination does not exhibit a strong relationship with voting registration and voting among the eligible, but it is associated with more participation in activities beyond voting. Experiences with discrimination increase the likelihood of Democratic partisanship only among immigrants, not the total sample. In predicting the acquisition and strength of partisanship, racial discrimination is a less influential factor than the sense of linked fate among Asian Americans.

Sense of Linked Fate

According to proponents of panethnicization or racial formation theory, politicized group consciousness, as measured by a sense of linked fate among racialized individuals, is key to the formation of panethnic or racial identity. This appears to be the case for predicting the acquisition of political partisanship among Asian Americans in the survey. A sense of linked fate with other Asian Americans also appears to facilitate the adoption of panethnicity as a forced choice among the foreign-born. However, linked fate is not as clearly associated with other sociopsychological indicators of ethnic-group attachment in predicting the preferred ethnic self-identity mode or panethnicity as a forced choice. A belief in a common fate among Asian Americans, on the other hand, is most consistently useful in predicting four of the five indicators of political orientations (greater political interest, trust, perceived responsiveness, and perceived influence). A sense of linked fate with other Asians is also positively associated with political participation beyond voting but not with voting or registration. This lack of impact on the formal channels of political participation may imply the limitations of using group identity as the basis of electoral coalitions.

Ethnic Origin

Reflecting in part the diversity of ethnic histories and cultures within the Asian American population as well as the close connections between Asian Americans and their personal or ancestral homeland in Asia, respondents' ethnic origin is the most consistently significant factor among the various sources of influence on the political attitudes and behavior of Asian Americans examined in this research. Significant ethnic differences that appear at the aggregate level in terms of how Asian Americans think and act politically often persists at the individual level after controlling for an extensive list of possible confounding factors informed by the literature. The persistence of ethnicity presents a resounding challenge to theories on assimilation and panethnicization. Nevertheless, it cannot be interpreted as supporting the argument of primordial determinism. Not only do ethnic differences vary in degree according to the sphere of behavior domain and the segment of the sample examined, but the significance of ethnic gaps suggests the need to identify additional factors rather than the failure of theories. One of the main tasks in future research is to identify those factors that can help account for ethnic differences among the Asian American population.

Gender

Although the persistence of ethnic gaps may recall a cat with nine lives, gender gaps between Asian American men and women often may be explained away after considering the same extended list of variables in this research. Although the relative insignificance of gender in structuring political attitudes and behavior represents a significant departure from the mainstream American behavioral research where non-Latino whites are often the research subjects, our findings at the aggregate level suggest that Asian American women also share many areas of commonality with white women in confronting barriers in political socialization and participation. Future research will need to collect comparison racial data in order to better assess the possible grounds for coalition-building. The remaining gender gaps among Asian Americans in ethnic self-identification and individual political mobilization, even after considering all other factors, also calls attention to the need for future research to identify sources of gender disparity in political socialization and the opportunity structure for Asian American men and women.

Central Tenets of a Proposed Model on Immigrant Political Adaptation and Incorporation

As a closing note to the argument that there is a need to reconsider current approaches to interpreting the political attitudes and behavior of Asian Americans—a non-European, nonwhite, multiethnic, relatively affluent, and majority-immigrant population—we propose the following as central tenets as the basis for understanding Asian Americans' political adaptation and incorporation. Importantly, the discussion below highlights *aspects* of current theories we find most useful, rather than a complete overhaul or replacement of existing theories. We argue that the conceptual frameworks introduced in Chapter 1—assimilation/acculturation, segmented assimilation, transnationalism, and racial formation/panethnicization—contribute to our understanding of important facets of Asian Americans' political adaptation and incorporation, but that none are adequate alone or in all cases.

Ethnic Origin and Identity

Although the survey is limited to the six largest of the twenty-five distinct ethnic Asian groups enumerated in the Census 2000 (Barnes and Bennett, 2002), our findings underscore the importance of distinguishing between these groups. For example, although only 15 percent of the sample as a whole initially self-identity as "Asian American" when asked about their preferred ethnic identity, responses to the question vary a great deal by ethnicity, ranging from 12 percent of Chinese respondents to 23 percent of South Asians. When the sample is disaggregated by gender, ethnicity remains an important determinant of identity. Each ethnic group in our study exhibits a different pattern of political party identification. At the most extreme ends, 44 percent of South Asians and 43 percent of Koreans, compared to 12 percent of Vietnamese, identify themselves as Democratic. Different ethnic groups participate in politics at different rates. Furthermore, levels of political interest, trust in local government, perceived political influence, and perceived government responsiveness all vary by ethnic origin. Even when we control for other factors in multivariate analyses, ethnic differences often remain important. These findings may underline the importance of primordial ties, but more likely they reveal the need to consider the additional factors that can help account for ethnic differences.

Experiences of International Migration and Resocialization

One reason that general studies of American politics come up short in terms of understanding Asian American politics is that they fail to consider the role of international migration and related processes. While European immigration came to a halt in the 1920s, the stream of immigrants into contemporary American communities is not predicted to end in the foreseeable future (Alba and Nee, 1997), even if the proportion of immigrants in high-immigration states such as California may soon stabilize (Myers and Pitkin, 2001). Throughout their history in the United States, changes in immigration flow have had a profound impact on the size and growth of the Asian American population. Because the majority of the contemporary Asian American population in the United States is adult immigrants, new conceptual models of Asian American political attitudes and behavior must take into account factors related to international migration and adult resocialization.

We incorporate a broad range of international migration-related variables in our analyses, including foreign-born status, place of education, citizenship status, English language preference, and length of permanent stay in the United States. Drawing on theories of transnationalism, we have also focused on connections with the homeland, prior experiences in the country of origin, and comparative attitudes toward the government in the country of origin and that in the United States. As seen throughout the book, international migration and resocialization processes are often crucial in the political lives of Asian Americans.

Race and Minority Group Status

Historically, nativist sentiment has served to reinforce the racial minority status of Asian Americans. As noted in Chapter 1, a predominant stereotype that continues to underline the racial minority status of Asian Americans today is that they are a perpetually foreign, inassimilable race (Perea, Delgado, Harris, Wildman, 2000; Lee, 2000; Wu, 2002). Robert Lee (1999: 164) contends that for

Asian Americans in the contemporary era, "well after the legal status of alien has been shed, no matter what their citizenship, how long they may have resided in the United States or how assimilated they are, the 'common understanding' that Asians are an alien presence in America is still the prevailing assumption in American culture."[4] Perhaps it is not surprising, then, that on average, four out of every ten respondents from each ethnic group in the survey had experienced racial and ethnic discrimination.

It is evident that race cannot be overlooked in research on Asian Americans and the political system. As a first preference, more Asian Americans identify with a racialized label ("Asian American") than as simply "American," even though most prefer an ethnic-specific label. After given a forced choice, about six in ten profess to identify with the panethnic, racialized label sometime in their life. Furthermore, experiences with racial discrimination and a sense of racial linked fate frequently emerge as relevant in our study.

Exposure to the Political System and Related Factors

The final tenet is related to factors associated with exposure to the political system over time, including political engagement (interest, knowledge, other political orientations), length of residence, having more money and education, political mobilization, media exposure, and connections with community institutions. These factors are conceivably linked, either directly or indirectly, to notions of political integration. Many factors related to increasing exposure to the political system are also considered critical according to assimilation theory and theories of acculturation. Those with more money and education are more likely to find themselves in workplace environments where political skills are learned and political topics are discussed (Verba, Schlozman, and Brady, 1995). One is exposed to more aspects of the political system as one's length of residence increases or as one pays more attention to the news media. Those who are more interested and knowledgeable about politics might also be more likely to seek out political information. Mobilization strategies by parties and other groups often include political information. And, as seen in Chapter 6, Asian American women are less likely to be mobilized to take part in politics than Asian American men, thus affecting women's opportunities of political exposure and participation.

Implications for Asian American Political Empowerment and Coalition Building

The PNAAPS, as the first multiethnic, multilingual, multi-city survey of its kind on Asian American public opinion, allows a more comprehensive and systematic overview of how individual Asian Americans across the nation act and feel about politics than has ever been possible before. What do the PNAAPS findings say about prospects for Asian American political empowerment in the

United States? Do they reveal possibilities in terms of coalition building within the multiethnic community and between Asian Americans and other groups in American society? These issues are explored below.

Prospects for Asian American Political Empowerment

In the United States, numbers matter for group representation in electoral politics. Thus, one source of potential political power for Asian Americans is their growing numbers in the population. Nearly 12 million people in the United States identified as "Asian" on the 2000 Census form (Barnes and Bennett, 2002). As mentioned in Chapter 1, Asian Americans also constitute one of the fastest-growing groups among the country's major racial and ethnic groups. From 1990 to 2000, the Asian American population grew by 72 percent. This exceptionally high growth rate may represent one of the most important sources of Asian American political empowerment. However, as the population rapidly expands (as has been the case for the last three decades), it is also becoming more diverse in terms of class, ethnicity, religion, nativity, mother tongue, immigration generation, and region of settlement. The internal diversity that accompanies population growth may threaten the ability of the community to act as a cohesive force in American politics. Prospects of empowerment for Asian Americans in the electoral arena, then, partly rest on whether or not they are able to forge and maintain a meaningful political community.

One indicator of the likelihood for Asian Americans to develop a meaningful political community is the extent to which members of different ethnic groups may identify themselves as part of a larger panethnic "Asian American" community. Using the PNAAPS, we are able to discern the contours of ethnic self-identity among Asian Americans. We also attempt to detect what might be interpreted as the foundations for a shared sense of panethnic identity among Asian Americans. As shown in Chapter 2, while only a minority of Asian Americans in the survey select "Asian American" as their first preferred group identity, the majority also acknowledge their identification with the panethnic label "Asian American" at some point of time in their lives—possibly under situations that call for the formation of a group identity that reaches beyond the ethnic-specific community. In addition, along with the traditional factors associated with political involvement, Asian Americans' political participation, especially in activities beyond voting, may be positively influenced by a number of group-related factors such as sense of linked fate with other Asian Americans, membership in an ethnic organization, and experiences with racial or ethnic discrimination.

In addition to shared identity, the creation of a meaningful political community is likely to depend upon the degree to which Asian Americans agree on critical political priorities and policies. The PNAAPS data show that approximately half of the respondents in the study identify a racial or ethnic issue (i.e., race relations, language barriers, discrimination, stereotyping, lack of ethnic political power, and interethnic relations) as one of the "most important problems" facing their communities. Furthermore, as noted in Chapter 1, Asian Americans generally agree on policies affecting the requisite opportunities and rights of members of the nonwhite, majority-immigrant community—such as affirmative action and bilingual services and, to a lesser extent, immigration control and campaign finance reform.

Finally, the PNAAPS data reveal some potential bases for pan-Asian American community building around political partisanship and vote choice. In terms of their political party loyalties, the PNAAPS data confirm past findings that many Asian Americans do not identify with the traditional American party categories. However, those who do are much more likely to be Democratic than Republican or Independent. In the November 2000 election, Asians voted for the Democratic candidate (Al Gore) by over a two to one margin over the Republican candidate (George W. Bush). When asked to choose between an Asian and a non-Asian candidate perceived as of equal qualification in any election, those who favor electing Asians greatly exceed those who do not by a three to one margin. This situation is reversed, however, when a less qualified Asian is pitted against a more qualified non-Asian—indicating that candidate quality is an important factor to consider in counting ethnic bloc vote among Asians.

The above findings leave open some interesting possibilities in terms of Asian American community building and political empowerment. One possibility is that because they are perceived as majority Democrat, as with other nonwhite groups, the Democratic Party may take the votes of Asian Americans for granted, while the Republican Party may forego any significant effort to mobilize the ethnic community, who are assumed to be "captured" by the opposing party (Frymer, 1999). The second, more optimistic possibility is that both parties may compete for the votes of the one-third of the Asian American voting-age population who have yet to express a commitment to either of the two parties. The third, and the most optimistic, possibility is that at least one of parties will consider Asian Americans as "swing votes" in hotly contested races, and as a consequence, each will invest heavily to turn out the community votes (Erie, 1988; Nakanishi, 1991, 1998). Alternatively, regardless of the attitudes toward and strategies of mainstream political parties, ethnic community concerns rather than political party affiliations may provide a stronger basis to direct the turnout patterns, vote choices, and candidate support among Asian Americans. In sum, while the diversity that characterizes the Asian American community may present multiple challenges to building a meaningful political coalition across ethnicities, the community's growing numbers, high growth rate, local concentration, and evidence of political consensus in candidate choice and policy support may serve as likely bases for panethnic community building and foundations for greater political empowerment.

As mentioned above, in terms of which political party Asian Americans are likely to throw their growing numbers behind, the answer lies with which party is able to produce a party platform that can reward loyalties or entice loyalties by capturing the hearts and minds of the large proportion of Asian Americans who do not express an identification with any American party. The success of any party is also likely to depend on their willingness to mobilize the Asian American votes. We find that mobilization by parties and individuals is associated positively with political participation.[5] Although mainstream institutions such as political parties have not engaged in mass mobilization efforts aimed at Asian Americans in the past, if they turn their attention toward the community in the future, party mobilization may have a dramatic effect on Asian Americans' partisanship and participation. Nevertheless, results from Table 4.8 show that the influence of major parties—channeled either through psychological attachment or institutional-mobilization efforts—on Asian American vote choice and policy preferences is not always evident. They suggest the importance for party organizations to work in concert with other socialization agents both within and outside of the ethnic community to achieve greater effect.

One final lesson to draw from the research here is that, barring a dramatic shift in U.S. immigration policies, the future direction of Asian American politics is likely to be heavily influenced by the reality of: 1) ethnicity remaining a central issue in the lives of Asian Americans and 2) a strong and continuous flow of new Asian immigration to the United States. Our study identifies a strong role for ethnicity in contemporary Asian Americans' political attitudes and behavior—a force that cannot be explained away in most cases by considering the influence of an extended list of possible confounding factors. However, we also find that identity as "Asian American" (versus "ethnic Asian") is associated with having a sense of shared culture with other Asian Americans, possessing or anticipating U.S. citizenship, and getting involved in Asian American causes. Thus, as more Asian Americans become citizens over time or if more Asian Americans join in projects or campaigns to promote Asian American causes, we might expect the role of ethnicity to diminish as panethnic identity develops or is activated more frequently and in a broader array of contexts. This study also establishes the importance of international migration-related factors, such as place of education, immigrant status, length of residence in the United States, and involvement in homeland politics for Asian Americans' political attitudes and behavior. If migration from Asia to the United States is curtailed or restricted, we would expect that the relative influence of immigration-related factors in Asian American politics as a whole to diminish—a scenario that appears to shape the political identity and behavior of Japanese Americans in our survey.

Asian Americans and the Larger Racial Context

Although Asian Americans have experienced marginalization in the political sphere, they are certainly not isolated in American politics. Asian Americans are part of a larger racial context and, therefore, our understanding of Asian American political attitudes and behavior is enriched by past research on other racial groups in the United States. A growing body of literature on the politics of other racial and ethnic minority communities has addressed issues of panethnic identity formation (Jackson, 1987; Lopez and Espiritu, 1990; Rodriguez and Cordero-Guzman, 1992; Jones-Correa and Leal, 1996), perceptions of linked fate (Miller, Gurin, Gurin, Malanchuk, 1981; Dawson, 1994), ethnic candidate vote choice (Lublin, 1997; Hill, Moreno, and Cue, 2001), participation in ethnic-specific causes (de la Garza et al., 1992), and race- and immigration-related policy attitudes (Segura, Falcon, Pachon, 1996; Kinder and Winter, 2001).

Past research on African Americans has emphasized that community and religious institutions may foster and support political participation (McAdam, 1982; Harris, 1999). Our results are consistent with those research conclusions. Consistent with findings on the importance of perceived panethnic linked fate in studies of African American political attitudes, we find a similarly strong role for linked fate among Asian Americans. Our research results also echo some of the findings in recent studies on Latinos. In particular, studies of Latino politics call attention to ethnic differences in political orientations and behaviors within the larger category of "Latinos" (Wrinkle et al., 1996). We find a similar need in studying the Asian American population. Our findings also support the centrality of nativity, language diversity, place of education, citizenship status, and transnational attachments in studying the political involvement and political attitudes of internally diverse, nonwhite, and majority-immigrant communities. These are the same factors emphasized by scholars on Latino politics and behaviors adopting either quantitative or qualitative research methods (e.g., Cain, Kiewiet, and Uhlaner, 1991; Arvizu and Garcia, 1996; Graham, 1997; Jones-Correa, 1998; Sierra, Carrillo, DeSipio, and Jones-Correa, 2000).

Crossracial Coalition Prospects

Sonenshein (2001) specifies that groups may take several paths in their attempts to gain political empowerment: They can go it alone, join forces with other minorities against the dominant majority, or forge alliances with elements within the majority group. Because they constitute a relatively small proportion of the U.S. population—Asian Americans made up no more than 5 percent of the total population in 2000—political empowerment for Asian Americans necessitates cooperation with other racial groups. Even in the cities that are home to the largest Asian American populations, such as New York and Los Angeles, Asian Americans do not have the numbers to go it alone.

According to Sonenshein (1993), one of the key aspects of coalition building is shared interests. In terms of common interests with other groups, Asian Americans may forge a coalition with Latinos based on their mutual interests about immigration-related issues. Together, Asian Americans and Latinos account for the vast majority of immigrants in the United States. In 2000, immigrants from Latin America comprised just about 50 percent of the foreign-born population and those from Asia make up over 25 percent (Lollock, 2001). We might expect Asian Americans and Latinos to coalesce around policies sensitive to immigrants and immigrants' needs, such as bilingual government services.[6]

Asian Americans may also join forces with black Americans and Latinos against the dominant majority group based on shared racial minority interests, especially interests that have to do with experiences with discrimination and hate crime. As reported in Chapter 1, an average of four in ten respondents from each Asian ethnic group in our study had experienced racial and ethnic discrimination. A recent national survey shows that 36 percent of Asian Americans, 40 percent of Latinos, and 46 percent of blacks reported experiencing racial discrimination in the past ten years compared to 18 percent of non-Latino whites.[7] In terms of policy attitudes, we might also anticipate that Asian Americans would join black Americans and Latinos in supporting affirmative action as a principle, even though there may be interracial differences in specific policy areas.

We might conclude from the discussion above that Asian Americans may find common ground (in the policies discussed above) with other minority groups in the future. It is also possible that Asian Americans may attempt to coalesce with non-Latino whites based on class interests, because both groups exhibit, on average, higher median household incomes than blacks and Latinos. In addition, because Asian Americans encompass a tremendous amount of socioeconomic diversity, we might see multiple coalitions forming, some between whites and those Asian American ethnic groups characterized by high levels of economic resources, and others between Asian American ethnic groups characterized by high poverty rates and low-income groups within the Latino and African-American communities. Different regional contexts may dictate the need for different crossracial (and crossethnic) formation, as well.

We find that, among those who identify with a party, Asian Americans tend to identify with the Democrats. Thus, our study leaves open the possibility that Asian Americans may also forge a coalition with other racial minority groups around shared political beliefs, particularly beliefs about which parties will best represent their interests. However, it should also be noted that while Asian Americans appear to be more Democratic in their partisan leanings than non-Latino whites, they are also slightly less likely to identify as Democrat than their Latino counterparts and much less likely than blacks.[8]

This study contends that Asian Americans are a critical component of American political life. The PNAAPS has allowed us important insights into the ways in which Asian Americans fit into the American political system in terms of processes of identity formation, political orientations, partisanship, participation, and gender role dynamics. In this final chapter, we have also examined prospects for Asian Americans' political empowerment and multiracial coalition building. Because Asian Americans are a fast-growing part of the American population, because of their historical and contemporary contributions to American politics, and because they offer a unique perspective in terms of viewing the larger political system, we hope we have shown that focusing on Asian Americans allows us to better understand racial and ethnic minority political behavior, and that this focus reveals insights related to the larger American political system at the dawn of the twenty-first century.

Question Wording and Coding Scheme of the Pilot National Asian American Political Survey

Ethnic and Panethnic Self-Identity

Ethnic Self-Identity

"People think of themselves in different ways. In general, do you think of yourself as an American, an Asian American, an Asian, a [R's ETHNIC GROUP]* American, or a [R's ETHNIC GROUP]?" Response categories include: American, Asian American, Asian, [R's ETHNIC GROUP] American (e.g., Filipino American, Korean American, etc.), [R's ETHNIC GROUP] (e.g., Filipino, Korean, etc.), not sure, refused

Panethnic Self-Identity

[If not self-identify as an Asian American in the previous question] *"Have you ever thought of yourself as an Asian American?"* 1=identify as Asian American either in the first question or provide a positive response in the follow-up question, 0=otherwise

Intensity of Panethnic Self-Identity

[For those who self-identify as Asian American either in the first or the follow-up question] *"How often do you think of yourself as an Asian American? Is it very often, often, or not that often?"* 3=very often, 2=often or not sure, 1=not very often, 0=do not identify as an Asian American even after the second question

Primordial Ethnic Ties

Ethnic Origin

"What country in Asia are you or your mother's side of the family from?" "What country in Asia are you or your father's side of the family from?"

Sociopsychological Engagement with Ethnic and Panethnic Community

Perceived Common Culture

"Some say that people of Asian descent in the U.S. have a great deal in common culturally, others disagree. Do you think groups of Asians in America are culturally

---

*Throughout the appendix *R* = respondent.

very similar, somewhat similar, somewhat different, or very different?" 1=very different, 2=somewhat different, 3=somewhat similar, 4=very similar

Panethnic Linked Fate

"Do you think what happens generally to other groups of Asians in this country will affect what happens in your life?" [IF YES] *Will it affect it a lot, some, or not very much?"* 0=No, 1=yes, will affect but not very much, 2=yes, will affect some or not sure how, 3=yes, will affect a lot

Ethnic Linked Fate

"What about the [R's ETHNIC GROUP] people in America, do you think what happens generally to ethnic group Americans will affect what happens in your life?" [IF YES] *"Will it affect it a lot, some, or not very much?"* 0=no, 1=yes, will affect but not very much, 2=yes, will affect some or not sure how, 3=yes, will affect a lot

Follow Asian American News

"How closely have you followed news stories and other information of Asians in the United States—very closely, fairly closely, not too closely, or not at all?" 1=not at all, 2=not too closely, 3=fairly closely, 4=very closely

Follow News in Asia

"How closely have you followed news stories and other information about what happened in Asia such as a story from Japan, Korea, China, India, Vietnam, and the Philippines—very closely, fairly closely, not too closely, or not at all?" 1=not at all, 2=not too closely, 3=fairly closely, 4=very closely

Political Participation

Voting Turnout

"Thinking about the November 2000 presidential election when Al Gore ran against George Bush, did you vote in the election?" *"Did you happen to vote in the 1998 Congressional elections, or didn't you get a chance to vote?"* 1=voted in 2000, 0=otherwise

Consistent Voting

0=R did not vote in 1998 or 2000, 1=R voted in both 1998 and 2000

Presidential Vote Choice

[IF voted in 2000] *"Which candidate did you vote for?"*

Participation Beyond Voting

"During the past four years, have you participated in any of the following types of political activity in your community?" (ACCEPT MULTIPLE ANSWERS) Response categories were 1) written or phoned a government official; 2) contacted an editor of a newspaper, magazine, or TV station; 3) donated money to a political campaign; 4) attended a public meeting, political rally, or fundraiser;

5) worked with others in your community to solve a problem; 6) signed a petition for a political cause; 7) served on any governmental board or commission; 8) taken part in a protest or demonstration; 9) worked for a political campaign. 0=no participation in any activity, 1=participation in one activity, . . . 8=participation in eight activities

Political Integration

Strength of Party Identification

"Generally speaking, do you usually think of yourself as a Republican, a Democrat, an Independent, or of another political affiliation?" [IF REPUBLICAN OR DEMOCRAT] *"Would you call yourself a strong (Republican/Democrat)?"* [IF INDEPENDENT] *"Do you think of yourself as closer to the Republican or Democratic Party?"* 0=no party identification, 1=Independent, closer to Democrat or Republican, 2=Democrat or Republican, but not a strong Democrat or Republican, 3=strong Democrat or Republican

Strong Democrat

0=no party identification, 1=Independent, closer to Democrat, 2=Democrat, but not a strong Democrat, 3=Strong Democrat

Strong Republican

0=no party identification, 1=Independent, closer to Republican, 2=Republican, but not a strong Republican, 3=Strong Republican

Political Ideology (Liberal)

"How would you describe your views on most matters having to do with politics? Do you generally think of yourself as very liberal, or somewhat liberal, or middle-of-the-road, or somewhat conservative, or very conservative?" 3=very liberal, 2=somewhat liberal, 1=middle of the road, 0=otherwise

Citizenship Status

[IF NOT A CITIZEN] *"Are you planning to apply for U.S. citizenship or to become a U.S. citizen?"* 0=no, 1=not a citizen, but expect to be one, 2=citizen

Political Interest and Knowledge

Political Interest

"How interested are you in politics and what's going on in government in general? Are you very interested, somewhat interested, only slightly interested, or not at all interested in politics and what goes on in government?" 4=very interested, 3=somewhat interested, 2=slightly interested, 1=not at all interested

Knowledge of U.S. Electoral Process

"How familiar are you with the current process of electing the U.S. president? Are you very familiar, somewhat familiar, or not familiar at all?" 1=somewhat familiar, 2=very familiar, 0=otherwise

Knowledge of Asian American Issues

"*To your best knowledge, have you heard of Dr. Wen Ho Lee, the nuclear scientist charged with downloading classified data and spent nine months in jail?*" 1=yes, 0=otherwise

Knowledge of Asian American movement

"*Have you heard of the 80-20 Initiative or a movement to help organize the presidential choice of Asian American voters?*" 1=yes, 0=otherwise

Civic Participation

Membership and Involvement in Ethnic Community Organizations

"*Do you belong to any organization or take part in any activities that represent the interests and viewpoints of [R'S ETHNIC GROUP] or other Asians in America?*" [IF YES] "*How active are you as a member? Are you very active, somewhat active, not too active, or not active at all?*" 0=no, 1=not active at all, 2=not too active, 3=somewhat active, 4=very active

Religious Attendance or Religiosity

"*How often do you attend religious services? Would you say—every week, almost every week, once or twice a month, a few times a year, or never?*" 1=never, 2=a few times a year, 3=once or twice a month, 4=almost every week, 5=every week

Participation in Activities Involving Asian Americans

"*Which of the following activities, that you participated in, involve/d an Asian American candidate or issue affecting Asian Americans?*" [read all responses from a previous question on participation beyond voting] 0=no participation in any Asian American activity, 1=participation in one Asian American activity, ... 8=participation in eight Asian American activities

Political Mobilization

Mobilization by Party

"*The political parties and candidate organizations, as well as other political groups, try to contact as many people as they can to get them to vote for particular candidates. During the past four years, have you received any letter, e-mail, or telephone call from a political party or candidate organization or other political group about a political campaign?*" 1=yes, 0=otherwise

Personal Recruitment

"*In the past four years, did someone you know try to request you to vote, or to contribute money to a political cause, or to engage in some other type of political activity?*" 1=yes, 0=otherwise

Attitudes toward Government

Political Trust

"Next, I have a few questions concerning your view of U.S. government officials: How much of the time do you think you can trust your local and state government officials to do what is right—just about always, most of the time, only some of the time, or none at all?" 4=just about always, 3=most of the time, 2=only some of the time, 1=none at all

Perceived Influence

"How much influence do you think someone like you can have over local government decisions—a lot, a moderate amount, a little, or none at all?" 4=a lot, 3=a moderate amount, 2=a little, 1=none at all

Perceived Government Responsiveness

"If you have some complaint about a government activity and you took that complaint to a local public official, do you think that he or she would pay a lot of attention to what you say, some attention, very little attention, or none at all?" 4=a lot of attention, 3=some attention, 2=very little attention, 1=none at all
*See question wording for comparative trust and comparative influence under **Homeland Ties.**

Acculturation

Language Use (Business/Home)

"What language do you usually speak when at home with family?" "What language do you usually use to conduct personal business and financial transactions?" 1=something else (language other than English), 2=mix of English and other language, 3=English

Media Use

"Compared to your usage of the English media, how often do you use [R'S ETHNIC GROUP'S] language media as a source of entertainment, news, and information? Would you say all of the time, most of the time, about the same time, not very often, or not at all?" 5=not at all, 4=not very often, 3=about the same time, 2=most of the time, 1=all of the time

Racial Integration

Attitude toward Interracial Marriage

"How would you feel if someone in your family married a person of a different ethnic background than yours? Would you strongly approve, approve, neither approve nor disapprove, disapprove, or strongly disapprove?" 1=strongly disapprove, 2=disapprove, 3=neither approve nor disapprove, 4=approve, 5=strongly approve

Neighborhood Racial Makeup

"How would you describe the ethnic makeup of the neighborhood where you live? Would you say it is mostly white, mostly black, mostly Latino, mostly Asian, or would you say the ethnic makeup is pretty evenly mixed?" 2=evenly mixed, 1=mostly white/mostly black/mostly Latino/mostly Asian, 0=otherwise

Crossracial Friendship

"Thinking for a moment of blacks, whites, Latinos and other Asians, do you yourself know any person who belongs to these groups whom you consider a close personal friend or not? [IF YES] What ethnic groups do they belong to? Any others? Any other group?" 0=no mixed friend, 1=one group of any race, 2=two groups, 3=three groups, 4=four groups, 5=five groups (Alternatively, we also create a dichotomous variable with 1=friendship with other Asian, 0=otherwise.)

Racial Discrimination

Experience with Personal Discrimination

"Have you ever personally experienced discrimination in the United States?" 2=yes, 1=not sure, 0=no

Ethnic Discrimination

[IF EXPERIENCED DISCRIMINATION] *"In your opinion, was it because of your ethnic background?"* 1=yes, 0=otherwise

Types of Discrimination

[IF EXPERIENCED DISCRIMINATION] *"In which of these ways, if any, have you experienced discrimination in ..."* 1=getting jobs or promotion, 2=getting education, 3=getting housing, 4=dealing with a government agency, 5=dealing with a business or retail establishment, 6=dealing with your neighbors, 7=dealing with strangers in a public place

Victim of Hate Crime

"Have you ever been the victim of a 'hate crime,' that is, have you had someone verbally or physically abuse you, or damage your property, specifically because you belong to a certain race or ethnic group?" 1=yes, 0=otherwise

Public Policy Opinion

Most Important Community Problem

"What's the most important problem facing [R's ETHNIC GROUP] people in the United States today? Is there another problem that is almost as important?" (ACCEPT UP TO TWO REPLIES)

Bilingual Services

"Government should provide public information and services important to the immigrant community in English as well as in the immigrants' native languages."

1=strongly disagree, ..., 4=neither agree nor disagree or no opinion, ..., 7=strongly agree

Limit Legal Immigration

"*Congress should pass laws limiting the number of legal immigrants admitted each year into this country.*" 1=strongly disagree, ..., 4=neither agree nor disagree or no opinion, ..., 7=strongly agree

Campaign Donations

"*Non-U.S. citizens who are legal permanent residents should be permitted to make donations to political campaigns.*" 1=strongly disagree, ..., 4=neither agree nor disagree or no opinion, ..., 7=strongly agree

Support Affirmative Action

"*Affirmative action refers to any measure, policy, or law used to increase diversity or rectify discrimination so that qualified individuals have equal access to employment, education, business, and contracting opportunities. Generally speaking, do you think affirmative action is a good thing or a bad thing for Asian Americans, or doesn't it affect Asian Americans much?*" 0=a bad thing, 1=does not affect or not sure, 2=a good thing

Job Training and Educational Assistance

"*Some people feel that because of past disadvantages there are some groups in society that should receive special job training and educational assistance. Others say that is unfair. What about you? Do you strongly favor, favor, neither favor nor oppose, oppose, or strongly oppose special job training and educational assistance for Asian Americans?*" 0=strongly oppose, 1=oppose, 2=neither favor/oppose or not sure, 3=favor, 4=strongly favor

Preferences in Hiring and Promotion

"*Some people feel that because of past disadvantages, there are some groups in society that should be given preferences in hiring and promotion. Others say that is unfair. What about you? Do you strongly favor, favor, neither favor nor oppose, oppose, or strongly oppose special preferences in hiring and promotion to Asian Americans?*" 0=strongly oppose, 1=oppose, 2=neither favor/oppose or not sure, 3=favor, 4=strongly favor

Ethnic Bloc Vote

Support Asian American Candidate

"*If you have an opportunity to decide on two candidates for political office, one of whom is Asian American, would you be more likely to vote for the Asian American candidate if the two are equally qualified?*" [IF YES] "*would you still vote for the Asian American, even if he or she is less qualified?*" 0=no, 1=no, if less qualified, 2=not sure, if less qualified, 3=yes, even if less qualified

Homeland Ties [asked only of immigrants]

Prior Partisanship

"Before you came to the United States, were you ever a member of any political party or political organization or a participant in any other type of political activities?" [IF YES] *"How active were you as a member? Very active, somewhat active, not too active, or not active at all?"* 0=do not belong, 1=belong but not active at all, 2=belong but not too active, 3=belong and somewhat active, 4=belong and very active

Active in Homeland Politics

"After arriving in the United States, have you ever participated in any activity dealing with the politics of your home country?" 1=yes, 0=otherwise

Maintain Homeland Contact

"How much contact either by phone or by mail or in person do you have with people in [R'S COUNTRY OF ORIGIN] during the past twelve months? Is it at least once a week, two or three times a month, once a month, once several months, once a year, or none?" 0=none, 1=once a year, 2=once several months, 3=once a month, 4=two or three times a month, 5=at least once a week

Plan to Return to Asia

"Generally speaking, where do you expect you and your children will end up living in the next fifteen to twenty years: in [R'S COUNTRY OF ORIGIN], somewhere in the United States, or elsewhere?" 1=in the U.S., 0=all else

Comparative Trust

"Do you feel you can generally trust U.S. government officials more, about the same, or less than government officials in your home country?" 1=more trust in U.S. officials, 0=otherwise

Comparative Influence

"Do you feel you can generally influence decisions made by U.S. government officials more, about the same, or less than those made by government officials in your home country?" 1=more influence, 0=otherwise

Sociodemographic Background

Gender

1=male, 2=female

Age

"In what year were you born?" raw score (−1 + year of interview minus birth year)

Nativity

"Were you born in Asia?" 1=born in Asia, 0=otherwise

Years of U.S. Stay

[IF BORN IN ASIA] *"How many years have you lived in the United States on a permanent basis?"* raw score in year

Length of Community Residence

"How long have you lived in you present city or town?" raw score in year

Proportion of Life in the U.S.

For the Asia-born, year of U.S. stay/age; for the U.S.-born, age/age or 1.

Homeownership

"Do you or your family own your own home or pay rent?" 1=own, 2=otherwise

Marital Status

"What is your marital status?" 1=married, 0=otherwise

Education

"What is the highest level of education or schooling you have completed?" 1=less than high school, 2=high school graduate, 3=vocational/technical training beyond high school or some college, 4=bachelor's degree, 5=some graduate school, 6=postgraduate degree (beyond college degree)

Non-U.S. Education

"Were you educated mainly in the United States?" 1=not in the United States, 0=otherwise

Income

"If you added together the yearly incomes of all the members of your family living at home last year, would the total of all their incomes be less than $20,000, or more than $40,000, or somewhere in between?" [IF LESS THAN $20,000] *"Would the total of all their incomes be less than $10,000?"* [IF IN-BETWEEN] *"Would the total of all their incomes be less than $30,000 or more than $30,000?"* [IF MORE THAN $40,000] *"Would the total of all their incomes be between $40,000 and $60,000, or between $60,000 and $80,000, or more than that?"* 1=less than $10,000, 2=$10,000 to $19,999, 3=$20,000 to $29,999, 4=$30,000 to $39,999, 5=$40,000 to $59,999, 6=$60,000 to $79,999, 7=$80,000 or over. (We use the grand mean of 4.47 to substitute the "not sure" and "refused" response categories); low income=less than or equal to $29,999

Employment

"What were you doing most of last week: working full-time, or working part-time, or were you self-employed, or keeping house, or going to school, or are you looking for work, or retired, or what?" [IF ILL, ON VACATION, OR ON STRIKE, RECORD AS "WORKING." IF LOOKING FOR WORK, ASK] *Have you looked for a full- or a part-time job in the past four weeks?"* 1=working full time, part time, or self-employed, 0=otherwise

Endnotes

Preface

1. Taken from the Organization of Chinese Americans press release on May 29, 2001, "Congressman Wu Denied Entry to DOE," which cites the Washington Post, "In The Loop" column, "DOE Trips on Security Blanket," printed on May 25, 2001.
2. From an Associated Press dispatch headlined, "TX Mayor Loses by a Hair after Racist Campaign Attacks Letters," July 10, 2002.
3. "Without having had the growing-up experience in Iowa, complete with the intrinsic basics of Midwest American life, how is this person adequately prepared to represent Midwest values and core beliefs, let alone understand and appreciate the constitutional rights guaranteed to us in writing by our Founding Fathers? (not her Founding Fathers)," Balderston wrote in an e-mail sent anonymously to a local newspaper. When contacted by a reporter from the newspaper, she responded with a rhetorical question: "Will a person raised to function in the upper caste of India, the most repressive form of discrimination on the planet, be able to shed such repressionist views and fully and effectively represent the citizens of House District 36?"(Dverak 2002).
4. This survey is also known as the MAAPS, the multicity Asian American Political Survey.
5. The grants were jointly proposed with her mentor and dissertation advisor M. Margaret Conway first to the NSF dissertation improvement grant and second to the Open Society Institute.

Chapter 1

1. According to Census 2000 PHC-T-1 Table 4, the Asian growth rate is higher than the 58 percent found among Latinos, the 22 percent found among blacks, or the 5 percent found among non-Hispanic whites. It is lower than the 110 percent found among American Indians and Alaska Natives and the 140 percent found among Native Hawaiian and Other Pacific Islanders over the 1990s. These calculations of population change are made using figures for "race alone or in combination" in Census 2000. If using figures for "race alone," the growth rate for U.S. persons who identified themselves as only of Asian but not other racial origin in 2000 is 48 percent, as compared to the 16 percent for blacks, 26 percent for American Indians, and 9 percent for Pacific Islanders. Direct, unqualified comparison of the 2000 and 1990 Census results is not always possible because of the allowance of reporting *one or more race* for mixed ancestry individuals and other changes in Census 2000 (Barnes and Bennett, 2002).

2. Asian Indians were classified as "white" and the number of Koreans was considered too small to justify a separate category in the censuses of 1950 and 1960.

3. For excellent and recent account of the Pacific Islander experience see Spickard, Rondilla, and Hippolite Wright (2002); for that of mixed-race Asians, see Williams-Leon and Nakashima (2001).

4. This historic act banned Chinese laborers from entering the United States and Chinese immigrants already in the States from naturalization. Entry of Chinese women was prohibited in an earlier legislation (the Page Act of 1875).

5. The Exclusion Act was repealed in 1943, but until 1965 only 105 Chinese were permitted to enter each year because of the racist quota set in the 1924 National Origin Act. For an excellent review of the numerous immigration policies and laws affecting Asians, see Hing (1993).

6. The 1790 Nationality Act permitted naturalization only to "free white" persons.

7. This annual quota was raised to 100 persons after the Philippines gained independence in 1946.

8. For a review of the origin and reinvention of the model minority thesis, see Woo (2000: 23–41).

9. A description of survey methodology and a profile of the respondents appear in a later section of the chapter.

10. It is also a population with multiple racial origins. According to the 2000 U.S. Census, 1.7 million or 14 percent of the 11.9 million people who identified themselves as Asian were of at least one other race than Asian, with the most common combination being "Asian and White" (52 percent). However, it is beyond the scope of this study to address issues dealing with persons of mixed ancestries.

11. Sources of information for calculating these figures are: U.S. Bureau of the Census, Census 2000 Tables DP-1, PHC-T-1; Census 2000 Summary File 1 (SF 1) Table QT-P7; Census 2000 Summary File 3 (SF 3); 1990 Census of Population, General Population Characteristics, Table CP-1; 1990 Summary Tape File 1 (STF 1) Table P007 Detailed Race.

12. It should be noted that Asian Americans have enjoyed a prolonged presence in the United States since the mid-eighteenth century.

13. U.S. Department of Commerce, *Current Population Survey: Voter Supplement File*, 1994, 1996, 1998, 2000 [computer files]. ICPSR version. Washington, D.C.: U.S. Department of Commerce, Bureau of the Census [producer], 1994, 1996, 1998, and 2000. Ann Arbor, Mich.: Inter-university Consortium for Political and Social Research [distributor], 1997, 1999, and 2001. See Lien (2001b) for details about the data source and findings.

14. The only exception is among the foreign-born Hmong population where only 49 percent indicated that they could speak English "well" or "very well."

15. In terms of this last point, the Asian American Legal Defense and Education Fund (AALDEF) found that during the 2000 presidential elections, Asian American voters in New York City encountered problems including the mistranslation of ballots (that flipped the party headings such that the "Democratic" label was translated as "Republican" and vice-versa for state offices), hostile poll workers, and the lack of interpreters to accommodate the heavy Asian voter turnout. During the 2001 New York City elections, numerous eligible Asian Americans lost their right to vote because of the omission of their names from the list of registered voters and improper police interference in election administration, among other issues (Magpantay, 2002). Similar problems were encountered by Vietnamese American voters in Orange County, California during the 2002 March primary election. The *Los Angeles Times* reported that Vietnamese-speaking voters were confused by the poor English-to-Vietnamese translation in the sample ballot (Reyes, 2002).

16. See source in note 15.

17. These measures may sum up to more than 100 percent because of multiple mentions.

18. The unusual situation in Florida following the 2000 election may account for the 18 percent of respondents who either refuse to report or are uncertain about the vote they cast.

19. For more of this point on the distinctiveness of the Asian American experience, see Kim (1999) and Lien (2001b). For a general discussion on the theories on racial and ethnic groups see Fuchs (1990), Hero (1992), and Feagin and Feagin (1999).

20. Note, however, that Filipinos were U.S. nationals between 1898 and 1946 through annexation. Also, native Hawaiians and other Pacific Islanders were colonized by various European

nations since as early as the sixteenth century and Hawaii was annexed by a joint resolution of Congress in 1898 (Kitano and Daniels, 1995).

21. Note historians contend that older waves of immigrants also lived transnational lives (Foner, 2001).

22. As mentioned earlier, other measures of socioeconomic status, such as per capita income and percent in poverty, show that Asian Americans continue to lag behind non-Latino whites. Further, socioeconomic status varies a great deal between specific Asian American ethnic groups. In *Observation 7*, we discuss the fact that Asian American voting rates rise substantially once the factor of eligibility is accounted for.

23. A detailed assessment of the constraints and strengths of extant archival survey data that may be used for conducting political research regarding Asian Americans is reported in the appendix section of Lien (2001b).

24. Because of the uncertainty in the 2000 election outcome, an unusually high percentage of our respondents who voted in the election were either uncertain (4 percent) or refused (14 percent) to state their presidential choice.

25. Prior to the passing away of Congresswoman Patsy Mink in September 2002, there were two Asian Americans in the Senate and six Asian American members in the House of Representatives (including one representing Guam and one representing Samoa) serving in the 107th Congress. There has been a consistent increase in the number of state and local officials over the past twenty years. Geron and Lai (2001) report that in 2000 there were more than three hundred Asian American elected officials in key local, state, and federal offices.

Chapter 2

1. See Chapters 3 to 5 in this book and Lien and Lee (2001) for details on how a panethnic identity affects Asian Americans in the survey.

2. We use the word "ethnic" as a generic term and treat panethnic or racial identity as one of the possible ways of identifying based on shared cultural practices, languages, behaviors, national or ancestral origins, physical attributes, and experiences. Furthermore, we use the terms "panethnic" and "racial" interchangeably to acknowledge the polyethnic origin of the American conception of race. Moreover, we do not address the complications on identity formation for individuals with mixed race or ethnicity (but see Root, 1992, 1996 and Williams-Leon and Nakashima, 2001 for a discussion).

3. It is also possible for an individual to not identify with any of the above. This situation may be related to a sense of dual marginalization or mixed identification or a refusal to express oneself in any of the suggested labeling. Although this issue is of great interest to social psychologists, an exploration of the phenomenon is beyond the scope of the current study.

4. We thank Chris Collet for this excellent point.

5. In rare cases where the respondent's father's and mother's side of the family came from two different countries, we assign ethnic origin based on the country on the mother's side.

6. A score of 3 is assigned to individuals who "very often" thought of themselves as Asian American; a score of 2 is assigned to those who either "often" thought of themselves to be Asian American or were uncertain about their level of frequency; a score of 1 is assigned to those who did not often think of themselves as Asian American; and a 0 score indicates an absence of pan–Asian American identification.

7. Interestingly, about 20 percent of Japanese Honolulu residents identify as "Asian American," with very few choosing to identify as ethnic American (12.5 percent) or by ethnicity alone (3 percent). When comparing across survey sites, the marginal distribution of responses to our ethnic identification question is remarkably similar across the four continental cities (Chicago, New York, Los Angeles, and San Francisco), but significantly different for Honolulu.

8. This is an issue much like the controversy over decennial census categories prior to Census 2000. PNAAPS may artificially dampen the levels of identification with different social group categories simply by question design.

9. The question wording in the questionnaire is: How do you identify, that is, what do you call yourself? (Examples: Asian, Hispanic, American, Latino, African-American, Black, Cuban, Cuban-American, Haitian, Haitian-America, etc.)

10.   The excluded categories are "Asian," "Other," "Don't know," and "Refused." They represent less than 9 percent of the survey respondents.
11.   For a majority immigrant population, this decision is logical and does not assume the process of assimilation or panethnicization.
12.   We measure the degree of integration into the mainstream political system with a 4-point scale of the strength of political partisanship. We test the possible partisan orientation effect by creating separate scales, one for the Democratic Party and the other for the Republican Party.
13.   For multivariate analysis, we create a three-item summed index of English language use weighted by the number of response categories in questions on respondents' preferred language used at home, in business transactions, and in consuming news and entertainment media (alpha=.68).
14.   We create a summed index of racial discrimination from positive responses of being a hate crime victim and of being discriminated based on ethnic background.
15.   We create a two-item summed index of comparative assessment of government by the level of immigrants' relative trust in government officials and self-efficacy in their ability to influence government decisions (alpha=.62).

Chapter 3

1.   This refers to Chinese from China, Hong Kong, or Taiwan; South Asians from India and Pakistan; and Filipinos, Japanese, Koreans, and the Vietnamese from each of the corresponding country in Asia.
2.   These labels are in the qualitative follow-up interviews of the survey participants conducted with selected Mandarin/English speaking Chinese immigrants in California (Lien, 2003).
3.   What is not so clear, however, is the exact meanings captured by the terms "liberalism" and "conservatism" (Flanigan and Zingale, 1991). Many Americans might agree with the general notion of liberalism as endorsing the idea of social change for greater equality and individual freedom and the greater involvement of government in effecting such change and that of conservatism as defending the status quo and prescribing a limited role for governmental intervention. Yet scholars of black and Latino politics contend that it may be problematic to assume that there is a shared understanding of the meanings of the liberal-moderate-conservative labels between whites and nonwhites and among nonwhite groups (Hero, 1992; Smith and Seltzer, 1992; Tate, 1993; DeSipio, 1996). Moreover, the simple application of the conventional ideological labels may miss the complexity and variability of attitudes within each of the nonwhite communities (McClain and Stewart, 1995).
4.   The independent impact of ideology on selected policy preferences among Asian Americans is assessed in Chapter 4 (Table 4.8).
5.   The knowledge level of racial discrimination against U.S. Asians among Chinese immigrants may be an exception because of political education under Chinese Communism, which criticizes U.S. human rights records.
6.   The seven areas in which to measure potential discrimination are: getting a job or promotion; education; housing; actions by a government agency; dealing with a business or retail establishment; interactions with neighbors; and actions by strangers in a public place.
7.   One reviewer of this manuscript raised the question of whether experiencing discrimination increases political interest or whether the causal arrow would run in the other direction, with those who have higher levels of political interest being more conscious of discriminatory actions in different situations. It is likely that the two may be mutually reinforcing of each other.
8.   These results are substantially the same as those produced using ordered logit, a multivariate method based on Baysesian statistical analysis that is used when the dependent variable is measured at the ordinal level. To facilitate interpretation and understanding of results, the OLS results are reported here.
9.   This is the full list of explanatory variables considered. Various sets of variables were dropped at one time or another from the models reported in this chapter because of concern over their theoretical relevance and empirical relationships to other variables in the models.
10.   Other regression equations were estimated, using a five-point ideology index as the dependent variable, with the dependent variable coded as 1 = very liberal, 2 = liberal, 3 = middle

of the road or not sure, 4 = somewhat conservative, and 5 = very conservative. Several differences in the variables contributing to predicting ideological patterns occurred. With the five-category ideology measure as the dependent variable, Japanese ethnic group was not significant for the entire sample. Examining ideological patterns among just the foreign born, neither attention to Asian-related news stories nor organizational activism in Asian American causes were significant predictors.

Chapter 4

1. This view of the remarkable stability of the distribution of political partisanship in the American electorate over the last half-century does not suggest that there are no fluctuations over time. The proportion of the Independents increased from less than a quarter before 1966 to over 35 percent between 1972 and 1978. In 1998 and 2000, it respectively accounts for 36 percent and 40 percent of the NES respondents. The majority of the Independents, however, are able to lean with a major party.

2. Numerous studies show that not only the acquisition of partisanship can be affected by issues positions, previous votes, and candidate evaluations, but the distribution of party identification in the electorate can be affected by question wording, availability of response categories, and coding (Niemi and Weisberg, 1993: 268–83; Sanders, Burton, and Kneeshaw, 2002).

3. To be sure, immigrants from some parts of Europe were not immediately accepted as full-fledged whites upon their arrival in the United States (Ignatiev, 1995; Jacobson, 1998). However, in their struggle toward acceptance as whites, less established groups from Europe, such as the Irish, often consolidated their racial position by distinguishing themselves from groups experiencing even greater racial hostility, such as Mexican Americans, blacks, and Asian Americans (Jacobson, 1998; Perea, Delgado, Harris, and Wildman, 2000). In addition, the role of parties and political machines in mobilizing immigrants has been somewhat romanticized in the past. While there is no doubt that parties were an important source of political mobilization for past waves of immigrants, their efforts to mobilize were heavily dependent on both the degree of party competition in a particular city (Erie, 1988) and historical political context (Mayhew, 1986; Sterne, 2001). In addition, political machines did not act in isolation, but were part of a complex array of organizations that included neighborhood organizations, unions, churches, and ethnic voluntary associations (Lin, n.d.; Sterne, 2001).

4. The same research finds 37 percent of the 84 Asians identified in a GSS (General Social Survey) pooled sample (1980–1989) are pure Independent; a comparable percentage of nonpartisanship is found among the 58 Asian respondents in the merged NES (1980–1988).

5. Elsewhere, the 1984 California Ethnicity Survey finds 42 percent of Asian American citizens are Democrat, while only 10 percent are Republican (Uhlaner, 2000). The same research finds 38 percent of the 84 Asians identified in a GSS pooled sample (1980–1989) are Democrat and 25 percent of them are Republican; Democrats outnumber Republicans by a two to one margin among the 58 Asian respondents in the merged NES sample (1980–1988).

6. There may be an age dimension, too. Collet and Selden (2003) find that the Bay area Vietnamese Americans who are over 45 are much more likely to register as Republican than the younger generation.

7. We call those who answer "do not think in these terms" ("no party") or "not sure" *nonidentifiers*. Respondents who did not indicate identification with any political party are called *no-partisans*. This is to distinguish from the term *nonpartisans*, which is conventionally used in American political behavior research to refer to those who are neither Democrat or Republican but maybe Independent.

8. In 2000 NES, 19 percent are strong Democrat, 15 percent each are weak or leaning Democrat, 12 percent are pure Independent, 13 percent are leaning Republican, 12 percent each are strong or weak Republican, less than 2 percent in total are either apolitical, uncertain, or of another orientation.

9. We treat third party identifiers as pure Independents in this research.

10. The percentages of respondents who possess either very high or somewhat high political interest range from 63 percent among weak Republican to 78 percent among strong Democrats. For more detail, see Table 4.3c.

11. Note, however, that those who score lower on minority status measure are not more likely to be Republicans.
12. For the Asia-born, the number of years of U.S. stay is divided by age; for the U.S.-born, the value is equal to 1 (or age/age). The measure is thus sensitive to not only the impact of nativity but also the learning capacity in relation to age. Given the same length of stay, immigrants who entered at a younger age are accorded a higher value than those who entered at an older age.
13. This explanation may apply to the observations on partisan strength reported in Table 4.6, too.
14. The indicators are prior membership and activism in political organizations, current level of contact with home country people and politics, intent to return to Asia to live, and assessment of relative personal influence on government decisions between the homeland and the adopted land.
15. A detailed discussion of the influence of partisanship as compared to other factors on political participation is found in the next chapter.
16. We thank the reviewers for suggesting this linkage.
17. The percent of respondents who claimed to be contacted by a party may seem high in light of our claims that parties have distanced themselves from the Asian American community throughout American history. However, it is important to keep in mind that we did not ask about direct mobilization by the parties. Thus, contact by the parties in this case may include very passive strategies rather than active mobilization. For instance, some respondents may have been contacted only through mass mailings and e-mail.

Chapter 5

1. However, see excellent discussions of the inappropriateness of using the average median household income to gauge the socioeconomic achievement of Asian Americans in Fong (2002) and Cheng and Yang (1996).
2. However, strength of partisanship is only a strong predictor of voting, not participation in time-based acts beyond voting.
3. We are aware that the direction of influence may be an issue. We address the issue of a possible causal relationship between mobilization and participation later in this chapter.
4. For other minority communities, such as black Americans, the church has long been considered a key source of political organization and mobilization (e.g., Morris, 1984; Dawson, Brown, and Allen, 1990; Wilcox, 1990; Calhoun-Brown, 1996; Harris, 1999). Among Latinos, Jones-Correa and Leal (2001) find that church attendance is important for political participation because churches provide a space for the sharing of political information and recruitment into political networks. Religious institutions in immigrant communities may not only serve as places of worship, but may also serve as civic associations that offer "a safe haven, connection with the home country, a place to exercise leadership abilities, and formal and informal social services" (Berndt, 2001: 72).
5. We are indebted to a reviewer for pointing out that the acquisition of partisanship among Asian Americans may not be strictly linear. Instead, there may be a length of residence "threshold" (around fifteen years) that is critical to the development of partisan attitudes. Further, he or she suggests that it is important to note that regardless of time spent in the U.S., 40–45 percent of Asian Americans are still Independent or nonidentifiers.
6. Correlation coefficients between citizenship and other variables of interest are presented later in the chapter.
7. Data are from the Kaiser Family Foundation/Harvard University/*Washington Post* survey report *Race and Ethnicity in 2001: Attitudes, Perceptions, and Experiences* (available online at www.kff.org/content/2001/3143).
8. We include a measure of income that substitutes the mean-value for missing values. Substituting this measure for the original income measure has no major effect on the results of the analyses and allows us to limit missing values and therefore avoid losing data.
9. As reported in a previous chapter, 41 percent of respondents claimed that they had been contacted during the past four years. Sixty-one percent of respondents who answered "yes" to this question specified that the Democrats had contacted them, 43 percent indicated that the Republicans had contacted them, and 21 percent were not sure which party had contacted

them. Results are similar if we modify the variable to include mobilization by the Democratic or Republican Party alone.

10. Once other variables were controlled in the full multivariate model, prior membership in a political party was not a statistically significant predictor of political participation.

11. Because the impact of any given factor in a MLE model is not constant across values and cannot be interpreted independently of other factor scores, discussion of results and comparison of effect size is facilitated by estimating the parameters with rescaled independent variables with scores varying between 0 and 1 such that lowest scores are all assigned a value of 0 and highest scores are rescaled to reflect a value of 1.

12. Data from the Current Population Survey show that among voting age *citizens*, 43 percent of Asian Americans voted in the November 2000 election compared to 45 percent of Latinos, 57 percent of African Americans, and 62 percent of non-Latino whites. Among the registered, all four groups voted at fairly similar rates (Jamieson, Shin, and Day, 2002).

13. These results are consistent with recent data from the November 2000 Current Population Survey showing that 83 percent of Asian American registered citizens of voting age turned out in the November 2000 election (compared to 86 percent of non-Latino whites, 84 percent of blacks, and 79 percent of Latinos who were registered citizens of voting age) (Jamieson, Shin, and Day, 2002).

14. Note that our claim here is not necessarily a causal one; rather we argue that political engagement and political participation are associated with one another among Asian Americans.

15. It may also be that the more politically active are more likely to join ethnic organizations.

16. Recently, scholars have attempted to address this causality issue by conducting field experiments that compare a randomly selected treatment group of individuals who are contacted to a randomly selected control group who are not contacted. Thus far, contemporary field experiment studies have focused on nonpartisan contacting and voter turnout (Green and Gerber, 2001; Ramirez, 2002). The results of the studies show some evidence that contacting leads to more participation (Green and Gerber, 2001; Ramirez, 2002). However, results of mobilization through contacting vary according to type of contact and sample. For example, in contrast to a more mixed-age turnout effort, Green and Gerber (2001) show that phone contacting of youth by other young people increases turnout. Based on data collected using an experimental design, Ramirez (2002) finds that phone contact among Latinos in a Los Angeles sample only marginally increased turnout overall. However, he found that among a restricted sample of U.S.-born Latinos, contact appeared to increase turnout dramatically. Among U.S.-born Latinos who registered for the first time before 1994, the effects of contact were even more striking.

17. We make this assertion with caution because those who are more politically active may also be most comfortable or compelled to report experience with discrimination.

18. Because the residency requirement for citizenship is five years, generally, we report the percent of citizens and registered voters who have been in the U.S. for six or more years (first two columns of Table 5.6).

19. One explanation for this unexpected result is that the close 2000 presidential race and a fair number of Asian American candidates running for state and local offices drew even those who were not exposed to the political system through the U.S. education system into the voting booth.

20. The Pearson correlation coefficient between the dependent variable (scale of nonvoting participation) and the variable measuring political activity related to the country of origin was .34 (one-tailed $p < .01$).

21. When we focus on specific types of political activity beyond voting, we see that the predictors of participation depend somewhat on type of political activity (Wong, Lien, and Conway, n.d.). For example, family income is a determinant of contacting an elected official, but not protesting. Being more liberal and perceiving a strong panethnic link are predictors of protesting, but not contacting an elected official or working with others in one's community. These three activities were selected for further analysis because they were the only activities in which foreignborn status affected participation.

22. However, though past studies have shown a strong relationship between strength of partisanship and voting, our findings do not suggest that strength of partisanship matters for participation once other political engagement measures are taken into account.

23. The movement for redress, led by Japanese Americans, resulted in the passage of the Civil Liberties Act of 1988. As a result of the movement, the U.S. government offered a formal

apology to Japanese Americans interned during the war and $20,000 to surviving internees. We are indebted to the reviewers for suggesting possible mobilization forces and their potential influence on participation rates among Japanese Americans.

Chapter 6

1. This is the full list of explanatory variables considered. Various sets of variables were dropped at one time or another from the final models reported in this chapter because of the concerns over their theoretical relevance and empirical relationships to other variables in the models.
2. Most of the statistical information and results regarding these models are reported in preceding chapters.
3. Multivariate tables for this and other variables dealing with political orientations are not shown but are available from the authors upon request.
4. Detailed discussion of the statistical models estimating the relative role of gender in deciding ethnic self-identity preference is found in Chapter 2, Tables 2.7 to 2.9.

Chapter 7

1. The forced choice question asked all those who did not initially identify as "Asian American" if they had *ever* identified as "Asian American."
2. However, the latter is not associated with either the adoption or the strength of panethnicity.
3. We are indebted to the reviewers for their valuable insights on this point.
4. Lee (2000) claims that, for example, stereotypes of Asian Americans as perpetual foreigners justified the Democratic National Committee's response to accusations that it had accepted illegal donations from foreigners in 1996 when the party contacted all Asian Pacific American donors with "foreign sounding" surnames to ask them to prove their citizenship or legal status in the United States.
5. Similar to this study, other studies using survey data conclude that mobilization predicts voter turnout. However, these studies are limited, as noted in Chapter 5, because researchers cannot be certain that higher rates of turnout among those who indicate that they have been mobilized are really attributable to contact, or whether they are due to other factors. Randomized field experiments do show evidence that mobilization leads to turnout (Gerber and Green, 2000; Green and Gerber, 2001; Michaelson, 2002).
6. A majority of Latinos who took part in a national survey in 2000 conducted jointly by the Kaiser Family Foundation, Harvard University, and the *Washington Post*, support bilingual education and a large proportion preferred Spanish-language instructions. On the other hand, a plurality of Asian Americans (45 percent) support a quota on legal immigration to the United States, even though a large proportion (approximately one in three) express no opinion on the matter. About 17 percent of Latinos in the same national survey of Latinos support a decrease in immigration in the United States, while 50 percent thought immigration levels should remain the same. Statistics and information on Latino public opinion are from the 2000 Kaiser Family Foundation/*Washington Post*/Harvard *2000 National Survey on Latinos in America.* Note that question wording varies between the PNAAPS and this survey. http://www.kff.org/content/2000/3023/LatinoFullToplineFinal.PDF
7. Statistics and information on Latino public opinion are from the Kaiser Family Foundation/*Washington Post*/Harvard survey *Race and Ethnicity in 2001: Attitudes, Perceptions, and Experiences.* Note that question wording varies between the PNAAPS and this survey. http://www.kff.org/content/2001/3143/RacialBiracialToplines.pdf
8. In the 2001 multiracial national survey mentioned above, non-Latino whites are the only major racial group for which the proportion of Republican identifiers (37 percent) is larger than the proportion of Democratic identifiers (29 percent). Approximately 37 percent of Asian Americans, 44 percent of Latinos, and 68 percent of blacks in the survey identified as Democrat.

References

Abelmann, Nancy, and John Lie. 1995. *Blue Dreams: Korean Americans and the Los Angeles Riots.* Cambridge, Mass.: Harvard University Press.

Abramson, Paul, John Aldrich, and David Rohde. 1998. *Change and Continuity in the 1996 Elections.* Washington, D.C.: Congressional Quarterly.

Akers, Joshua. 2002. "Kansas Repeals Law Banning Asian Immigrants From Inheriting Property." Associated Press. June 4.

Alba, Richard D., and Victor Nee. 1997. "Rethinking Assimilation Theory for a New Era of Immigrants." *International Migration Review* 31: 826–75.

Alex-Assensoh, Yvette, and A. B. Assensoh. 2001. "Inner-City Contexts, Church Attendance, and African-American Political Participation." *Journal of Politics* 63: 886–901.

Anderson, Kristi. 1979. *The Creation of a Democratic Majority, 1928–1936.* Chicago: University of Chicago Press.

Atkin, Charles. 1981. "Communication and Political Socialization." In *Political Communication Handbook,* edited by Dan Nimmo and Keith Sanders, 299–328. Beverly Hills, Calif.: Sage.

Arvizu, John R., and F. Chris Garcia. 1996. "Latino Voting Participation: Explaining and Differentiating Latino Voting Turnout." *Hispanic Journal of Behavioral Sciences* 18: 104–28.

Barkan, Elliott R. 1983. "Whom Shall We Integrate: A Comparative Analysis of the Immigration and Naturalization Trends of Asians before and after the 1965 Immigration Act (1951–1978)." *Journal of American Ethnic History* 3: 29–55.

Barnes, Jessica S., and Claudette Bennett. 2002. *The Asian Population: 2000.* Census 2000 Brief (C2KBR/01-16). Washington, D.C.: U.S. Department of Commerce, Bureau of the Census.

Bartels, Larry. 2000. "Partisanship and Voting Behavior, 1952–1996." *American Journal of Political Science* 44: 35–50.

Basch, Linda, Nina Glick Schiller, and Christina Szanton Blanc. 1994. *Nations Unbound.* Langhorne, Pa.: Gordon and Breach.

Baxter, Sandra, and Marjorie Lansing. 1983. *Women and Politics: The Visible Majority.* Rev. ed. Ann Arbor, Mich.: University of Michigan Press.

Beck, Paul Allen. 1974. "A Socialization Theory of Partisan Realignment." In Richard G. Niemi and Associates, *The Politics of Future Citizens.* San Francisco: Jossey Bass Publishers.

Beck, Paul Allen, and M. Kent Jennings. 1991. "Family Traditions, Political Periods, and the Development of Partisan Orientations." *Journal of Politics* 53: 742–63.

Bell, David. 1985. "The Triumph of Asian Americans." *The New Republic,* July 15–22: 24–31.

Bennett, Linda L. M., and Stephen Earl Bennett. 1989. "Enduring Gender Differences in Political Interest: The Impact of Socialization and Political Dispositions." *American Politics Quarterly* 17: 105–22.

Berndt, Jerry. 2001. "The Soul of Los Angeles." *Cross Currents* 51: 71–82.

Black, Jerome H., and Leithner, C. 1988. "Immigrants and Political Involvement in Canada: The Role of the Ethnic Media." *Canadian Ethnic Studies* 20 (1): 1–20.

Blais, Andre, Elisabeth Gidengil, Richard Nadeau, and Neit Nevitte. 2001. "Measuring Party Identification: Britain, Canada, and the United States." *Political Behavior* 23: 5–22.

Blalock, Hubert M., Jr. 1967. *Toward a Theory of Minority-Group Relations.* New York: John Wiley & Sons.

Burns, Nancy, Kay Lehman Schlozman, and Sidney Verba. 2001. *The Private Roots of Public Action.* Cambridge, Mass.: Harvard University Press.

Cain, Bruce. 1991. "The Contemporary Context of Ethnic and Racial Politics in California." In *Racial and Ethnic Politics in California,* edited by Byran O. Jackson and Michael B. Preston, 9–24. Berkeley: IGS Press.

Cain, Bruce E., D. Roderick Kiewiet, and Carole J. Uhlaner. 1991. "The Acquisition of Partisanship by Latinos and Asian Americans." *American Journal of Political Science* 35: 390–422.

Calhoun-Brown, Allison. 1996. "African-American Churches and Political Mobilization: The Psychological Impact of Organizational Resources." *Journal of Politics* 58: 935–53.

Campbell, Angus, Philip E. Converse, Warren E. Miller, and Donald E. Stokes. 1960. *The American Voter.* Chicago: University of Chicago Press.

Caplan, N., J. K. Whitmore, and M. H. Choy. 1989. *The Boat People and Achievement in America: A Study of Family Life, Hard Work, and Cultural Values.* Ann Arbor, Mich.: University of Michigan Press.

Carnes, Tony, and Fenggang Yang, eds. 2003. *Asian American Religions: Borders and Boundaries.* New York: New York University Press.

Chaffee, Steven H., Clifford I. Nass, and Seung-Mock Yang. 1990. "The Bridging Role of Television in Immigrant Political Socialization." *Human Communication Research* 17: 266–88.

Chaffee, Steven H., and Seung-Mock Yang. 1990. "Communication and Political Socialization." In *Political Socialization, Citizenship, Education, and Democracy,* edited by O. Ichilov, 137–57. New York: Teachers College Press.

Chan, Sucheng. 1991. *Asian Americans: An Interpretive History.* Boston: Twayne Publishers.

Chang, Gordon. 2001. "Asian Americans and Politics: Some Perspectives From History." In *Asian Americans and Politics: Perspectives, Experiences, Prospects,* edited by Gordon Chang, 13–38. Stanford, Calif.: Stanford University Press.

Cheng, Lucie, and Edna Bonacich, eds. 1984. *Labor Immigration under Capitalism: Asian Workers in the United States before World War II.* Berkeley, Calif.: University of California Press.

Cheng, Lucie, and Philip Yang. 1996. "The 'Model Minority' Deconstructed." In *Ethnic Los Angeles,* edited by Roger Waldinger and Mehdi Bozorgmmehr, 305–44. New York: Russell Sage Foundation.

Chin, Tung Pok. 2000. *Paper Son: One Man's Story.* Philadelphia, Pa.: Temple University Press.

Cho, Wendy K. Tam. 1999. "Naturalization, Socialization, Participation: Immigrants and (Non-) Voting." *Journal of Politics* 61: 1140–55.

———. 2001. "Foreshadowing Strategic Pan-Ethnic Politics: Asian American Campaign Finance Activity in Varying Multicultural Contexts." *State Politics & Policy Quarterly* 1 (3): 273–94.

Cho, Wendy Tam, and Bruce Cain. 2001. "Asian Americans as the Median Voters: An Exploration of Attitudes and Voting Patterns on Ballot Initiatives." In *Asian Americans and Politics: Perspectives, Experiences, Prospects,* edited by Gordon Chang, 133–52. Stanford, Calif.: Stanford University Press.

Chow, Esther Ngan-Ling. 1987. "The Development of Feminist Consciousness Among Asian American Women." *Gender and Society* (3): 284–99.

Clark, Janet, and Cal Clark. 1996. "The Gender Gap: A Manifestation of Women's Dissatisfaction with the American Polity." In *Broken Contract? Changing Relationships between Americans and Their Government,* edited by Stephen Craig, 167–82. Boulder, Colo.: Westview Press.

Collet, Christian, and Nadine Selden. 2003. "Separate Ways . . . Worlds Apart?: The 'Generation Gap' in Vietnamese America as Seen through *The San Jose Mercury News* Poll." *Amerasia Journal.* (forthcoming)

Converse, Philip E. 1969. "Of Time and Partisan Stability." *Comparative Political Studies* 2: 139–71.

———. 1976. *The Dynamics of Party Support: Cohort-Analyzing Party Identification.* Beverly Hills, Calif.: Sage.

Conway, M. Margaret. 1991. *Political Participation in the United States,* 2d ed. Washington, D.C.: Congressional Quarterly Press.

———. 2000. *Political Participation in the United States*, 3d ed. Washington, D.C.: CQ Press.

———. 2001a. "Political Participation in American Elections: Who Decides What." In *America's Choice,* edited by William J. Crotty, 79–94. New York: Westview Press.

———. 2001b. "Political Mobilization in America." In *The State of Democracy in America,* edited by William J. Crotty, 31–46. Washington, D.C.: Georgetown University Press.

Conway, M. Margaret, and Alfonso J. Damico. 2000. "Patterns of Socialization to Community and Political Participation: A Longitudinal Study." Paper presented at the Annual Meeting of the International Society of Political Psychology, July 1–4. Seattle, Wash.

Conway, M. Margaret, Gertrude A. Steuernagel, and David W. Ahern. 1997. *Women and Political Participation.* Washington, D.C.: CQ Press.

Dahl, Robert. 1961. *Who Governs? Democracy and Power in an American City.* New Haven, Conn.: Yale University Press.

Damico, Alfonso J., M. Margaret Conway, and Sandra Bowman Damico. 1998. "The Democratic Education of Women." *Women and Politics* 19 (2): 1–31.

———. 2000. "Patterns of Political Trust and Mistrust: Three Moments in the Lives of Democratic Citizens." *Polity* 32 (spring): 377–400.

Daniels, Roger. 1971. *Concentration Camps USA: Japanese Americans and World War II.* Hinsdale, Ill.: Dryden Press.

———. 1988. *Asian America: Chinese and Japanese in the United States since 1850.* Seattle: University of Washington Press.

Dawson, Michael. 1994. *Behind the Mule: The Roots of Contemporary African-American Political Ideologies.* Chicago: University of Chicago Press.

Dawson, Michael, Ronald Brown, and Richard Allen. 1990. "Racial Belief Systems, Religious Guidance, and African American Political Participation." *National Political Science Review* 2: 22–44.

de la Garza, Rodolfo, Angelo Falcon, F. Chris Garcia, and John A. Garcia. 1992. *Latino Voices: Mexican, Puerto Rican, and Cuban Perspectives on American Politics.* Boulder, Colo.: Westview.

de la Garza, Rodolfo, Martha Menchaca, and Louis DeSipio. 1994. *Barrio Ballots: Latino Politics in the 1990 Elections.* Boulder, Colo.: Westview.

de Tocqueville, Alexis. 1969. *Democracy in America.* Edited by J. P. Mayer. George Lawrence (trans). New York: Doubleday.

DeSipio, Louis. 1996. *Counting the Latino Vote: Latinos as a New Electorate.* Charlottesville, Va.: University of Virginia Press.

DeSipio, Louis, and Jennifer Jerit. 1998. "Voluntary Citizens and Democratic Participation: Political Behaviors among Naturalized U.S. Citizens." Paper presented at the Annual Meeting of the Midwest Political Science Association, Chicago.

Delli Carpini, Michael X., and Scott Keller. 2000. "Gender and Knowledge." In *Gender and American Politics,* edited by Jyl Josephson and Sue Tolleson-Rinehart, 21–52. Armonk, N.Y.: M.E. Sharpe.

Dinnerstein, Leonard, Roger L. Nichols, and David M. Reimers. 1996. *Natives and Strangers: A Multicultural History of Americans.* New York: Oxford University Press.

Dirlik, Arif. 1996. "Asians on the Rim: Transnational Capital and Local Community in the Making of Contemporary Asian America." *Amerasia* 22 (3): 1–24.

———. 1998. "The Asia-Pacific in Asian-American Perspective." In *What Is in a Rim? Critical Perspectives on the Pacific Region Idea.* 2d ed., edited by Arif Dirlik, 283–308. Lanham, Md.: Roman and Littlefield Publishers, Inc.

Dvorak, Todd. 2002. "GOP Pulls Support for Iowa Hopeful." Associated Press. October 27.

Edmonston, Barry, and Charles Schultze, eds. 1995. *Modernizing the U.S. Census.* Washington, D.C.: National Academy Press.

Eldersveld, Samuel J., Hanes Walton, Jr. 2000. *Political Parties in American Society.* 2d ed. Boston: Bedford/St. Martin's.

Erie, Steven P. 1988. *Rainbow's End.* Berkeley: University of California Press.

Erie, Steven P., and Harold Brackman. 1993. *Paths to Political Incorporation for Latinos and Asian Pacifics in California.* Berkeley: University of California and the California Policy Seminar.

Espiritu, Yen Le. 1992. *Asian American Panethnicity.* Philadelphia, Pa.: Temple University Press.

———. 1997. *Asian American Women and Men: Labor, Laws, and Love.* Thousand Oaks, Calif.: Sage Publications.

Espiritu, Yen Le, and Michael Omi. 2000. "Who Are You Calling Asian?" In *The State of Asian Pacific America, Volume IV: Transforming Race Relations,* edited by Paul M. Ong, 43–101. Los Angeles, Calif.: LEAP and UCLA Asian American Studies Center.

Eveland, William P., Jr. 2002. "News Information Processing as Mediator of the Relationship between Motivation and Political Knowledge." *Journalism and Mass Communication Quarterly* 79 (1): 26–40.

Eveland, William P., Jr., and Dietram A. Scheufele. 2000. "Connecting News Media Use with Gaps in Knowledge and Participation." *Political Communication* 17: 215–37.

Eveland, William P., Jr., Jack M. McLeod, and Edward M. Horowitz. 1998. "Communication and Age in Childhood Political Socialization: An Interactive Model of Political Development." *Journalism and Mass Communication* 75 (4): 699–718.

Faist, Thomas. 2000. "Transnationalization in International Migration: Implications for the Study of Citizenship and Culture." *Ethnic and Racial Studies* 23: 189–222.

Feagin, Joe R., and Clairece Feagin. 1999. *Racial and Ethnic Relations.* 6th ed. Upper Saddle River, N.J.: Prentice Hall.

Finifter, Ada W., and Bernard M. Finifter. 1989. "Party Identification and Political Adaptation of American Migrants in Australia." *Journal of Politics* 51: 599–630.

Finkel, Steven E. 1986. "Reciprocal Effects of Participation and Political Efficacy: A Panel Analysis." *American Journal of Political Science* 29: 891–913.

Fiorina, Morris. 1981. *Retrospective Voting in American National Elections.* New Haven, Conn.: Yale University Press.

Flanigan, William H., and Nancy H. Zingale. 1994. *Political Behavior of the American Electorate.* 8th ed. Washington, D.C.: CQ Press.

Flexner, Eleanor. 1975. *Century of Struggle,* rev. ed. Cambridge, Mass.: Harvard University Press.

Foner, Nancy. 2001. "Transnationalism Then and Now: New York Immigrants Today and at the Turn of the Twentieth Century." In *Migration, Transnationalization, and Race in a Changing New York,* edited by Hector Cordero-Guzman, Robert C. Smith, and Ramon Grosfoguel, 35–57. Philadelphia, Pa.: Temple University Press.

Fong, Timothy. 1998. *The Contemporary Asian American Experience.* Upper Saddle River, N.J.: Prentice Hall.

———. 2002. *The Contemporary Asian American Experience.* 2d ed. Upper Saddle River, N.J.: Prentice Hall.

Freedman, Amy. 2000. *Political Participation and Ethnic Minorities.* New York: Routledge.

Frymer, Paul. 1999. *Uneasy Alliances: Race and Party Competition in America.* Princeton, N.J.: Princeton University Press.

Fuchs, Lawrence H. 1990. *The American Kaleidoscope: Race, Ethnicity, and the Civic Culture.* Hanover, Conn.: Wesleyan University Press.

Gans, Herbert. 1992. "Second Generation Decline: Scenarios for the Economic and Ethnic Futures of the Post-1965 American Immigrants." *Ethnic and Racial Studies* 15: 173–92.

Gerber, Alan S., and Donald P. Green. 2000. "The Effects of Canvassing, Direct Mail, and Telephone Contact on Voter Turnout: A Field Experiment." *American Political Science Review* 94: 469–86.

Geron, Kim, and James Lai. 2001. "Transforming Ethnic Politics: A Comparative Analysis of Electoral Support for and Policy Priorities of Asian American and Latino Elected Officials." Paper presented at the Annual Meeting of the American Political Science Association, San Francisco.

Gerstle, Gary, and John Mollenkopf, eds. 2001. *E Pluribus Unum? Contemporary and Historical Perspectives on Immigrant Political Incorporation.* New York: Russell Sage Foundation.

Gibson, Margaret. 1988. *Accommodation without Assimilation: Sikh Immigrant Children in an American High School.* Ithaca, N.Y.: Cornell University Press.

Gilroy, Paul. 1993. *The Black Atlantic.* Cambridge, Mass.: Harvard University Press.

Gitelman, Zvi. 1982. *Becoming Israelies: Political Socialization of Soviet and American Immigrants.* New York: Praeger.

Glazer, Nathan, and Daniel Patrick Moynihan. 1963. *Beyond the Melting Pot.* Cambridge, Mass.: MIT Press.

Glenn, Evelyn Nakano. 1985. "Racial Ethnic Women's Labor: The Intersection of Race, Gender, and Class Oppression." *Review of Radical Political Economics* 17: 86–108.

Glick-Schiller, Nina, Linda Basch, and Cristina Blanc-Szanton. 1995. "From Immigrant to Transmigrant: Theorizing Transnational Migration." *Anthropological Quarterly* 68: 48–63.

Gordon, Milton. 1964. *Assimilation in American Life: The Role of Race, Religion, and National Origins.* New York: Oxford University Press.

Graham, Pamela M. 1997. "Reimagining the Nation and Defining the District: Dominican Migration and Transnational Politics." In *Caribbean Circuits: New Directions in the Study of Caribbean Migration,* edited by Patricia Pessar, 91–126. New York: Center for Migration Studies.

Green, Donald P., and Alan S. Gerber. 2001. "Getting Out the Youth Vote in Local Elections: Results from Six Door-to-Door Canvassing Experiments." Institution for Social and Policy Studies, Yale University. www.yale.edu/isps/publications/doortodoor.pdf (accessed July 26, 2003).

Green, Donald, Bradley Palmquist, and Eric Schickler. 2002. *Partisan Hearts and Minds: Political Parties and the Social Identities of Voters.* New Haven, Conn.: Yale University Press.

Groves, Robert M., and Robert L. Kahn. 1979. *Surveys by Telephone: A National Comparison with Personal Interviews.* New York: Academic Press.

Groves, Robert M., P. N. Biemer, L. E. Lyberg, J. T. Massey, W. L. Nicholas II., and J. Waksberg, eds. 1988. *Telephone Survey Methodology.* New York: Wiley.

Gurin, Patricia, Shirley Hatchett, and James Jackson. 1989. *Hope and Independence: Blacks' Response to Electoral and Party Politics.* New York, N.Y.: Russell Sage Foundation.

Gyory, Andrew. 1998. *Closing the Gate: Race, Politics, and the Chinese Exclusion Act.* Chapel Hill: University of North Carolina Press.

Hajnal, Zoltan, and Mark Baldassare. 2001. "Finding Common Ground: Racial and Ethnic Attitudes in California." Report, Public Policy Institute of California, San Francisco, Calif.

Hall, Patrica Wong, and Victor Hwang, eds. 2001. *Anti-Asian Violence in North America.* Walnut Creek, Calif.: AltaMira.

Hardy-Fanta, Carol. 1993. *Latina Politics, Latino Politics: Gender, Culture, and Political Participation in Boston.* Philadelphia, Pa.: Temple University Press.

Harles, John C. 1993. *Politics in the Lifeboat: Immigrants and the American Democratic Order.* Boulder, Colo.: Westview Press.

Harris, Fredrick. 1999. *Something Within: Religion in African-American Political Activism.* New York: Oxford University Press.

Henig, Jeffrey, and Dennis E. Gale. 1987. "The Political Incorporation of Newcomers to Racially Changing Neighborhoods." *Urban Affairs Quarterly* 22: 399–419.

Hero, Rodney. 1992. *Latinos and U.S. Political System: Two-Tiered Pluralism.* Philadelphia, Pa.: Temple University Press.

Hill, Kevin A., Dario Moreno, and Lourdes Cue. 2001. "Racial and Partisan Voting in a Tri-Ethnic City." *Journal of Urban Affairs* 23: 291–307.

Hing, Bill Ong. 1993. *Making and Remaking Asian America through Immigration Policy 1850–1990.* Stanford, Calif.: Stanford University Press.

Hong, Joann, and Pyong Gap Min. 1999. "Ethnic Attachment among Second Generation Korean Adolescents." *Amerasia Journal* 25 (1): 165–178.

Hoskin, Marilyn. 1989. *New Immigrants and Democratic Society: Minority Integration in Western Democracies.* New York: Praeger.

Houghland, James, and James Christenson. 1983. "Religion and Politics: The Relationship of Religious Participation to Political Efficacy and Involvement." *Sociology and Social Research* 67: 406–420.

Huckfeldt, Robert, and John Sprague. 1995. *Citizens, Politics, and Social Communication.* New York: Cambridge University Press.

Hum, Tarry, and Michaela Zonta. 2000. "Residential Patterns of Asian Pacific Americans." In *The State of Asian Pacific America: Transforming Race Relations,* edited by Paul M. Ong, 191–242. Los Angeles, Calif.: LEAP Asian Pacific American Policy Institute and UCLA Asian American Studies Center.

Hune, Shirley. 2000. "Doing Gender with a Feminist Gaze: Toward a Historical Reconstruction of Asian America." In *Contemporary Asian America: A Multidisciplinary Reader,* edited by Min Zhou and James V. Gatewood, 413–30. New York: New York University Press.

Huntington, Samuel P. 1968. *Political Order in Changing Societies.* New Haven, Conn.: Yale University Press.

Ichioka, Yuji. 1988. *The Issei: The World of the First Generation Japanese Immigrants, 1885–1924.* New York: The Free Press.

Ignatiev, Noel. 1995. *How the Irish Became White.* London: Verso.

Isajiw, Wsevolod W. 1990. "Ethnic-Identity Retention." In *Ethnic Identity and Equality,* edited by Raymond Breton et al., 34–91. Toronto, Canada: University of Toronto Press.

Iwamura, Jane, and Paul Spickard, eds. 2003. *Revealing the Sacred in Asian and Pacific America*. New York: Routledge.

Jackson, Byran O. 1987. "The Effects of Racial Group Consciousness on Political Mobilization in American Cities." *Western Political Quarterly* 40: 631–46.

Jackson, Jay W., and Eliot R. Smith. 1999. "Conceptualizing Social Identity." *Personality & Social Psychology Bulletin* 25 (1): 120–35.

Jacobson, Matthew F. 1998. *Whiteness of a Different Color: European Immigrants and the Alchemy of Race*. Cambridge, Mass.: Harvard University Press.

Jamieson, Amie, Hyon B. Shin, and Jennifer Day. 2002. *Voting and Registration in the Election of November 2000*. Current Population Reports (P20-542). Washington, D.C.: U.S. Department of Commerce, Bureau of the Census.

Jennings, M. Kent. 1987. "Residues of a Movement: The Aging of the American Protest Generation." *American Political Science Review* 81 (June): 367–82.

———. 1996. "Political Knowledge across Time and Generations." *Public Opinion Quarterly* 60: 223–52.

Jennings, M. Kent, and Richard G. Niemi. 1981. *Generations and Politics*. Princeton, N.J.: Princeton University Press.

Jennings, M. Kent, and Gregory Markus. 1984. "Political Orientations over the Long Haul: Results from the Three Wave Political Socialization Panel Study." *American Political Science Review* 78: 1000–18.

Jiobu, Robert M. 1996. "Recent Asian Pacific Immigrants: The Demographic Background." In *The State of Asian Pacific America: Reframing the Immigration Debate: A Public Policy Report*, edited by Bill Ong Hing and Ronald Lee, 35–57. Los Angeles, Calif.: LEAP Asian Pacific American Public Policy Institute and UCLA Asian American Studies Center.

Jones-Correa, Michael. 1998. *Between Two Nations: The Political Predicament of Latinos in New York City*. Ithaca, N.Y.: Cornell University Press.

Jones-Correa, Michael, and David L. Leal. 1996. "Becoming 'Hispanic': Secondary Panethnic Identification among Latin American-Origin Populations in the United States." *Hispanic Journal of Behavioral Sciences* 18: 214–54.

———. 2001. "Political Participation: Does Religion Matter?" *Political Research Quarterly* 54: 751–70.

Josephson, Jyl, and Sue Tolleson-Rinehart. 2000. "Introduction. Gender, Sex, and American Political Life." In *Gender and American Politics* edited by Josephson and S. Tolleson-Rinehart. Armonk, N.Y.: M.E. Sharpe.

Junn, Jane. 1999. "Participation in a Liberal Democracy: The Political Assimilation of Immigrants and Ethnic Minorities in the United States." *The American Behavioral Scientist* 42: 1417–38.

Karpathakis, Anna. 1999. "Home Society Politics and Immigrant Political Incorporation: The Case of Greek Immigrants in New York City." *International Migration Review* 33: 55–79.

Keith, Bruce E., David Magleby, Candice Nelson, Elizabeth Orr, Mark Westlye, and Raymond Wolfinger. 1992. *The Myth of the Independent Voter*. Berkeley: University of California Press.

Kibria, Nazli. 1990. "Power, Patriarchy, and Gender Conflict in the Vietnamese Immigrant Community." *Gender and Society* 4 (1): 9–24.

———. 1997. "The Construction of 'Asian American'." *Ethnic and Racial Studies* 20: 523–44.

———. 2000. "Race, Ethnic Options, and Ethnic Binds: Identity Negotiations of Second-Generation Chinese and Korean Americans." *Sociological Perspectives* 43: 77–96.

Kim, Claire. 1999. "The Racial Triangulation of Asian Americans." *Politics and Society* 27: 105–38.

———. 2000. *Bitter Fruit: The Politics of Black-Korean Conflict in New York City*. New Haven, Conn.: Yale University Press.

Kim, Claire, and Taeku Lee. 2001. "Interracial Politics: Asian Americans and Other Communities of Color." *PS: Political Science and Politics* 34: 631–38.

Kim, Hyung-chan. 1994. *A Legal History of Asian Americans, 1790–1990*. Westport, Conn.: Greenwood Press.

———. 1996. *Asian Americans and Congress: A Documentary History*. Westport, Conn.: Greenwood Press.

Kim, Thomas P. 2000. "Why Parties Fail Asian Americans." Paper delivered at the Annual Meeting of the American Political Science Association, August 31–September 3, Washington, D.C.

Kinder, Donald R., and Nicholas Winter. 2001. "Exploring the Racial Divide: Blacks, Whites, and Opinion on National Policy." *American Journal of Political Science* 45: 439–56.

Kitano, Harry L., and Roger Daniels. 1995. *Asian Americans: Emerging Minorities.* 2d ed. Englewood Cliffs, N.J.: Prentice-Hall.

Kraus, Sidney, and Dennis Davis. 1976. *The Effects of Mass Communication on Political Behavior.* University Park. Pa.: The Pennsylvania State University Press.

Kwoh, Stewart, and Mindy Hui. 1993. "Empowering Our Communities: Political Policy." In *The State of Asian Pacific America: Policy Issues to the Year 2020, 189–98.* Los Angeles, Calif.: LEAP Asian Pacific American Policy Institute and UCLA Asian American Studies Center.

Kwong, Peter. 1987. *The New Chinatown.* New York: Hill & Wang.

———. 1997. *Forbidden Workers: Illegal Chinese Immigrants and American Labor.* New York: New Press.

Lai, Him Mark. 1992. *From Overseas Chinese to Chinese Americans.* (In Chinese). Hong Kong: Joint Publishing Co.

Lai, James. 2000. Beyond Voting: The Recruitment of Asian Pacific American Elected Officials and Their Impact on Group Political Mobilization. Ph.D. Dissertation. Department of Political Science, University of Southern California.

Lai, James, Wendy Cho, Thomas Kim, and Okiyoshi Takeda. 2001. "Asian Pacific American Campaigns, Elections, and Elected Officials." *PS: Political Science and Politics* 34: 611–18.

Lee, Robert. 1999. *Orientals: Asian Americans in Popular Culture.* Philadelphia, Pa.: Temple University Press.

Lee, Stacey. 1996. "Perceptions of Panethnicity Among Asian American High School Students." *Amerasia Journal* 22: 109–25.

Lee, Taeku. 2000. "Racial Attitudes and the Color Line(s) at the Close of the Twentieth Century." In *The State of Asian Pacific America: Transforming Race Relations,* edited by Paul M. Ong, 103–58. Los Angeles, Calif.: LEAP Asian Pacific American Policy Institute and UCLA Asian American Studies Center.

Leighley, Jan. 2001. *Strength in Numbers? The Political Mobilization of Racial and Ethnic Minorities.* Princeton, N.J.: Princeton University Press.

Lien, Pei-te. 1994. "Ethnicity and Political Participation: A Comparison between Asian and Mexican Americans." *Political Behavior* 16: 237–64.

———. 1997. *The Political Participation of Asian Americans: Voting Behavior in Southern California.* New York, N.Y.: Garland Publishing.

———. 1998. "Does the Gender Gap in Political Attitudes and Behavior Vary across Racial Groups?" *Political Research Quarterly* 51: 869–94.

———. 2000. "Who Votes in Multiracial America? An Analysis of Voting and Registration by Race and Ethnicity, 1990–96." In *Black and Multiracial Politics in America,* edited by Yvette Alex-Assensoh and Lawrence Hanks, 199–224. New York: New York University Press.

———. 2001a. "Race, Gender, and the Comparative Status of Asian American Women in Voting Participation." In *Asian Americans and Politics: Perspectives, Experiences, and Prospects,* edited by Gordon Chang, 173–93. Stanford, Calif.: Stanford University Press.

———. 2001b. *The Making of Asian America through Political Participation.* Philadelphia, Pa.: Temple University Press.

———. 2003. "Comparing the Voting Participation of Chinese to Other Asian Americans in U.S. Elections." *Chinese America: History and Perspectives* 17: 1–13.

———. 2003. "Religion and Political Adaptation among Asian Americans: An Empirical Assessment From the Multi-Site Asian American Political Survey." In *Asian American Religions: Borders and Boundaries,* edited by Tony Carnes and Fenggeng Yang. New York: New York University Press. (forthcoming)

———. 2003. "Behind the Numbers: Talking Politics with Immigrant Chinese Americans." Paper presented at the Annual Meeting of the American Political Science Association, August 26–31, Philadelphia.

Lien, Pei-te, Christian Collet, Janelle Wong, and Karthick Ramakrishnan. 2001. "Asian Pacific American Politics Symposium: Public Opinion and Political Participation." *PS: Political Science and Politics* 34: 625–30.

Lien, Pei-te, M. Margaret Conway, Taeku Lee, and Janelle Wong. 2001a. "The Mosaic of Asian American Politics: Preliminary findings from the Five-City Post-Election Survey." Paper presented at the Annual Meeting of the Midwest Political Science Association, Chicago.

———. 2001b. "The Pilot Asian American Political Survey: Summary Report." In *The National Asian Pacific American Political Almanac, 2001-02,* edited by James Lai and Don Nakanishi, 80–95. Los Angeles, Calif.: UCLA Asian American Studies Center.

Lien, Pei-te, and Taeku Lee. 2001. "The Political Significance of Group Dynamics among Asians in America." Paper presented at the Annual Meeting of the American Political Science Association, August 30–September 2, San Francisco.

Lin, Jan. 1998. *Reconstructing Chinatown: Ethnic Enclave, Global Change.* Minneapolis: University of Minnesota Press.

Lin, Ann Chih. n.d. "Group Inclusion or Group Rights? Ethnic Advocacy Groups and the Political Incorporation of Immigrants." Unpublished manuscript.

Ling, Huping. 1998. *Surviving on the Gold Mountain: A History of Chinese American Women and Their Lives.* Albany, N.Y.: State University of New York.

Liu, Eric. 1998. *The Accidental Asian: Notes of a Native Speaker.* New York: Random House.

Liu, John, and Lucie Cheng. 1994. "Pacific Rim Development and the Duality of Post-1965 Asian Immigration to the United States." In *The New Asian Immigration in Los Angeles and Global Restructuring,* edited by Paul Ong, Edna Bonacich, and Lucie Cheng, 74–99. Philadelphia, Pa.: Temple University Press.

Lollock, Lisa. 2001. "The Foreign-Born Population in the United States: March 2000. Current Population Reports, P20-534." Washington, D.C.: U.S. GPO.

Lopez, David, and Yen Espiritu. 1990. "Panethnicity in the United States: A Theoretical Framework." *Ethnic and Racial Studies* 13: 199–224.

Lott, Juanita T. 1997. *Asian Americans: From Racial Category to Multiple Identities.* Walnut Creek, Calif.: Alta Mira Press.

Lowe, Lisa. 1996. *Immigrant Acts: On Asian American Cultural Politics.* Durham, N.C.: Duke University Press.

Lublin, David. 1997. "The Election of African Americans and Latinos to the U.S. House of Representatives, 1972–1994." *American Politics Quarterly* 25: 269–87.

Magpantay, Glenn. 2002. "Asian American Access to Democracy in the NYC 2001 Elections." New York: Asian American Legal Defense and Education Fund.

Mayhew, David R. 1986. *Placing Parties in American Politics: Organization, Electoral Settings, and Government Activity in the Twentieth Century.* New Jersey: Princeton University Press.

Mazumdar, Sucheta. 1989. "General Introduction: A Woman-Centered Perspective on Asian American History." In *Making Waves: An Anthology of Writings by and about Asian American Women,* edited by Asian Women United of California, 1–22. Boston: Beacon Press.

McAdam, Doug. 1982. *Political Process and the Development of Black Insurgency, 1930–1970.* Chicago: University of Chicago Press.

McClain, Paula, and Joseph Stewart, Jr. 1995. *"Can We All Get Along?" Racial and Ethnic Minorities in American Politics.* Boulder, Colo.: Westview Press.

McLeod, Jack M. 2000. "Media and Civic Socialization of Youth." *Journal of Adolescent Health.* Society for Adolescent Medicine, Conference Proceedings, 27S: 45–51.

McLeod, Jack M., Deitram A. Scheufele, and Patricia Moy. 1999. "Community, Communication, and Participation: The Role of Mass Media and Interpersonal Discussion in Local Political Participation." *Political Communication* 16: 315–36.

Michaelson, Melissa R. 2002. "Turning Out Latino Voters." Paper delivered at the 2002 Annual Meeting of the American Political Science Association, August 29–September 1, Boston.

Miller, Arthur H., Patricia Gurin, Gerald Gurin, and Oksana Malanchuk. 1981. "Group Consciousness and Political Participation." *American Journal of Political Science* 25: 494–511.

Miller, Warren E., and Shanks, J. Merrill. 1996. *The New American Voter.* Cambridge, Mass.: Harvard University Press.

Min, Pyong Gap. 1990. "Problems of Korean Immigrant Entrepreneurs. *International Migration Review* 24: 436–55.

———. ed. 1995. *Asian Americans: Contemporary Trends and Issues.* Thousand Oaks, Calif.: Sage.

———.1999. "Ethnicity: Concepts, Theories, and Trends." In *Struggle for Ethnic Identity,* edited by Pyong Gap Min and Rose Kim, 16–46. Walnut Creek, Calif.: AltaMira Press.

Min, Pyong Gap, and Jung H. Kim, eds. 2002. *Religions in Asian America.* Walnut Creek, Calif.: AltaMira Press.

Montoya, Lisa. 2002. "Gender and Citizenship in Latino Participation." In *Latinos: Remaking America,* edited by Marcelo M. Suarez-Orozco and Mariela M. Paez. Berkeley, Calif.: University of California Press and DRCLAS.

Morris, Aldon. 1984. *The Origins of the Civil Rights Movement.* New York: Free Press.

Myers, Dowell, and John Pitkin. 2001. *Demographic Futures for California.* Population Dynamics Group. School of Policy, Planning, and Development, University of Southern California.

Nakanishi, Don T. 1986. "Asian American Politics: An Agenda for Research." *American Journal* 12 (2): 1–27.

———. 1991. "The Next Swing Vote? Asian Pacific Americans and California Politics." In *Racial and Ethnic Politics in California*, edited by Byran O. Jackson and Michael B. Preston, 25–54. Berkeley, Calif.: IGS Press.

———. 1998. "When the Numbers Do Not Add Up: Asian Pacific Americans and California Politics." In *Racial and Ethnic Politics in California*. Volume 2, edited by Michael Preston, Bruce E. Cain, and Sandra Bass, 3–43. Berkeley, Calif.: IGS Press.

———. 2001. "Beyond Electoral Politics: Renewing a Search for a Paradigm of Asian Pacific American Politics." In *Asian Americans and Politics: Perspectives, Experiences, and Prospects*, edited by Gordon Chang, 102–32. Stanford: Stanford University Press.

Neckerman, Karthryn, Prudence Carter, and Jennifer Lee. 1999. "Segmented Assimilation and Minority Cultures of Mobility." *Ethnic and Racial Studies* 22: 945–65.

New York Times, 2001. "Bungled Ballots in Chinatown," A-1, Editorial Desk. January 1, 2001.

Ngin, ChorSwang, and Rodolfo D. Torres. 2001. "Racialized Metropolis: Theorizing Asian American and Latino Identities and Ethnicities in Southern California." In *Asian and Latino Immigrants in a Restructuring Economy: The Metamorphosis of Southern California*, edited by Marta Lopez-Garza and David R. Diaz, 368–90. Stanford, Calif.: Stanford University Press.

Nie, Norman, Sidney Verba, and Jae-on Kim. 1974. "Political Participation and the Life Cycle." *Comparative Politics* 6: 319–40.

Niemi, Richard G., and M. Kent Jennings. 1991. "Issues and Inheritance in the Formation of Party Identification." *American Journal of Political Science* 35 (4): 970–88.

Niemi, Richard G., and Herbert F. Weisberg. 1993. *Controversies in Voting Behavior*. 3d ed. Washington, D.C.: Congressional Quarterly.

Niemi, Richard G., G. Bingham Powell, Jr., Harold W. Stanley, and C. Lawrence Evans. 1985. "Testing the Converse Partisanship Model with New Electorates." *Comparative Political Studies* 18: 300–22.

Office of Management and Budget. 1997. "Revisions to the Standards for the Classification of Federal Data on Race and Ethnicity." Washington, D.C.: OMB, Executive Office of the President.

Okihiro, Gary. 1994. *Margins and Mainstream*. Seattle: University of Washington Press.

———. 2001. *The Columbia Guide to Asian American History*. New York: Columbia University Press.

Omi, Michael, and Howard Winant. 1994. *Racial Formation in the United States: From the 1960s to the 1990s*. 2d ed. New York: Routledge.

Ong, Paul, and Suzanne Hee. 1994. "Economic Diversity." In *The State of Asian Pacific America: Economic Diversity, Issues, and Policies*, 31–56. Los Angeles, Calif.: LEAP Asian Pacific American Public Policy Institute and UCLA Asian American Studies Center.

Ong, Paul, and Don T. Nakanishi. 1996. "Becoming Citizens, Becoming Voters: The Naturalization and Political Participation of Asian Pacific Immigrants." In *Reframing the Immigration Debate*, edited by Bill Ong Hing and Ronald Lee, 275–303. Los Angeles: LEAP Asian Pacific American Public Policy Institute and UCLA Asian American Studies Center.

Ong, Paul, Edna Bonacich, and Lucie Cheng, eds. 1994. *The New Asian Immigration in Los Angeles and Global Restructuring*. Philadelphia, Pa.: Temple University Press.

Pantoja, Adrian, Ricardo Ramirez, and Gary Segura. 2001. "Citizens by Choice, Voters by Necessity: Patterns in Political Mobilization in Naturalized Latinos." *Political Research Quarterly* 54: 729–50.

Park, Robert Ezra. 1928. "Human Migration and the Marginal Man." *American Journal of Sociology* 33: 881–93.

———. 1950. *Race and Culture*. New York: Free Press.

Pelissero, John P., Timothy Krebs, and Shannon Jenkins. 2000. "Asian Americans, Political Organizations, and Participation in Chicago Electoral Precincts." *Urban Affairs Review* 35: 750–69.

Perea, Juan, Richard Delgado, Angela P. Harris, and Stephanie Wildman. 2000. *Race and Races*. New York: West Wadsworth.

Petersen, William. 1966. "Success Story, Japanese American Style." *New York Times Magazine*, January 9.

Phinney, Jean. 1990. "Ethnic Identity in Adolescents and Adults: Review of Research." *Psychological Bulletin* 108: 499–514.

Poole, Keith, and Harmon Ziegler. 1985. *Women, Public Opinion, and Politics*. New York: Longman.

Portes, Alejandro, and Robert Bach. 1985. *Latin Journey: Cuban and Mexican Immigrants in the United States.* Berkeley, Calif.: University of California Press.

Portes, Alejandro, and Rubén G. Rumbaut. 1996. *Immigrant America: A Portrait.* 2d ed. University of California Press.

———. 2001. *Legacies: The Story of the Immigrant Second Generation.* Berkeley and New York: University of California Press and Russell Sage Foundation.

Portes, Alejandro, and Min Zhou. 1994. "The New Second Generation: Segmented Assimilation and Its Variants." *The Annals of the American Academy of Political and Social Science* 530: 74–97.

Putnam, Robert. 2000. *Bowling Alone.* New York: Touchstone (Simon and Schuster).

Ramirez, Ricardo. 2002. "Getting out the Vote: The Impact of Non-partisan Voter Mobilization Efforts on Low Turnout Latino Precincts." Public Policy Institute of California. Unpublished manuscript.

Reyes, David. 2002. "Orange County Vietnamese Voters Fault Sample Ballot Election." *The Los Angeles Times*, B-3, March 21.

Rodriguez, Clara, and Hector Cordero-Guzman. 1992. "Placing Race in Context." *Ethnic and Racial Studies* 15: 523–20.

Rogers, Reuel. 2000. Between Race and Ethnicity: Afro-Caribbean Immigrants, African Americans, and the Politics of Incorporation. Ph.D. Diss., Princeton University.

Root, Maria P., ed. 1992. *Racially Mixed People in America.* Newbury Park, Calif.: Sage.

———, ed. 1996. *The Multiracial Experience.* Thousand Oaks, Calif.: Sage.

Rosenstone, Steven J. 1982. "Economic Adversity and Voter Turnout." *American Journal of Political Science* 26: 25–46.

Rosenstone, Steven J., and John Mark Hansen. 1993. *Mobilization, Participation, and Democracy in America.* Macmillan Publishing.

Rumbaut, Ruben. 1997. "Assimilation and Its Discontents: Between Rhetoric and Reality." *International Migration Review* 31: 923–60.

Said, Edward W. 1978. *Orientalism.* New York: Pantheon Books.

Saito, Leland. 1998. *Race and Politics: Asian Americans, Latinos, and Whites in a Los Angeles Suburb.* Urbana, Ill.: University of Illinois Press.

Salamon Lester M., Stephen Van Evera. 1973. "Fear, Apathy, and Discrimination: A Test of Three Explanations of Political Participation." *The American Political Science Review* 67: 1288–1306.

Salyer, Lucy E. 1995. *Laws Harsh as Tigers: Chinese Immigrants and the Shaping of Modern Immigration Law.* Chapel Hill and London: The University of North Carolina Press.

Sanders, David, Jonathan Burton, and Jack Kneeshaw. 2002. "Identifying the True Party Identifiers." *Party Politics* 8 (2): 193–205.

Sandmeyer, Elmer C. 1973. (1939). *The Anti-Chinese Movement in California.* Urbana, Ill.: University of Illinois Press.

Sanjek, Roger. 1998. *The Future of Us All: Race and Neighborhood Politics in New York City.* Ithaca, N.Y.: Cornell University Press.

Sapiro, Virginia. 1983. *The Political Integration of Women.* Urbana, Ill.: University of Illinois Press.

Schlozman, Kay Lehman. Sidney Verba, and Henry Brady. 1999. "Civic Participation and the Equality Problem. In *Civic Engagement in American Democracy,* edited by Theda Skocpal and Ydorris Fiorina, 427–461. Washington, D.C.: Brookings Institution Press/New York: Russell sage foundation.

Schier, Steven. 2000. *By Invitation Only: The Rise of Exclusive Politics in the United States.* Pittsburgh, Pa.: University of Pittsburgh Press.

Seelye, Katharine. 2001. "Poverty Rates Fell in 2000, but Income Was Stagnant." *The New York Times.* September 26, Section A, p. 12.

Segura, Gary, Dennis Falcon, and Harry Pachon. 1996. "Dynamics of Latino Partisanship in California: Immigration, Issue Salience, and Their Implications." *Harvard Journal of Hispanic Policy* 10: 62–80.

Shah, Dhavan V., Jack M. McLeod, and So-Hyang Yoon. 2001. "Communication, Context, and Community." *Communication Research* 28 (4): 464–506.

Shapiro, Robert J., and Harpreet Mahajan, 1986. "Gender Differences in Policy Preferences: A Summary of Trends from the 1960s to the 1980s." *Public Opinion Quarterly* 50: 42–61.

Sierra, Christine Marie, Teresa Carrillo, Louis DeSipio, and Michael Jones-Correa. 2000. "Latino Immigration and Citizenship." *PS: Political Science and Politics* 33: 535–40.

Sigel, Roberta, ed. 1988. *Political Learning in Adulthood.* Chicago: University of Chicago Press.

Sigel, Roberta, and Krista Jenkins. 2001. "Acceptance of the Women's Movement across Time and

Generations: A Mother/Daughter Study." Paper presented at the American Political Science Association Meeting, August 30–September 2, San Francisco.

Smith, Rogers M. 1997. *Civic Ideals: Conflicting Visions of Citizenship in U.S. History.* New Haven, Conn.: Yale University Press.

Smith, Tony. 2000. *Foreign Attachments: The Power of Ethnic Groups in the Making of American Foreign Policy.* Cambridge, Mass.: Harvard University Press.

Smith, Daniel, and Caroline Tolbert. 2001. "The Initiative to Party: Partisanship and Ballot Initiatives in California." *Party Politics* 7 (6): 781–99.

Smith, Robert C., and Richard Seltzer. 1992. *Race, Class, and Culture.* Albany, N.Y.: State University of New York Press.

Sonenshein, Raphael. 1993. *Politics in Black and White.* Princeton: Princeton University Press.

———. 2001. "When Ideologies Agree and Interests Collide, What's a Leader to Do? The Prospects for Latino-Jewish Coalitions in Los Angeles." In *Governing American Cities: Inter-Ethnic Coalitions, Competition, and Conflict,* edited by Michael Jones-Correa, 210–29. New York: Russell Sage Foundation.

Sowell, Thomas. 1981. *The Economics and Politics of Race.* New York: Quill.

Spickard, Paul, Joanne Rondilla, and Debbie Hippolite Wright, eds. 2002. *Pacific Diaspora: Island Peoples in the United States and Across the Pacific.* Honolulu: University of Hawaii Press.

Sterne, Evelyn S. 2001. "Beyond the Boss: Immigration and American Political Culture from 1880 to 1940." In *E Pluribus Unum? Contemporary and Historical Perspectives on Immigrant Political Incorporation,* edited by Gary Gerstle and John Mollenkopf, 33–66. New York: Russell Sage Foundation.

Stoll, Michael. 2001. "Race, Neighborhood Poverty, and Participation in Voluntary Associations." *Sociological Forum* 16: 529–57.

Tajfel, Henri. 1978. *The Social Psychology of Minorities.* London: Minority Rights Group.

———. 1981. *Human Groups and Social Categories.* New York: Cambridge University Press.

———, ed. 1982. *Social Identity and Intergroup Relations.* New York: Cambridge University Press.

Takaki, Ronald. 1989. *Strangers from a Different Shore.* Boston: Little, Brown.

Tang, Eric. 2000. "Collateral Damage: Southeast Asian Poverty in the United States." *Social Text* 18 (1): 55–79.

Tate, Katherine. 1993. *From Protest to Politics: The New Black Voters in American Elections.* New York: Harvard University Press.

Thai, Hung C. 1999. " 'Splitting Things in Half Is So White!': Conceptions of Family Life, Friendship, and the Formation of Ethnic Identity among Second Generation Vietnamese Americans." *Amerasia Journal* 25 (1): 53–88.

Tuan, Mia. 1998. *Forever Foreigners or Honorary Whites?* New Brunswick, N.J.: Rutgers University Press.

Uhlaner, Carole, J. 1991. "Perceived Discrimination and Prejudice and the Coalition Prospects of Blacks, Latinos, and Asian Americans." In *Racial and Ethnic Politics in California,* edited by Byran O. Jackson and Michael B. Preston, 339–96. Berkeley, Calif.: IGS Press.

———. 1996. "Latinos and Ethnic Politics in California: Participation and Preference." In *Latino Politics in California,* edited by Anibal Yanez-Chavez, 33–72. Center for U.S.-Mexican Studies.

———. 2000. "Political Activity and Preferences of African Americans, Latinos, and Asian Americans." In *Race and Immigration: New Challenges for American Democracy,* edited by Gerald Jaynes, 217–54. New Haven: Yale University Press.

Uhlaner, Carole J., Bruce Cain, and D. Roderick Kiewiet. 1989. "Political Participation of Ethnic Minorities in the 1980s." *Political Behavior* 17: 195–231.

U.S. Bureau of the Census. 1993. *1990 Census of Population, Asians and Pacific Islanders in the United States.* Washington, D.C.: U.S. GPO.

———. 1998. *Current Population Survey: Voter Supplement File, 1998* [computer file]. ICPSR version. Washington, D.C.: U.S. Department of Commerce, Bureau of the Census [producer], 1998. Ann Arbor, Mich.: Inter-university Consortium for Political and Social Research [distributor].

———. 1999. *Current Population Reports, Series P23-205, Population Profile of the United States: 1999.* Washington, D.C.: U.S. GPO.

U.S. Immigration and Naturalization Service. 2002. *Statistical Yearbook of the Immigration and Naturalization Service: 2000.* U.S. Deparment of Justice. www.bcis.gov/graphics/shared/aboutus/statistics/IMM00yrbk/IMM2000list.htm (accessed July 30, 2003).

Verba, Sidney, and Norman H. Nie. 1972. *Participation in America: Political Democracy and Social Equality.* New York: Harper Row.

Verba, Sidney, Nancy Burns, and Kay Lehman Schlozman. 1997. "Knowing and Caring about Politics: Gender and Political Engagement." *Journal of Politics* 59: 1051–72.

Verba, Sidney, Kay Lehman Schlozman, and Henry E. Brady. 1995. *Voice and Equality: Civic Voluntarism in American Politics.* Cambridge, Mass.: Harvard University Press.

Vertovec, Steven. 1999. "Conceiving and Researching Transnationalism." *Ethnic and Racial Studies* 22: 447–62.

Viswanath, K., and Pamela Arora. 2000. "Ethnic Media in the United States: An Essay on Their Role in Integration, Assimilation, and Social Control." *Mass Communication & Society* 3 (1): 39–56.

Wald, Kenneth, Dennis Owen, and Samuel Hill, Jr. 1988. "Church as Political Communities." *American Political Science Review* 82: 531–48.

Wald, Kenneth. 1997. *Religion and Politics in the United States.* 3d ed. Washington, D.C.: CQ Press.

Wang, Ling-chi. 1991. "The Politics of Ethnic Identity and Empowerment: The Asian American Community since the 1960s." *Asian American Policy Review* 2: 43–56.

———. 1995. "The Structure of Dual Domination: Toward a Paradigm for the Study of the Chinese Diaspora in the United States." *Amerasia Journal* 21 (1&2): 149–70.

———. 1998. "Race, Class, Citizenship, and Extraterritoriality: Asian Americans and the 1996 Campaign Finance Scandal." *Amerasia Journal* 24 (1): 1–21.

Warner, W. L. and L. Srole. 1945. *The Social Systems of American Ethnic Groups.* New Haven, Conn.: Yale University Press.

Waters, Mary C. 1999. *Black Identities: West Indian Immigrant Dreams and American Realities.* New York: Russell Sage Foundation and Cambridge, Mass.: Harvard University Press.

Wattenberg, Martin P. 1998. *The Decline of American Political Parties: 1952–1996.* Cambridge, Mass.: Harvard University Press.

Weglyn, Michi. 1976. *Years of Infamy: The Untold Story of America's Concentration Camps.* New York: William Morrow.

Wei, William. 1993. *The Asian American Movement.* Philadelphia, Pa.: Temple University Press.

Wilcox, Clyde. 1990. "Religious Sources of Politicization among Blacks in Washington, D.C." *Journal for the Scientific Study of Religion* 29: 387–94.

Williams-Leon, Teresa, and Cynthia Nakashima. 2001. *The Sum of Our Parts: Mixed-Heritage Asian Americans.* Philadelphia, Pa.: Temple University Press.

Wolfinger, Raymond, and Steven J. Rosenstone. 1980. *Who Votes?* New Haven, Conn.: Yale University Press.

Wong, Janelle S. 2000. "The Effects of Age and Political Exposure on the Development of Party Identification among Asian American and Latino Immigrants in the United States." *Political Behavior* 22: 341–71.

———. 2001. "The New Dynamics of Immigrants' Political Incorporation: A Multi-Method Study of Political Participation and Mobilization among Asian and Latino Immigrants in the United States." Department of Political Science, Yale University. Unpublished dissertation manuscript.

———. 2003. "Gender and Political Involvement among Chinese Americans in Southern California." In *Asian Pacific Americans and American Politics: Law, Participation, and Policy,* edited by Don Nakanishi and James Lai, 211–30. Blue Ridge Summit, Pa.: Rowman and Littlefield.

Wong, Janelle, Pei-te Lien, and M. Margaret Conway. n.d. "Political Participation among Asian Americans: Evidence from the Multi-Site Asian American Political Survey." Unpublished manuscript.

Woo, Deborah. 2000. *Glass Ceilings and Asian Americans: The New Face of Workplace Barriers.* Walnut Creek, Calif.: AltaMira Press.

Wrinkle, Robert D., Joseph Stewart, Jr., J. L. Polinard, Kenneth J. Meirer, and John R. Arvizu. 1996. "Ethnicity and Nonelectoral Political Participation." *Hispanic Journal of Behavioral Sciences* 18: 142–43.

Wu, Frank. 2002. *Yellow: Race in America Beyond Black and White.* New York: Basic Books.

Wu, Frank, and May Nicholson. 1997. "Have You No Decency? An Analysis of Racial Aspects of Media Coverage on the John Huang Matter." *Asian American Policy Review* VII: 1–37.

Yoo, David K. Ed. 1999. *New Spiritual Homes: Religion and Asian Americans.* Honolulu: University of Hawaii Press, in association with UCLA Asian American Studies Center, Los Angeles.

Zaller, John R. 1992. *The Nature and Origins of Mass Opinion.* Cambridge, U.K.: Cambridge University Press.

Zeigler, Harmon. 1993. *Political Parties in Industrial Democracies: Imagining the Masses.* Itasca, Ill.: F. E. Peacock Publishers, Inc.

Zhou, Min. 1997. "Segmented Assimilation: Issues, Controversies, and Recent Research on the New Second Generation." *International Migration Review* 31: 975–1009.

———. 2001. "Straddling Different Worlds: The Acculturation of Vietnamese Refugee Children." In *Ethnicities: Children of Immigrants in America,* edited by Ruben G. Rumbaut and Alejandro Portes, 187–228. Berkeley and New York: California/Russell Sage Foundation.

Zhou, Min, and Carl Bankston III. 1998. *Growing up American: How Vietnamese Children Adapt to Life in the United States.* New York: Russell Sage.

Zhou, Min, and James Gatewood. 2000. "Introduction: Revisiting Contemporary Asian America." In *Contemporary Asian America: A Multi-Disciplinary Reader,* edited by Min Zhou and James Gatewood, 1–46. New York: New York University Press.

Zia, Helen. 2000. *Asian American Dreams.* New York: Farrar, Straus, and Giroux.

Index